THE LETTERS
of
JOHN *and* JUDE

THE LETTERS

of

JOHN *and* JUDE

Translated,
with Introductions and Interpretations
by

WILLIAM BARCLAY

THE WESTMINSTER PRESS
PHILADELPHIA

First published by The Saint Andrew Press
Edinburgh, Scotland
I, II, and III John: First Edition, April, 1958
Second Edition, May, 1960
Jude: First Edition, July, 1958
Second Edition, May, 1960

Library of Congress Catalog Card No. 61–10838

Typeset in Great Britain
Printed in the United States of America

To
My Friend
P. M. S.
A Great Encourager

GENERAL INTRODUCTION

It may truly be said that this series of Daily Bible Studies began almost accidentally. A series which the Church of Scotland was using came to an end, and another series was immediately required. I was asked to write a volume on *Acts*, and, at the moment, had no intention beyond that. But one volume followed another, until the demand for one volume became a plan to write on the whole New Testament.

The translation which is given in each volume claims no special merit. It was included in order that the reader might be able to carry both the text of the New Testament and the comments on it wherever he went, and that he might be able to read it anywhere. While I was making the translation, the translations of Moffatt, Weymouth, and Knox were ever beside me. *The American Revised Standard Version, The Twentieth Century New Testament,* and *The New Testament in Plain English,* by Charles Kingsley Williams, have been in constant use. Since its publication, I have consistently consulted *The Authentic New Testament,* translated by Hugh J. Schonfield.

I cannot see another edition of these books going out to the public without expressing my very deep and sincere gratitude to the Church of Scotland Publications Committee for allowing me the privilege of first beginning, and then continuing, this series. And in particular I wish to express my very great gratitude to the convener, Rev. R. G. Macdonald, O.B.E., M.A., D.D., and to the committee's secretary and manager, Rev. Andrew McCosh, M.A., S.T.M., for constant encouragement and never-failing sympathy and help.

As these volumes went on, the idea of the whole series developed. The aim is to make the results of modern scholarship available to the non-technical reader in a form that it does not require a theological education to understand; and then to seek to make the teaching of the New Testament books relevant to life and work to-day. The whole aim of these books is summed up in Richard of Chichester's famous prayer; they are meant to enable men and women to know Jesus Christ more clearly, to love Him more dearly, and to follow Him more nearly. It is my prayer that they may do something to make that possible.

FOREWORD

The Letters of John are of the greatest importance for the light they shed on the thought and on the theology of the New Testament, and for the information they supply on the administration of the growing Church. And there are few books which show more clearly the threats of the heresies and the misguided thinking which came from within the Church itself.

Although there are not a great many outstanding commentaries on these Letters, the commentaries which do exist are of the first rank. There are those on the Greek text. That of A. E. Brooke in the *International Critical Commentary* is a mine of information. That of B. F. Westcott in the Macmillan Commentaries is distinguished by Westcott's almost unique combination of exactly scholarship and warm devotion. There are those on the English text. That of A. Plummer in the *Cambridge Bible for Schools and Colleges* was published as far back as 1883, but it is still a most useful and excellent volume. But the outstanding volume on these letters is that by C. H. Dodd in the *Moffatt Commentary*. It is without question one of the best commentaries in the English language, even although it is based on the English text and not on the Greek text. It would have been tedious to detail every one of my debts to C. H. Dodd; I can only say here and now that there is hardly a page in this book which does not contain its debt to him.

It may be that the Letters of John are not among the most widely read of New Testament books. It is my hope and prayer that this book may do something to show how valuable and relevant they are.

The little letter of *Jude* is a largely neglected book. It is very closely connected with *Second Peter*, for *Second Peter* very largely took it over and included it. It is a very difficult letter to understand, even for biblical students.

ix

The reason for this is that it moves in a quite different world of thought and imagery. It draws much of its thought and imagery and illustrative material, not from the Old Testament, but from the books which were written between the Old and the New Testament, books which are to us largely unknown, but which in their own day were immensely popular. For that reason some considerable space has been necessary to interpret it, and it must be read in close conjunction with *Second Peter*. But it will be found that the mental toil of reading through it is more than worthwhile.

Jude is not commonly dealt with alone. It is usually taken along with *First* and *Second Peter*. In the *International Critical Commentary* the three books are dealt with by C. Bigg. In the *Moffatt Commentary* it is included in the volume on *The General Epistles* by James Moffatt himself. The three letters are again dealt with together by E. H. Plumptre in *The Cambridge Bible for Schools and Colleges*. The most massive commentary on it is in J. B. Mayor's volume on *Second Peter* and *Jude* in the Macmillan Commentaries. In *The Cambridge Greek Testament for Schools and Colleges* there is an excellent short volume by M. R. James.

If *Jude* is neglected, it is unjustly neglected, for there are few New Testament books which, when properly understood, more vividly show the dangers which threatened the early Church from false doctrine and from misguided ethical teaching.

I hope that this little book will enable its readers to understand *Jude* better and to value it more.

WILLIAM BARCLAY.

TRINITY COLLEGE,
   GLASGOW,
      March, 1960.

CONTENTS

CONTENTS

THE LETTERS OF JOHN

THE LETTERS OF JOHN

INTRODUCTION

A Personal Letter and its Background

THE First Letter of John is entitled a letter, and yet it neither begins nor ends as such. It has no opening address, and it has no closing greetings, such as the letters of Paul have. And yet no one can read it without feeling its intensely personal character. Beyond all doubt the man who wrote it had in his mind's eye a quite definite situation and a quite definite group of people. Both the form and the personal character of I *John* will be explained, if we think of it as what someone has called " a loving and anxious sermon " written by a pastor who loved his people, and sent out to the various Churches over which he had charge. It is a homily written out of a devoted pastor's love and care and concern for his people.

Any such letter or homily is provoked and produced by an actual situation; and it cannot be fully understood apart from its situation. If, then, we wish to understand I *John* we have first of all to try to reconstruct the situation which produced it and which moved John to write it. To understand I *John* we must remember *when* and *where* it was written. It was written some time a little after A.D. 100, and it was written in Ephesus.

The Falling Away

By A.D. 100 certain things had almost inevitably happened within the Church, and especially within the Church in a place like Ephesus.

(i) Many of the Christians were now second or even third generation Christians. The thrill of the first days, and of the new discovery, had, to some extent at least, passed away. Wordsworth said of one of the great moments of modern history:

" Bliss was it in that dawn to be alive."

In the very first days of Christianity there was a glory and a splendour, a magnificence and a radiance in life.

3

But now Christianity had become a thing of habit; it had become, as it has been put, " traditional, half-hearted, nominal." Men had grown used to it, and something of the wonder had gone lost. Jesus knew men, and Jesus had Himself said: " The love of many shall grow cold " (*Matthew* 24: 12). John was writing at a time when, for some at least, the first thrill was gone, and when the flame of devotion had died to a flicker. It was to this very Church at Ephesus that the Risen Christ had said, " Nevertheless I have somewhat against thee, because thou hast left thy first love " (*Revelation* 2: 4).

(ii) One result of this was that there were members of the Church who found the standards which Christianity demanded a burden and a weariness. They did not want to be *saints* in the New Testament sense of the term. The New Testament word for *saint* is *hagios*, which is the word which is also commonly translated *holy*. Its basic meaning is *different*. The Temple was *hagios* because it was *different* from other buildings; the Sabbath was *hagios* because it was *different* from other days; the Jewish nation was *hagios* because it was *different* from other peoples; and the Christian was called to be *hagios* because he was called to be *different* from other men. There was always a distinct cleavage between the Christian and the world. In the Fourth Gospel Jesus says, " If ye were of the world, the world would love its own; but because ye are not of the world, but I have chosen you out of the world, therefore the world hateth you " (*John* 15: 19). " I have given them Thy word," said Jesus in His prayer to God, " and the world hath hated them, because they are not of the world, even as I am not of the world " (*John* 17: 14). But all this involved an ethical demand. It demanded a new standard of moral purity, a new sexual ethic, a new kindness, a new service, a new forgiveness— and it was difficult. And once the first thrill and enthusiasm were gone it became harder and harder to stand out against the world, to deny oneself the things which the world habitually allowed itself, to refuse to conform to the generally accepted social standards and practices of the society of the age. What had once been an uplifting challenge had become a wearisome burden.

(iii) It is to be noted that I *John* shows no signs that the Church to which it was written is being persecuted. At that time no danger of violence from outside the Church was threatening. The peril, as it has been put, was not persecution but seduction; for the peril came from within. That, too, Jesus had foreseen. " Many false prophets," He said, " shall arise, and shall deceive many " (*Matthew* 24: 11). This was a danger of which Paul had warned the leaders of this very Church of Ephesus, when he made his farewell address to them. " I know this," he said, " that after my departing shall grievous wolves enter among you, not sparing the flock. Also of your own selves shall men arise, speaking perverse things to draw away disciples after them " (*Acts* 20: 29, 30).

The trouble which I *John* seeks to combat did not come from men who were out to destroy the Christian faith; it came from men who thought that they were improving the Christian faith. It came from men whose aim was to make Christianity intellectually respectable. It came from men who knew the intellectual tendencies and currents of the day, and who wished to express Christianity in terms of these current philosophical ideas. It came from men who felt that the time had come for Christianity to come to terms with secular philosophy and with contemporary thought.

The Contemporary Philosophy

What, then, was this contemporary thought and philosophy with which the false prophets and mistaken teachers wished to align the Christian faith? All throughout the Greek world there was an ever-developing tendency of thought to which the general name of Gnosticism is given. The basic belief of all Gnostic thought is that only spirit is good, and that matter is essentially evil. If this be so, the Gnostic inevitably despises the world, for the world is matter, and all things created out of matter are essentially evil. In particular the Gnostic despises the body. The body is matter, and therefore the body is evil. Now imprisoned within this body there is the spirit, the mind, the reason of man. That spirit is a seed, an effluence of the spirit who is God, and who is altogether good. So, then, the aim of life must be to release this heavenly seed which is imprisoned in the evil of the body. And that can only be done by an elaborate and secret knowledge and ritual and initiation which only the true Gnostic can supply. Here was a tendency of thought which was written deep into Greek thinking—and which, truth to tell, has not even yet ceased to exist. The basis of it is the conviction that all matter is evil, and that spirit alone is good, and that the one real aim in life is to liberate man's spirit from the vile prison-house of the body.

The False Teachers

With that in our minds let us turn to I *John*, and let us gather from it the evidence as to who these false teachers were, and what they taught. They had been within the Church, but they had seceded from the Church. " They went out from us, but they were not of us " (I *John* 2: 19). They are men of influence for they claim to be prophets. " Many false prophets are gone out into the world " (I *John* 4: 1). Although they have left the Church, they still try to disseminate their teaching within the Church, and to seduce the members of the Church from the true faith (I *John* 2: 26).

The Denial of Jesus' Messiahship

At least some of these false teachers denied that Jesus was the Messiah. " Who is a liar," demands John, " but he that denieth that Jesus is the Christ? " (I *John* 2: 22). It is most likely that these false teachers were not Gnostics

proper, but Jews. Things had always been difficult for
Jewish Christians, but the events of history made them
doubly difficult. It was very difficult for a Jew to come to
believe in a crucified Messiah. But suppose he had begun
so to believe his difficulties were by no means finished.
The Christians believed in the speedy return of Jesus,
a return in which he would come to save and to vindicate
His people. Clearly that would be a hope that would be
specially near and dear to the heart of the Jews. And
then what happened? In A.D. 70, Jerusalem was captured
by the Romans, and so infuriated were the Romans with
the long intransigence and the suicidal resistance of
the Jews, that they literally tore the Holy City stone
from stone and drew a plough across the midst of it. In
view of that how could a Jew easily accept the hope that
Jesus would come and save His people? The Holy City
was desolate; the Jews were dispersed throughout the
world. The city of God was shattered, and the people
of God were utterly subjected. In face of that how could
it be true that the Messiah had come? So long as Jewish
thought had any remnants of the nationalistic hope in it,
it could not possibly accept the Messiahship of Jesus,
for Jesus had come and gone, and the Jewish nation was
destroyed. There were doubtless Jews who had looked
to Jesus to return to be the Saviour of the Jewish people,
and doubtless these Jews denied that Jesus could be the
Messiah.

The Denial of the Incarnation

But there was something even more serious than that.
There was false teaching which came directly from an
attempt from within the Church to bring Christianity
into line with Gnosticism. We must remember the Gnostic
point of view that spirit alone is good and matter is utterly
evil. *Given that point of view any real incarnation is impossible.*
Given that point of view, it is impossible that God should
ever take human flesh upon Himself. That is exactly

what centuries later Augustine was to point out. Before Augustine became a Christian, he was skilled in the philosophies of the various schools. In the *Confessions* (6: 9) he tells us that, somewhere or other in the heathen writers, he had read in one form or another nearly all the things which Christianity says; but there was a great Christian saying which he had never found in any pagan author, and which no one would ever find, and that saying was: " The Word became flesh and dwelt among us " (*John* 1: 14). Since the heathen thinkers believed in the essential evil of matter, and therefore the essential evil of the body, that is one thing which they could never say.

It is clear that the false teachers against whom John was writing in this First Letter denied the reality of the incarnation and the reality of Jesus' physical body. "Every spirit," writes John, " that confesseth that Jesus Christ is come in the flesh is of God; and every spirit that confesseth not that Jesus Christ is come in the flesh is not of God " (*John* 4: 2, 3).

In the early Church this refusal to admit the reality of the incarnation took, broadly speaking, two forms.

(i) In its most radical and wholesale form it is called *Docetism,* which Goodspeed suggests might be translated *Seemism.* The Greek verb *dokein* means *to seem*; and the Docetists taught that Jesus only *seemed* to have a body. They declared that His body was an unsubstantial phantasm. They insisted that He never had a flesh and blood, physical, human body; but that He was a purely spiritual being, who had nothing but the appearance of having a body. One of the apocryphal and heretical books written from this point of view is the *Acts of John,* which dates from about A.D. 160. In it John is made to say that sometimes when he touched Jesus he seemed to meet with a material and solid body, but at other times, " the substance was immaterial, as if it did not exist at all." And John is made to say that when Jesus walked He never left any footprint upon the ground. The simplest form of Docetism is the complete denial that Jesus ever had a human, physical body of any kind.

(ii) There was a more subtle, and perhaps even more dangerous, variant of this theory connected with the name of Cerinthus. In tradition John and Cerinthus were sworn enemies. Eusebius (*Ecclesiastical History* 4.14.6) hands down a story which shows how John felt about Cerinthus. He tells how John went to the public bath-house in Ephesus to bathe. He saw Cerinthus inside, and refused even to enter the building. " Let us flee," he said, " lest even the bathhouse fall, because Cerinthus the enemy of truth is within." Cerinthus drew a definite distinction between the human Jesus and the divine Christ. He said that Jesus was a man, born in a perfectly natural way. He lived in special obedience to God, and after His baptism, the Christ in the shape of a dove descended upon Him, from that power which is above all powers, and then Jesus brought to men news of the Father who had been as yet unknown. Nor did Cerinthus stop there. He said that at the end of Jesus' life, the Christ again withdrew from Him, and that the Christ never suffered at all, but that it was the human Jesus who suffered, died, and rose again, while the divine Christ remained absolutely incapable of suffering, and in purely spiritual existence. This again comes out in the stories of the apocryphal and heretical gospels written under the influence of this point of view. In the *Gospel of Peter*, written about A.D. 130, it is said that Jesus showed no pain upon the Cross, and that His cry was: " My power! My power! Why has thou forsaken me? " It was at that moment that the divine Christ left the human Jesus. The *Acts of John* go further. They tell how, when the human Jesus was being crucified on Calvary, John was actually talking to the divine Christ in a cave in the hillside, and that the divine Christ said to him, " John, unto the multitude down below in Jerusalem I am being crucified, and pierced with lances and with reeds, and gall and vinegar are given me to drink. But I am speaking to you, and listen to what I say. . . . Nothing, therefore, of the things they will say of me have I suffered " (*Acts of John* 97).

We may see how widespread this way of thinking was from the Letters of Ignatius. Ignatius was writing to a group of Churches in Asia Minor which must have been much the same group as that to which I *John* was written. When Ignatius wrote he was a prisoner and was being conveyed to Rome to be martyred by being flung to the beasts in the arena. He writes to the Trallians: " Be deaf, therefore, when anyone speaks to you apart from Jesus Christ, who was of the family of David, and Mary, who was truly born, both ate and drank, was truly persecuted under Pontius Pilate, was truly crucified and died . . . who also was truly raised from the dead. . . . But if, as some affirm, who are without God—that is, who are unbelievers—His suffering was only a semblance . . . why am I a prisoner? " (Ignatius, *To the Trallians* 9 and 10). To the Christians at Smyrna he writes: " For He suffered all these things for us that we might attain salvation, and He truly suffered even as He also truly raised Himself, not as some unbelievers say, that His passion was merely in semblance " (*To the Smyrnaeans* 2). Polycarp writing to the Philippians uses John's very words: " For everyone who does not confess that Jesus Christ has come in the flesh is an anti-Christ " (*To the Philippians* 7: 1).

This teaching of Cerinthus is also rebuked in I *John*. John writes of Jesus: " This is He that came by water and blood, even Jesus Christ; *not by water only, but by water and blood* (I *John* 5: 6). The point of that verse is that the Gnostic teachers would have agreed that the divine Christ came by *water*, that is, at the Baptism of Jesus; but they would have denied that He came by *blood*, that is, by the Cross, for they would have insisted that the divine Christ left the human Jesus before His crucifixion, and thus never suffered at all.

The great and grave danger of this heresy is that it comes from what can only be called a mistaken reverence. It is afraid to ascribe to Jesus full and true humanity. It regards it as irreverent to think that Jesus had a really human and truly physical body as all men have. It is a heresy which is by no means dead; in fact, it is a heresy which to this day is held, usually quite unconsciously, by not a few devout Christians. But it must be remembered, as John so clearly saw, that unless Jesus truly became man He could not save man, that, in fact, man's salvation is dependent on the full identification of Jesus Christ with man. As one of the great early fathers unforgettably put it: " He became what we are to make us what He is."

(iii) This Gnostic belief had certain practical and ethical consequences in the lives of those who held it.

(a) The Gnostic attitude to matter and to all physical and created things begot a certain attitude to the body, and to the things of the body. That attitude could take any one of three different forms. (1) Since the body was altogether evil, it might take the form of asceticism. It might take the form of fasting and of celibacy and of the rigid control, and even deliberate ill-treatment of, the body. The view that celibacy is better than marriage, and the identification of sex with sin, go back to Gnostic influence and belief—and they are views which still linger on in certain quarters. There is no trace of that view in this letter at all. (2) Since the body is altogether evil, it might take the form of a contention that the body did not matter; therefore, its appetites and its lusts might be gratified without control and without limit. Since the body is in any event evil, then it makes no difference what a man does with it. In such a view physical chastity, purity and immorality did not matter, for it is not of the slightest importance what is done with the evil body. There are echoes of this in this letter. John condemns as a liar the man who says that he knows God, and who yet does not keep God's commandments; the man who says

that he abides in Christ ought to walk as Christ walked
(I *John* 1: 6; 2: 4-6). There were clearly Gnostics in
these communities who claimed special knowledge of
God, and whose conduct was very far removed from the
demand of the Christian ethic. In certain quarters this
Gnostic belief could go even further. The Gnostic is the
wise man, the man who has *gnōsis*, *knowledge*, the man who
knows. Now certain Gnostics held that the real Gnostic
must, therefore, know the best as well as the worst; he
must know the depths as well as the heights; he must
enter into every experience of life at its highest or at its
deepest level, as the case may be. It might almost be
said that such men held that it was an obligation to sin.
The idea is something like the idea that it is good for a
young man " to sow his wild oats." Only the Gnostics,
who held this view, went further, and looked on sin as a
kind of religious duty. There is a reference to this kind
of belief in the letter to Thyatira in the *Revelation*, where
the Risen Christ refers to those who have known " the
depths of Satan " (*Revelation* 2: 24). And it may well
be that John is referring to these people when he insists
that " God is light, and in Him is no darkness at all "
(I *John* 1: 5). The Gnostics, who held this view, would
have held that there is in God not only blazing light but
deep darkness—and that a man must penetrate into both.
It is easy to see the disastrous consequences of such a
belief. (3) There was a third kind of Gnostic belief. Clearly
the true Gnostic would regard himself as an altogether
spiritual man; he would regard himself as having shed
all the material things of life, and as having released his
spirit from the bondage of matter. Such Gnostics held
that they were completely above sin; that sin for them
had ceased to exist; that they were so spiritual that they
were above and beyond sin, and that they had reached
spiritual perfection. It is to them that John refers when he
speaks of those who deceive themselves by saying that
they have no sin (I *John* 1: 8-10).

It is quite clear that whichever of these three ways Gnostic belief took its ethical consequences were perilous in the extreme; and it is clear that the last two lines of belief and conduct were to be found in the society to which John wrote.

(b) Still further, this Gnosticism issued in an attitude to men which was the necessary destruction of Christian fellowship. We have seen that the Gnostic aimed at the release of the spirit from the prison house of the evil matter of the physical body by means of an elaborate, secret and esoteric knowledge. Clearly such a knowledge was not for every man. Ordinary people were too involved in the everyday life and work of the world ever to have time for the study and training and discipline which were necessary; and, even if they had such time, there were many who were intellectually quite incapable of grasping and understanding the involved and elaborate mysteries and speculations of Gnostic theosophy and philosophy so-called. This produced a quite inevitable result. It divided men into two classes—those who were capable of a really spiritual life, and those who were not. The Gnostics had names for these two classes of men. The ancients commonly divided the being of man into three parts. There was the *sōma*, the *body*, which is the physical part of man. There was the *psuchē*, which we generally translate *soul*, but here we must have a care, for the word does not mean what we mean by soul. To the Greeks the *psuchē* is the principle of physical life. Everything which has physical life has *psuchē*; an animal has *psuchē* just as much as a man has, for *psuchē* is no more than the life principle which makes creatures alive. *Psuchē* is that physical life which a man shares with all that lives. There was the *pneuma*, the spirit; and it is the spirit which is the real thing, which is possessed only by man, which makes a man kin to God. The whole aim of Gnosticism was the release of the *pneuma* from the *sōma*; but that release could only be won by long and arduous and painful

13

study, which only the leisured intellectual could ever undertake and complete. The Gnostics, therefore, divided men into two classes—the *psuchikoi*, men who could never advance beyond the principle of physical life, men who could never attain to anything else than what was to all intents and purposes animal living; and the *pneumatikoi*, those who were truly spiritual, and who were truly akin to God.

The result of this was clear. The Gnostics produced a spiritual aristocracy who looked down with contempt and disgust and even hatred on those who were lesser men. The *peumatikoi* regarded the *psuchikoi* as contemptible, earthbound creatures who could never at any time know what real religion was, and who could never know or approach God. The consequence of this is obviously the annihilation of Christian fellowship. That is why, again and again, John insists all over his letter that the true test of real Christianity is love for the brethren. If we really are walking in the light we have fellowship one with another (1: 7). He who says he is in the light, and hates his brother, is in fact in darkness (2: 9-11). The proof that we have passed from dark to light is that we love the brethren (3: 14-17). The marks of Christianity are belief in Christ and love for the brethren (3: 23). God is love, and he who does not love does not know God at all (4: 7, 8). Because God loved us, we ought to love each other; it is when we love each other that God dwells in us (4: 10-12). The commandment is that he who loves God must love his brother also, and he who says he loves God, and at the same time hates his brother, is branded as a liar (4: 20, 21). The Gnostic, to put it bluntly, would have said that the mark of true religion is contempt for ordinary men; John insists in every chapter of his letter that the mark of true religion is love for every man.

It is quite clear that, if the Gnostics had had their way, there could never have been any such thing as a Christian fellowship, for there can never be a fellowship in a society where there is a small religious aristocracy which despises every one else.

Here, then, is a picture of these Gnostic heretics. They talked of being born of God, of walking in the light, of having no sin, of dwelling in God, of knowing God. These were their catch phrases. They had no idea of destroying the Church and the faith; by their way of it they were going to cleanse the Church of what they regarded as dead wood, and they were going to make Christianity an intellectually respectable philosophy, fit to stand beside the great systems of the day. But the effect of their teaching was to destroy the incarnation, to eliminate the Christian ethic, and to make fellowship within the Church impossible. It is little wonder that John, with such fervent pastoral devotion, seeks to defend the Churches he loved from such an insidious and threatening attack from within, for this was a threat which was far more perilous than the threat of any heathen persecution. The very existence of the Christian faith and of the Christian Church was at stake.

The Message of John

1 John is a short letter, and, even if it had been John's aim, he could not in it have gone through the whole gamut of orthodox Christian belief; we cannot look within it for a systematic exposition of the Christian faith; but nonetheless it will be of the greatest interest to examine this letter to see with what basic underlying beliefs John confronts those who were threatening to be the wreckers of the Christian faith.

The Object of Writing

John's object in writing is two-fold, yet one. He writes that the joy of his people may be full (1: 4), and that they may not sin (2: 1). He sees clearly that however fascinating and attractive the wrong way may be, it is not in its nature to bring happiness. To bring them joy and to preserve them from sin is one and the same thing.

The Idea of God

John has two great things to say about God. God is light and in Him there is no darkness at all (1: 5). God is love, and that love made Him love us, before we loved Him, and made Him send His Son as a remedy for our sins (4: 7-10, 16). That is to say, John's conviction is that God is a self-revealing and a self-giving God. He is light, and not darkness; He is love, and not anger or hate.

The Idea of Jesus

Because the main attack of the heretics and the false teachers was on the Christian conviction of the person of Christ, this letter, which answers them, is specially rich and helpful in what it has to say about Jesus Christ.

(i) Jesus is He who was from the beginning (1: 1; 2: 14). When a man is confronted with Jesus, he is confronted with the eternal.

(ii) Another way of putting the same conviction is to say that Jesus is the Son of God, and, for John, it is essential to be convinced of that (4: 15; 5: 5). The relationship of Jesus to God is unique; in Jesus is seen the ever-seeking and ever-forgiving heart of God.

(iii) For John, Jesus was the Christ, or, to use the more familiar word, the Messiah (2: 22; 5: 1). That again for John was an essential article of belief. It may seem that here we have come into a region of ideas which is much narrower, and which is, in fact, Jewish. But there is something essential here. To say that Jesus is from the beginning, and to say that He is the Son of God is to conserve His connection with *eternity*; but to say that He is the Christ, the Messiah, is to conserve his connection with *history*. It is to see His coming as the event towards which God's plan, working itself out in His chosen people, was moving; and it is to see Him as the culmination and the realization of the hopes and prayers and dreams and visions of the prophets, and of the longings of the people of God. When John says that Jesus is from the beginning, the Son of God, then he rightly lays it down that Jesus did not emerge from history, but that He came from beyond history; but, when he lays it down that Jesus is the Messiah, he lays it down that at the same time all history leads up to Him

(iv) It is the conviction of John that Jesus was most truly and fully man. To deny that Jesus came in the flesh is to be moved by the spirit of anti-Christ (4: 2, 3). It is John's witness that Jesus was so truly man that he himself had known, and touched, and handled Him (1: 1, 3). No writer in the New Testament holds with greater intensity the full reality of the incarnation. Not only did He become man, He also suffered for men. It was by water and blood that He came (5: 6); and He laid down His life for men (3: 16).

(v) The coming of Jesus, His incarnation, His life, His death, His resurrection and His ascension all combine to deal with the sin of man. Jesus was without sin (3: 5); and man is essentially a sinner, even though in his arrogance he may claim to be without sin (1: 8-10); and yet the sinless one came to take away the sin of sinning men (3: 5). In regard to man's sin Jesus is two things.

(a) Jesus is our *advocate* with the Father (2: 1). The word is *paraklētos*. A *paraklētos* is someone who is called in to help. The word could be used of a doctor called in to help. It can be used, and is often used, of a witness called in to give evidence in favour of someone on trial, or a defending lawyer or orator called in to defend someone under accusation. Jesus, then, pleads our case with God; He, the sinless one, is the defender of sinning men.

(b) But Jesus is more than that. Twice John calls Him the *propitiation* for our sins (2: 2; 4: 10). When a man sinned, the relationship which should exist between him and God is broken and interrupted. A propitiatory sacrifice is a sacrifice which restores that relationship, or, rather, a sacrifice in virtue of which that relationship is restored. It is an *atoning* sacrifice, that is a sacrifice which once again makes man and God *at one*. So, then, through what Jesus was and did the relationship between God and man, broken by sin, is restored. Jesus does not only plead the case of the sinner; He sets the sinner at one, at home, with God. The blood of Jesus Christ cleanses us from all sin (1: 7).

(vi) In consequence of all this, through Jesus Christ, men who believe have life (4: 9; 5: 11, 12). This is true in a double sense. They have life in the sense that they are saved from death; and they have life in the sense that life has ceased to be mere existence, and has become life indeed.

(vii) All this may be summed up by saying that Jesus is the Saviour of the world (4: 14). And here we have something which has to be set out in full. " The Father sent the Son to be the Saviour of the world " (4: 14). We have already talked of Jesus as pleading men's case before God, as being their defender, as being their advocate. If we were to leave that without any further addition, it might be argued that God wished to condemn men, and that Jesus wished to save men, and that God was deflected from His dire purpose by the pleading and the self-sacrifice of Jesus Christ. But that is not so because, with John, as with every writer in the New Testament, the whole initiative is with God. It was God who sent His Son to be the Saviour of men.

It can be seen that within the short compass of this letter the wonder and the glory and the grace of Christ are most fully set out.

The Spirit

In this letter John has less to say about the Spirit; for his highest teaching about the Spirit we must turn back to the Fourth Gospel. It may be said that in 1 *John* the function of the Spirit is in some sense to be the liaison between God and man. It is the Spirit who makes us conscious that there is within us the abiding presence

of God through Jesus Christ (3: 24; 4: 13). We may say
that it is the Spirit who enables us to grasp and to realize
the precious fellowship with divine life, with God Himself,
which is being offered to us.

The World

The world within which the Christian lives is a hostile
world; it is a world without God. The world does not
know the Christian, because it did not know Christ (3: 1).
The world hates the Christian, just as it hated Christ
(3: 13). The false teachers are of the world, and not of
God, and it is because they speak the world's language
that the world is ready to hear them and to listen to them
and to accept them (4: 4, 5). The whole world, says
John sweepingly, lieth in wickedness (5: 19). It is for that
reason that the Christian has to overcome the world,
and his weapon in his struggle with the world is faith
(5: 4).

But hostile as the world is, it remains true that the
world is doomed. The world and all its desires are passing
away (2: 17). That, indeed, is why it is folly to give one's
heart to the world; the world is on the way to dissolution.

But although the Christian lives in a hostile world,
and although the present world is passing away, there is
no need for despair and fear. In Christ the new age has
come. The darkness is past, and the true light now shines
(2: 8). God in Christ has broken into time; the new
age has come. It is not yet fully realized, but the consummation is sure.

The Christian lives in an evil and a hostile world, but he
possesses that by which he can overcome the world;
and, when the destined end of the world comes, he is
safe, because he already possesses that which makes him a
member of the new community in the new age.

The Fellowship of the Church

John does more than move in the high realms of theology;
he has certain most practical things to say about the

Christian Church and the Christian life. No New Testament writer stresses more consistently and more strenuously the necessity of Christian fellowship. Christians, John was convinced, are not only bound to God, they are also bound to each other. When we walk in the light, we have fellowship with each other (I: 7). The man who claims to walk in the light, but who hates his brother, is in reality walking in darkness; it is the man who loves his brother who is in the light (2: 9-11). The Christian demand is that we should love our brother. The proof that a man has passed from darkness to light is the fact that he does love his brother. To hate one's brother man is in essence to be a murderer, as Cain was. If any man is able out of his fulness to help his brother's poverty, and does not do so, it is ridiculous for him to claim that the love of God dwells in him. The essence of religion is to believe on the name of the Lord Jesus Christ, and to love one another (3: 11-17, 23). God is love; and, therefore, the man who loves is kin to God. God has loved us, and that is the best reason why we should love each other (4: 7-12). If a man says that he loves God, and at the same time hates his brother, he is a liar. The command is that he who loves God must love his brother also (4: 20, 21).

It was John's conviction that the only way in which a man can prove that he loves God is by loving his fellowmen; and that that love must not be only a sentimental emotion, but that it must be a dynamic towards practical help.

The Righteousness of the Christian

No New Testament writer makes a stronger ethical demand than John does, and no New Testament writer more strongly condemns a so-called religion which fails to issue in ethical action. God is righteous and every one who knows God must reflect in his life the righteousness of God (2: 29). Whoever abides in Christ, and whoever

is born of God, does not sin; whoever does not do righteousness is not of God (3: 3-10); and the characteristic
of this righteousness is that it issues in love for the brethren
(3: 10, 11). We show our love to God and to men by
keeping God's commandments (5: 2). Whoever is born
of God does not sin (5: 18).

For John knowledge of God and obedience to God
must ever go hand in hand. It is by keeping His commandments that we prove that we really do know God. The
man who says that he knows God, and who does not keep
God's commandments is a liar (2: 3-5).

It is, in fact, this obedience which is the basis of effective
prayer. We receive what we ask of God, because we keep
His commandments, and do that which is pleasing in His
sight (3: 22).

The two marks which characterize genuine Christianity
are love of the brethren and obedience to the revealed
commandments of God.

Such, then, were the basic beliefs and demands with
which John confronted the heretics who were threatening
the Christian theology, and undermining the Christian
ethic.

The Destination of the Letter

There remains one problem at which we must look to
complete the introduction to this letter. There are certain
baffling problems in regard to its destination. The letter
itself gives us no clue as to where it was sent. Tradition
strongly connects it with Asia Minor, and especially with
Ephesus, where, according to tradition, John lived for
long. But there are certain other odd facts which somehow
have to be explained.

Cassiodorus says that the First Letter of John was
written *Ad Parthos*, which means To the Parthians; and
Augustine has a series of ten tractates written on The
Epistle of John *ad Parthos*, again To the Parthians. One
Geneva manuscript still further complicates the matter

by entitling the letter *Ad Sparthos*. There is no such word as *Sparthos*. There are two possible explanations of this impossible title. (i) Just possibly it is meant for *Ad Sparsos*, which would mean To the Christians scattered abroad; (ii) In Greek the title would be *Pros Parthous*. Now in the early manuscripts there was no space between the words; the words were all run together; and they were all written in capital letters. So, then, the title would run PROSPARTHOUS. If a scribe was writing to dictation, he could quite easily copy that as PROSSPARTHOUS, especially if he did not in any event know what the title meant. The title *Ad Sparthos* can be eliminated as a mere mistake.

But where did the title *Ad Parthous*, To the Parthians, come from? There is one possible explanation. 2 *John* does tell us of its destination. It is written to *The elect lady and her children* (2 *John* 1). Now let us turn to the end of 1 *Peter*. The Authorized Version has: " The Church that is at Babylon, elected together with you, saluteth you " (1 *Peter* 5: 13). No doubt the Authorized Version has correctly given the sense; but the reader of the New Testament will note that the phrase *the church that is* is printed in the Authorized Version in italic print. That, of course, means that it has no equivalent in the Greek. In the Greek there is, in fact, no actual mention of a *church* at all. This the Revised Standard Version accurately indicates: " She who is at Babylon, who is likewise chosen (elect), sends you greetings." As far as the Greek goes it would be perfectly possible, and indeed natural, to take that as referring, not to a *Church*, but to a *lady*. That is precisely what certain of the scholars in the very early Church did; they took the greeting at the end of 1 *Peter* to be a greeting from an elect lady whose home was in Babylon. Now we get this phrase *the elect lady* again in 2 *John*. It was easy to identify the two elect ladies, and to assume that 2 *John* was also written to Babylon. The natural title for the inhabitants of Babylon was Parthians, and hence we have the explanation of this title. The process went even further. The Greek for *the elect lady* is *hē elektē*. We have already seen that the early manuscripts were written all in capital letters; and it would be just possible to take *Elektē*, not as an adjective meaning *elect*, but as a proper name, *Elekta*; and this is, in fact, what Clement of Alexandria may have done, for we have information that he said that the Johannine letters were written to a certain Babylonian lady, Elekta by name, and to her children.

So, then, it may well be that the title *Ad Parthos*, To the Parthians, arose from a whole series of misunderstandings. *The elect one* in I *Peter* is quite certainly the Church, as the Authorized Version rightly saw. Moffatt translates: " Your sister Church in Babylon, elect like yourselves, salutes you." And, further, it is almost certain that in any event *Babylon* there stands for *Rome*, for the early writers identified Rome with Babylon, the great harlot, drunk with the blood of the saints (cp. *Revelation* 17: 5). Clearly, the title *Ad Parthos* has a most interesting history, but equally clearly it arose from an ingenious misunderstanding.

There is still one further complication. It is related that Clement of Alexandria referred to John's letters as being " written to virgins." On the face of it that is improbable, for that would not be a specially relevant title for the letters. How could that arise? The Greek for that would be *Pros Parthenous*. Now that closely resembles *Pros Parthous*; and, it so happens, John was regularly himself called *Ho Parthenos*, the Virgin, because he never married, and because of the purity of his life. This further title must have come from a still further confusion between the mistaken title, *Ad Parthos*, and John's own title, *Ho Parthenos*.

This is a case where we may take it that tradition is certainly right, and all the ingenious theories mistaken.

We may take it that these letters were written in Ephesus and to the surrounding Churches in Asia Minor; it is Ephesus with which John's name is always connected, and he is never mentioned in connection with Babylon. When John wrote, it would certainly be to the district where his writ ran, and that was Ephesus and the surrounding territory.

In Defence of the Faith

John wrote his great letter to meet a threatening situation and in defence of the faith. The heresies which he attacked are by no means altogether echoes of " old unhappy far off things and battles long ago." They are still beneath the surface, and sometimes they even still raise their heads. To study his letter will confirm us in the true faith, and will enable us to have a defence against that which would seduce us from it.

JOHN

THE PASTOR'S AIM

I *John* I: I-4

> What we are telling you about is that which was
> from the beginning, that which we heard, that which
> we saw with our eyes, that which we gazed upon,
> and which our hands touched. It is about the word
> of life that we are telling you. (And the life appeared
> to us, and we saw it, and testify to it; and we are
> now bringing you the message of this eternal life,
> which was with the Father and which appeared to us).
> It is about what we saw and heard that we are bringing
> the message to you, that you too may have fellowship
> with us, for our fellowship is with the Father, and
> with Jesus Christ, the Son. And we are writing these
> things to you that your joy may be completed.

EVERY man when he sits down to write a letter, or when
he rises to preach a sermon, has some object in view.
By his writing or his preaching he wishes to produce some
effect in the minds and in the hearts and in the lives of
those to whom his message is addressed. And here at the
very beginning of his letter John sets down his objects in
writing to his people.

(i) It is his wish to produce fellowship with men and
fellowship with God (verse 3). The aim of every preacher
and of every teacher must always be to bring men closer
to one another and closer to God. Any message which is
productive of schism and division is a false message.
The pastor's aim must always be to bring men into friendship with one another and into friendship with God. The
Christian message can be summed up in two great aims—
love for men, and love for God.

(ii) It is his wish to bring his people joy (verse 4). He
writes in order that their joy may be completed. The
essence of Christianity is joy. A message whose only
effect is to depress and to discourage those who hear it
has stopped halfway. It is quite true that often the aim

25

of the preacher and the teacher must be to awaken a godly sorrow which will lead to a true repentance. But after the sense of deep need has been awakened, men must be led to the one place where that need can be supplied; and, after the agonizing sense of sin has been produced, men must be led to the Saviour in whom sins are all forgiven. The ultimate note of the Christian message is joy.

(iii) To that end his aim is to set Jesus Christ before them. A great teacher always used to tell his students that their one aim as preachers must be " to speak a good word for Jesus Christ "; and it was said of another great saint that, wherever his conversation began it cut straight across country to Jesus Christ.

The simple fact is that if men are ever to find fellowship with one another and fellowship with God, and if they are ever to find true joy, they will find them nowhere else than in Jesus Christ.

THE PASTOR'S RIGHT TO SPEAK

I *John* I: I-4 (*continued*)

HERE at the very beginning of his letter John sets down his right to speak; and that right consists in one thing—in personal experience of Jesus Christ (verses 2 and 3).

(i) He says that he has *heard* Christ. Long ago Zedekiah had said to Jeremiah: " Is there any word from the Lord? " (*Jeremiah* 37: 17). What men are interested in is not someone's opinions and speculations and ingenious guesses, but in a word from the Lord. It was said of one great preacher that first he listened to God, and then he spoke to men; and it was said of John Brown of Haddington that, when he preached, he paused ever and again, as if listening for a voice. The true teacher is the man who has a message from Jesus Christ, because he has heard His voice.

(ii) He says that he has *seen* Christ. It is told of Alexander Whyte, the great preacher, that, after a great sermon, someone once said to him, " You preached today as if you had come straight from the presence." And Whyte answered, " Perhaps I did." It is quite true that we cannot see Christ in the flesh as John saw Him; but we can still see Him with the eye of faith.

> " And, warm, sweet, tender, even yet
>   A present help is He;
> And faith has still its Olivet,
>   And love its Galilee."

(iii) He says that he has *gazed* on Christ. What, then, is the difference between *seeing* Christ, and *gazing* upon Him? In the Greek the verb for *to see* is *horan*, and it means simply to see with physical sight and with the physical eye. The verb for *to gaze* is *theasthai*, and it means to gaze at someone, or at something, until a long look has grasped something of the meaning and the significance of that person or thing. So Jesus, speaking to the crowds of John the Baptist, asked: " What did you go out into the wilderness *to see* (*theasthai*)? " (*Luke* 7: 24); and in that word he describes how the crowds flocked out to gaze in wonder at John, and to ask themselves and each other who and what this man might be. Speaking of Jesus in the prologue to his gospel, John says, " We beheld His glory " (*John* I: 14). The verb is again *theasthai*, and the idea is not that of a passing glance, and a quick look, but of a steadfast searching gaze, which seeks to discover something of the meaning of the mystery of Christ. A quick glance at Christ never made a man a Christian, for the eyes of the Christian are fixed in wondering love on Jesus Christ.

(iv) He says that his hands actually *touched* Christ. Luke tells of how Jesus came back to His disciples, when He had risen from the dead, and said, " Behold my hands and feet, that it is I myself: handle me and see, for a spirit hath not flesh and bones as ye see me have " (*Luke* 24: 39). Here John is thinking of the people who were called the Docetists. These people were so spiritually-minded that they held that Jesus never at any time had a flesh and blood body, but that He was only a phantom appearing in human form. They refused to believe that the God, who was pure spirit, could ever soil Himself by taking human flesh and blood upon Himself. But John here insists that the Jesus he had known was, in truth, a man amongst men. To John there was nothing in all the world more dangerous—as we shall see—than to doubt that Jesus Christ was fully man.

THE PASTOR'S MESSAGE

I John I: I-4 (*continued*)

JOHN'S message was of Jesus Christ; and of Jesus he has three great things to say. First, he says that Jesus was *from the beginning*. That is to say, in Jesus Christ eternity entered time; in Jesus Christ the eternal God personally entered the world of men. Second, he insists that that entry into the world of men was a real entry; he insists that it was real manhood that God took upon Himself. God did not act the part of manhood; He in the most literal sense became man. Third, through that action there came to men the word of life, the word which is life, and which brings life, the word which can change death into life, and mere existence into real life. Here John calls the message of the Gospel the word of life. Again and again in the New Testament the gospel is called a *word*; and it is of the greatest interest to see the various connections in which this word is used.

(i) Oftener than anything else the gospel message is called the *word of God* (*Acts* 4: 3I; 6: 2, 7; II: I; I3: 5, 7, 44; I6: 32; *Philippians* I: I4; I *Thessalonians* 2: I3; *Hebrews* I3: 7; *Revelation* I: 2, 9; 6: 9; 20: 4). The message of the gospel is not a human discovery; it is not the product of the mind of man or of the thought of man. It is not human speculation. It is a word which comes from God and which tells of God. It is news of God which man could not have discovered for himself.

(ii) Very frequently the gospel message is called the *word of the Lord* (*Acts* 8: 25; 12: 24; 13: 49; 15: 35; 1 *Thessalonians* 1: 8; 2 *Thessalonians* 3: 1). It is not always certain whether the Lord is God or Jesus, but more often than not it is Jesus who is meant. The gospel is, therefore, the word of God which came to men through Jesus Christ. It is a message which God could have sent to men in no other way than through His Son.

(iii) Twice the gospel message is called the *word of hearing* (*logos akoēs*) (1 *Thessalonians* 2: 13; *Hebrews* 4: 2). That is to say, the gospel message depends on two things; it depends on a voice that is ready to speak it, and an ear that is ready to hear it.

(iv) The gospel message is the *word of the Kingdom* (*Matthew* 13: 19). The gospel message is the announcement of the kingship of God, and the summons to man to render to God the obedience which will make him a citizen of that kingdom.

(v) The gospel message is the *word of the gospel* (*Acts* 15: 7; *Colossians* 1: 5). The word *gospel* means *good news*; and the gospel is essentially good news to man about God.

(vi) The gospel is the *word of grace* (*Acts* 14: 3; 20: 32). The gospel is the good news which tells of God's generous and undeserved love for man; it is the news that man is not saddled with the impossible task of earning the love of God; he is freely offered that love.

(vii) The gospel is the *word of salvation* (*Acts* 13: 26). The gospel is the offer of forgiveness for past sin, and of strength and power to overcome sin in the future. It is the news of liberation from the penalty of sin and emancipation from the power of sin.

(viii) The gospel is the *word of reconciliation* (2 *Corinthians* 5: 19). It is the message that the lost relationship between man and God is restored in Jesus Christ. The gospel is that which breaks down the barrier between man and God which the sin of man had erected.

(ix) The gospel is the *word of the Cross* (I *Corinthians* I: 18). At the heart of the gospel there is the Cross on which there is shown to man the final proof of the forgiving, sacrificing, seeking love of God.

(x) The gospel is the *word of truth* (2 *Corinthians* 6: 7; *Ephesians* I: 13; *Colossians* I: 5; 2 *Timothy* 2: 15). With the coming of the gospel it is no longer necessary to guess and to grope, for Jesus Christ brought to us the truth about God.

(xi) The gospel is the *word of righteousness* (*Hebrews* 5: 13). It is by the power of the gospel that a man is enabled to break from the power of evil, and to rise to the righteousness which is pleasing in the sight of God.

(xii) The gospel is *the health-giving word* (2 *Timothy* I: 13; 2: 8). The gospel is the antidote which cures the poison of sin, and the medicine which defeats the disease of evil.

(xiii) The gospel is the *word of life* (*Philippians* 2: 16). It is through its power that a man is delivered from death and enabled to enter into a life which is life at its best.

GOD IS LIGHT

I *John* I: 5

> And this is the message which we have heard from Him, and which we pass on to you, that God is light, and there is no darkness in Him.

A MAN'S own character will necessarily be determined by the character of the god whom he worships; and, therefore, John begins by laying down the nature of the God, who is the God and Father of Jesus Christ, and whom all Christians worship. God, he says, is light, and there is no darkness in Him. What, then, does this statement that God is light tell us about God?

(i) It tells us that God is splendour and glory. There is

nothing so glorious as a blaze of light piercing the darkness. There is nothing so dazzling and nothing so unapproachable as burning and shining light. To say that God is light tells us of the sheer splendour and the radiant glory of God.

(ii) It tells us that God is self-revealing. Above all things light is seen; and it is the very characteristic of light to diffuse itself, so that it illumines the darkness which is round about it. To say that God is light is to say that there is nothing secretive, furtive, concealed about God. God wishes to be seen and to be known by men.

(iii) It tells us of the purity and the holiness of God. White light is the very symbol of radiant purity. There is none of the darkness which cloaks hidden evil in God; there are none of the shadows of the things which fear the light. That God is light speaks to us of the white purity and the stainless holiness of the all-holy God.

(iv) It tells us of the guidance of God. It is one of the great functions of light to guide and to make the road easy. It is a light which points the way to go; it is a light on the far horizon to which men will direct their steps in the dark. The road that is lit is the road that is plain. To say that God is light is to say that God is the God who offers His guidance for the footsteps of men.

(v) It tells us of the revealing quality in the presence of God. Light is the great revealer. Flaws which are hidden in the shade are obvious in the light. Soilings and stains which would never be seen in the shadows are obvious in the light. Light reveals the imperfections in any piece of workmanship or material. So the imperfections of life are seen in the presence of God. Whittier wrote:

> " Our thoughts lie open to Thy sight;
>   And naked to Thy glance;
> Our secret sins are in the light
>   Of Thy pure countenance."

We can never know either the depth to which life has fallen, or the height to which life can rise, until we see it in the revealing light of God.

THE HOSTILE DARK

I John 1: 5 (*continued*)

In God, says John, there is no darkness at all. All over the New Testament darkness stands for the very opposite of the Christian life; it stands for all that the Christian life is not, and that it must never be.

(i) Darkness stands for the Christless life. It represents the life that a man lived before he met Christ, or the life that he lives, if he strays away from Christ. John writes to his people that, now that Christ has come, the darkness is past and the true light shines (*I John* 2: 8). Paul writes to his Christian friends that once they were darkness, but now they are light in the Lord (*Ephesians* 5: 8). God, he says, has delivered us from the power of darkness, and has brought us into the Kingdom of His dear Son (*Colossians* 1: 13). Christians are not in darkness, for they are children of the day (*I Thessalonians* 5: 4). Those who follow Christ shall not walk in darkness, as others must, but they will have the light of life (*John* 8: 12). God has called the Christians out of darkness into His marvellous light (*I Peter* 2: 9). Always in the New Testament the dark stands for the Christless life, and for the life without God.

(ii) The dark is hostile to the light. In the prologue to his gospel, John writes, as it ought to be translated, that the light shines in the darkness, and the darkness has not overcome it (*John* 1: 5). It is the picture of the darkness seeking to strangle and to obliterate the light—but unable to overpower it. The dark and the light are natural and inevitable enemies.

(iii) The darkness stands for the ignorance of life apart from Christ. Jesus summons His friends to walk in the light, lest the darkness come upon them, for the man who walks in the darkness does not know where he is going (*John* 12: 35). Jesus is the light, and He has come that

32

those who believe in Him should not walk in darkness (*John* 12: 46). The dark stands for the ignorance, the blind groping, the essential lostness of life without Christ.

(iv) The darkness stands for the chaos of life without God. God, says Paul, thinking of God's first act of creation, commanded His light to shine out of the darkness (2 *Corinthians* 4: 6). Without God's light the world is a chaos, without form and void, a disordered emptiness, in which life has neither order nor sense.

(v) The darkness stands for the immorality of the Christless life. It is Paul's appeal to men that they should cast off the works of darkness (*Romans* 13: 12). Men, because their deeds are evil, loved the darkness rather than the light (*John* 3: 19). The darkness stands for the immorality of the Christless life, the life which is filled with things which seek the shadows, because they cannot stand the light of day.

(vi) The darkness is characteristically unfruitful. Paul speaks of the unfruitful works of darkness (*Ephesians* 5: 11). If growing things are despoiled of the light, their growth is stunted and arrested. The darkness is the Christless atmosphere in which no fruit of the Spirit will ever grow.

(vii) The darkness is connected with lovelessness and hate. If a man hates his brother, it is a sign that he walks in darkness (I *John* 2: 9-11). Love is sunshine, and hatred is the dark.

(viii) The dark is the abode of the enemies of Christ and the final goal of those who will not accept Him. The struggle of the Christian and of Christ is against the hostile rulers of the darkness of this world (*Ephesians* 6: 12). And consistent and rebellious sinners are those for whom the mist of darkness is reserved (2 *Peter* 2: 9; *Jude* 13). The darkness is the life which is separated from God.

THE NECESSITY OF WALKING IN THE LIGHT

I *John* I: 6, 7

> If we say that we have fellowship with Him, and if
> at the same time we walk in darkness, we lie and we
> are not doing the truth. But, if we walk in the light,
> as He is in the light, we have fellowship with each other,
> and the blood of Jesus Christ is steadily cleansing
> us from all sin.

HERE John is writing to counteract one heretical and
mistaken way of thought. There were those who claimed
to be specially intellectually and spiritually advanced,
but whose lives showed no sign of that. They claimed to
have advanced so far along the road of knowledge that for
them sin had ceased to matter. They claimed to be so
spiritual that sin was of no account at all. They claimed
to be so far on that for them the laws had ceased to exist.
It is on record that Napoleon once said that laws were
made for ordinary people, but were never meant for the
like of him. So these heretics claimed to be so far on that,
even if they did sin, it was of no importance whatsoever.
In later days Clement of Alexandria tells us that there
were heretics who said that it makes no difference how
a man lives. They said that nothing brought any risk to a
really spiritual man. Irenaeus tells us that they declared
that a truly spiritual man was quite incapable of ever
incurring any pollution or infection, no matter what kind
of deeds he did. These people in effect said that they had
risen to a height in which sin did not matter.

In answer to this John insists on certain things.

(i) He insists that to have fellowship with the God who
is light a man must walk in the light, and that, if he is
still walking in the moral and ethical darkness of the
Christless life, then he can have no fellowship with God.
This is precisely what the Old Testament had said centuries
before. God said, " Ye shall be holy; for I the Lord your God
am holy " (*Leviticus* 19: 2; cp. 20: 7, 26). He who would

34

find fellowship with God is committed to a life of goodness which reflects the goodness of God. C. H. Dodd writes: " The Church is a society of people, who, believing in a God of pure goodness, accept the obligation to be good like Him." This does not mean that a man must be perfect before he can have fellowship with God; if that were the case, all of us would be shut out. But it does mean that he will spend his whole life in the awareness of his obligations, in the effort to fulfil them, and in penitence when he fails. It will mean that he will never think that sin does not matter; it will mean that the nearer he comes to God, the more terrible sin will be to him.

(ii) He insists that these mistaken thinkers have the wrong idea of truth. He says that, if people who claim to be specially advanced still walk in darkness, they are not *doing* the truth. Exactly the same phrase is used in the Fourth Gospel, when it speaks of him that *doeth* the truth (*John* 3: 21). This means that for the Christian truth is never only intellectual truth; truth is always moral truth. Truth is not something which exercises only the mind; truth is something which exercises the whole personality. Truth is not the discovery of abstract truth; it is concrete living. Truth is not only thinking; it is also acting. The words which the New Testament uses along with *truth* are very significant. It speaks of *holding* the truth (*Romans* 1: 18); of *obeying* the truth (*Romans* 2: 8; *Galatians* 3: 7); of *walking according* to the truth (*Galatians* 2: 14; *3 John* 4); of *resisting* the truth (*2 Timothy* 3: 8); of *erring from* the truth (*James* 5: 19). There is such a thing as might be called " discussion circle Christianity." It is possible to look on Christianity as a series of intellectual problems to be solved, and it is possible to look on the Bible as a book about which illuminating information is to be amassed. But for the Christian Christianity is something to be followed, and the Bible is a book to be obeyed. It is perfectly possible for intellectual eminence and moral failure to go hand in hand.

For the Christian the truth is something first to be discovered and then to be obeyed.

THE TESTS OF TRUTH

I *John* I: 6, 7 (*continued*)

As John sees it there are two great tests of truth.

(i) Truth is the begetter of fellowship. If men are really walking in the light, they have fellowship one with another. No belief can be fully Christian, if it separates a man from his fellow-men. No Church can be exclusive and be the Church of Christ at one and the same time. Fellowship is the test of the reality of truth. That which destroys fellowship cannot be true.

(ii) He who really knows the truth is daily more and more cleansed from sin by the blood of Jesus Christ. The translation of the Authorized Version is correct enough here, but it can very easily be misunderstood. It runs: " The blood of Jesus Christ cleanseth us from all sin." That can be read as a general statement of a general principle. But that is not what it is; it is a statement of what ought to be happening in the particular individual life. The meaning is that all the time, day by day, constantly and consistently, the blood of Jesus Christ ought to be carrying out a cleansing process in the life of the individual Christian.

The word in the Greek for *to cleanse* is *katharizein*; that was originally a ritual word, and described the ritual and ceremonies and washings and so on which qualified a man to approach his gods. But the word, as religion developed, came to have a moral sense; and it describes the goodness which enables a man to enter into the presence of God. So what John is saying is, " If you really know what the sacrifice of Christ has done, if you are really experiencing its power, day by day you will be adding loveliness and holiness to your life, and day by day you will be becoming more fit to enter the presence of God.

Here indeed is a great conception. It looks on the sacrifice of Christ, not only as something which atones for the sin of the past, but as something which equips a man in holiness day by day.

Here is a tremendous conception of religion. True religion is that by which every day in life a man comes closer to his fellow-men and closer to God. Religion is that which produces fellowship with God and fellowship with men—and we can never have the one without the other.

THE THREEFOLD LIE

I *John* I: 6, 7 (*continued*)

FOUR times in his letter John bluntly accuses the false teachers of being liars; and the first of these occasions is in this present passage.

(i) Those who claim to have fellowship with the God, who is altogether light, and who yet themselves walk in the dark, are lying (verse 6). A little later he repeats this charge in a slightly different way. The man who says that he knows God, and who yet does not keep God's commandments, is a liar (I *John* 2: 4). Here John is laying down the blunt truth that the man whose practice does not fit his profession is in fact a liar. The man who says one thing with his lips and entirely another thing with his life is a liar. The man who contradicts his claims by his living is a liar. John is not thinking of the man who tries his hardest and who yet often fails. He is not thinking of the man who genuinely loves Jesus Christ, and who is bitterly conscious that his life is very far from showing the love which he feels. " A man," said H. G. Wells, " may be a very bad musician, and may yet be passionately in love with music "; and a man may be very conscious of his failure, and may yet be passionately in love with Christ and the way of Christ. John is thinking of the man who makes the highest possible claims to knowledge, to intellectual eminence, and to spirituality, and who yet deliberately allows himself things which he well knows are forbidden. The man who professes to love Christ, and who yet deliberately disobeys Him, is guilty of a lie.

(ii) The man who denies that Jesus is the Christ is a liar (I *John* 2: 22). Here is something which runs through the whole New Testament. The ultimate and final test of any man is his reaction to Jesus Christ. The ultimate and soul-searching question which Jesus asks every man is: "Whom say ye that I am?" (*Matthew* 16: 13). A man confronted with Christ cannot but see the greatness that is there; and, if he denies it, he is a liar, refusing to admit even to himself the pre-eminence of Christ.

(iii) The man who says that he loves God, and who at the same time hates his brother is a liar (I *John* 4: 20). Love of God and hatred of man cannot exist in the same person. If a man hates his fellow-men, if he is at variance with any one of them, if there is bitterness in his heart towards any man, that is the proof that he does not really and truly and fully love God. All our protestations of love to Christ and love to God are useless, if in our hearts there is hatred towards any man.

THE SINNER'S SELF-DECEPTION

I *John* 1: 8-10

> If we say that we have no sin, we deceive ourselves, and the truth is not in us. If we confess our sins, we can rely on Him in His righteousness to forgive us our sins, and to make us clean from all unrighteousness.
> If we say that have not sinned, we make Him a liar, and His word is not in us.

IN this passage John describes and condemns two further mistaken ways of thought.

(i) There is, first, the man who says that he has no sin. That may mean either of two things. It may describe the man who says that he has no responsibility for his sin.

It is easy enough to find all kinds of defences behind which to seek to hide. We may blame our sins on our heredity, on our environment, on our temperament, on our physical condition. We may claim that someone misled us and that we were led astray. It is characteristic of us all that we seek to shuffle out of the responsibility for sin. Or, this may describe the man who claims that sin has no effect upon him; who says that he can sin and take no harm; who insists that he can take his pleasures, and, if need be, make his mistakes and emerge none the worse for them. It is John's insistence that, when a man has sinned, defences and excuses and self-justifications are completely irrelevant. The only thing which will meet the situation is humble and pentitent confession to God, and, if need be, to men.

Then John says a very surprising thing. He says that we can depend on God *in his righteousness* to forgive us, if we confess our sins. On the face of it, we might well have thought that God in His righteousness would have been much more likely to condemn than to forgive. But the point is that God, just because He is righteous, never breaks His word; and Scripture is full of the promise of mercy to the man who comes to God with the broken, the contrite, and the penitent heart. God has promised that He will never despise the penitent heart; God will not break His word; and, if we humbly and sorrowfully confess our sins, God will forgive. The very fact of making excuses and seeking for self-justification debars us from forgiveness, because it debars us from penitence; the very fact of humble confession opens the door to forgiveness, for the man with the penitent heart can claim the promises of God.

(ii) There is, second, the man who says that he has not in actual fact sinned. That attitude is not nearly so uncommon as we might think. There are any number of people who do not really believe that they have sinned. They rather resent being called sinners. Their mistake is that they think of sin as the kind of thing which everyone sees and which gets into the newspapers; and they forget that sin is *hamartia*; and *hamartia* literally means a *missing of the target*. To fail to be as good a father, mother, wife, husband, son, daughter, workman, person as we might have been is to sin; and that includes and involves us all.

In any event the man who says that he has not sinned, is in effect doing nothing less than call God a liar, for God has said that all have sinned.

So John condemns the man who claims that he is so far advanced in knowledge and in the spiritual life, that sin for him has ceased to matter; he condemns the man who evades the responsibility for his sin, or who holds that sin has no effect upon him; he condemns the man who has never even realized that he is a sinner. The essence of the Christian life is, first, to realize our sin; and then to go to God for that forgiveness which can wipe out the past, and for that cleansing which can make the future new.

A PASTOR'S CONCERN

I *John* 2: 1, 2

> My little children, I am writing these things to you that you may not sin. But, if anyone does sin, we have one who will plead our cause to the Father, Jesus Christ the righteous. For He is the propitiating sacrifice for our sins, and not for ours only, but also for the whole world.

SURELY the first thing to note in this passage is the sheer affection of it. John begins with the address, " My little children." Both in Latin and in Greek diminutives have a special affection in them. Diminutives are words which are used, as it were, with a caress. When John writes, he is a very old man; he must have been, in fact, the last survivor of his generation, maybe the last man alive who had walked and talked with Jesus in the days of His flesh. So often age gets out of sympathy with youth; so often in age there is an un-understanding severity, even an impatient irritableness with the new ways and the lax ways of the younger generation. But it is not so in John; in him, in his old age, there is nothing but tenderness for those who are his little children in the faith. Again, he is writing to tell them that they must not sin. But he does not scold; there is no cutting edge in his voice; he does not deal in invective and lash them with his tongue. He seeks to love them into goodness. In this opening address there is the yearning, affectionate tenderness of a pastor for his people, whom he has known for long in all their wayward foolishness, and whom he still loves.

As we have said, his object in writing is that they may not sin. There is a two-fold connection of thought here, a connection with what has gone before and a connection with what comes afterwards. There is a two-fold danger that they may indeed think lightly of sin. John says two things about sin. First, he has just said that sin is universal; no man escapes it; anyone who says that he has not sinned is a liar, and the truth is not in him. Everyone is involved in the fact of sin. Second, although that is so, there is forgiveness of sins, through what Jesus Christ has done, and still does, for men. Now it would be possible to use both these statements as an excuse to think lightly of sin. If all have sinned, why make a fuss about it, and what is the use of struggling against something which is in any event an inevitable part of the human situation? Again, if there is forgiveness of sins, why worry about it? If Jesus Christ has won forgiveness for men, and if He is there to plead our cause with God, then does sin after all matter so very much?

In face of that, John, as Westcott points out, has two things to say?

First, the Christian is one who has come to know God; and the inevitable accompaniment of knowledge must be *obedience*. We shall return to this more fully; but at the moment we note that to know God and to obey God must, as John sees it, necessarily be twin parts of the same experience.

Second, the man who claims that he abides in God (verse 6) and in Jesus Christ, must necessarily live the same kind of life as Jesus lived. That is to say, union with Christ necessarily involves *imitation* of Christ. So John lays down his two great ethical principles; knowledge involves obedience, and union involves imitation; and, therefore, in the Christian life there can never be any inducement to think lightly of sin.

JESUS CHRIST THE PARACLETE

1 *John* 2: 1, 2 (*continued*)

IT will take us some considerable time to deal with these two verses, for there are hardly any other two verses in the New Testament which so succinctly set out the work of Christ.

Let us first set out the problem. It is clear that Christianity is above all an ethical religion; that is what John is concerned above all to stress. But it is also clear that man is so often an ethical failure. Confronted with the demands of God, man admits them and accepts them— and then universally fails to keep them. Here, then, there is a barrier erected between man and God. How can man, the sinner, ever enter into the presence of God, the all-holy? The problem is how the sin of man can ever find fellowship with the holiness of God. That problem is solved in Jesus Christ. And in this passage John uses two great words about Jesus Christ, which we must study and understand, not simply to acquire intellectual knowledge, but to understand, and thus to enter into, the benefits of Christ.

He calls Jesus Christ our *Advocate with the Father*. The word is *paraklētos*, and it is the word which in the Fourth Gospel the Authorized Version translates *Comforter*. It is so great a word, and has behind it so great a thought, that we must examine it in all detail. The word *paraklētos* comes from the verb *parakalein*. There are occasions when *parakalein* means *to comfort*. It is, for instance, used with that meaning in *Genesis* 37: 35, where it is said that all Jacob's sons and daughters rose up to *comfort* him at the loss of Joseph; in *Isaiah* 61: 2, where it is said that the function of the prophet is to *comfort* all that mourn; and in *Matthew* 5: 4, where it is said that those who mourn will be *comforted*.

But that is neither the commonest nor the most literal sense of the verb *parakalein*; the commonest sense of *parakalein* is *to call someone to one's side* in order to use that person in some way as a helper and a counsellor. In ordinary Greek that is a very common usage. Xenophon (*Anabasis* 1.6.5) tells how Cyrus *summoned* (*parakalein*) Clearchos into his tent to be his counsellor, for Clearchos was a man who was held in the highest honour by Cyrus and by the Greeks. Aeschines, the Greek orator, protests against his opponents calling in Demosthenes. his great rival, and says: " Why need you *call* Demosthenes *to your support?* To do so is *to call in* a rascally rhetorician to cheat the ears of the jury? " (*Against Ctesiphon* 200). So, then, *parakalein* regularly and naturally means to call someone to one's side for help and counsel and support.

Paraklētos itself is a word which is passive in its form, and it literally means *someone who is called to one's side*; but since it is always the reason for the calling in that is uppermost in the mind, the word, although passive in form, has an active sense, and it comes to mean a helper, a supporter, and, above all, a witness in someone's favour, a supporter of someone's cause, an advocate in someone's defence. Here again it is a very common word in ordinary secular Greek. Demosthenes (*De Fals. Leg.* I) speaks of the importunities and the party spirit of *advocates* (*paraklētoi*), serving the ends of private ambition instead of public good. Diogenes Laertius (4: 50) tells of a caustic saying of the philosopher Bion. A very talkative person sought his help in some matter. Bion said, " I will do

43

what you want, if you will only send someone to me to plead your case (i.e., send a *paraklētos*), and stay away yourself." When Philo is telling the story of Joseph and his brethren, he says that, when Joseph forgave them for the wrong that they had done him, he said, " I offer you an amnesty for all that you did to me; you need no other *paraklētos* " (*Life of Joseph* 40). That is to say, they did not need anyone to plead for mercy for them. Philo tells how the Jews of Alexandria were being oppressed by a certain governor and determined to take their case to the emperor. " We must find," they said, " a more powerful *paraklētos, advocate*, by whom the Emperor Gaius will be brought to a favourable disposition towards us " (*Leg. in Flacc.* 968 B).

So common was this word that it came into other languages just as it stood. Other languages did not have a translation for it; they simply adopted the word. In the New Testament itself the Syriac, Egyptian, Arabic, and Ethiopic versions all keep the word *paraklētos* just as it stands. The Jews especially adopted the word, and used it in this sense of *advocate*, someone to plead one's cause. They used it as the opposite of the word *accuser*. So the Rabbis had a saying about what would happen in the day of God's judgment. " The man who keeps one commandment of the Law has gotten to himself one *paraklētos*; the man who breaks one commandment of the Law has gotten to himself one accuser." They said, " If a man is summoned to court on a capital charge, he needs powerful *paraklētoi* (the plural of the word) to save him; repentance and good works are his *paraklētoi* in the judgment of God." " All the righteousness and mercy which an Israelite does in this world are great peace and great *paraklētoi* between him and his father in heaven." So they said that the sin-offering is a man's *paraklētos* before God; the sin-offering pleads a man's cause with God.

So the word came into the Christian ordinary vocabulary. The word could be used quite literally. In the days of the persecutions and the martyrs, a Christian pleader called Vettius Epagathos ably pled the case of those who were accused of being Christians. " He was an advocate (*paraklētos*) for the Christians, for he had the Advocate within himself, even the Spirit " (Eusebius, *The Ecclesiastical History* 5: 1). The Letter of Barnabas (20) speaks of evil men who are the *advocates* of the wealthy, and the unjust judges of the poor. The writer of Second Clement asks: " Who shall be your *paraklētos* if it is not clear that your works are righteous and holy? " (2 *Clement* 6: 9).

A *paraklētos* has been defined as " one who lends his presence to his friends." More than once in the New Testament there is this great and precious conception of Jesus as the friend, the advocate and the defender of man. In a military court-martial the officer who defends the soldier who is under accusation is called the prisoner's friend. Jesus is our friend. Paul writes of that Christ who is at the right hand of God, and " who also maketh intercession for us " (*Romans* 8: 34). The writer of the Letter to the Hebrews speaks of Jesus Christ as the one who " ever liveth to make intercession " for men (*Hebrews* 7: 25); and he also speaks of Him as " appearing in the presence of God for us " (*Hebrews* 8: 24).

The tremendous thing about Jesus is that Jesus has never lost His interest in, or His love for, men. We are not to think of Him as having gone through His life upon the earth, and His death upon the Cross, and then being finished with men. He still bears His concern for men upon His heart; He still pleads for men; Jesus Christ is the prisoner's friend for all men.

JESUS CHRIST THE PROPITIATION

I John 2: 1, 2 (*continued*)

JOHN goes on to say that Jesus is *the propitiation for our sins*. The word is *hilasmos*. This is a more difficult picture for us fully to grasp and to understand. The picture of the *advocate* is a universal picture, for all men have the experience of a friend who comes to their aid and to their support. But the picture in *propitiation* comes from *sacrifice*, and is more natural to the Jewish mind than it is to ours. To understand it we must get at the basic ideas behind it.

The great aim of all religion is fellowship with God; the great aim of religion is to know God as friend, and to enter with joy, and not with fear, into His presence. It therefore follows that the supreme problem of religion is sin, for it is sin that interrupts fellowship with God; and it is sin which makes it impossible to enter into the presence of God. It is to meet that problem that all sacrifice arises. By sacrifice fellowship with God is restored. We never think of religion aright unless we think of it in terms of personal relationship. The aim of religion is a perfect personal relationship with God; sin interrupts that relationship; and sacrifice is designed to restore that relationship when it is interrupted. So the Jews offered, night and morning, the sin-offering in the Temple. That was the offering, not for any particular sin, but for man as a sinner; and so long as the Temple lasted that offering was made to God in the morning and in the evening. The Jews offered their trespass-offerings to God; these were the offerings for particular sins, and for particular breaches of the Law. The Jews had their Day of Atonement, whose ritual was designed to atone for *all* sins, sins known and sins unknown, sins of which men were conscious and sins of which they were not conscious. It is with that background that we must come at this picture of propitiation.

As we have said, the Greek word for *propitiation* is *hilasmos*, and the corresponding verb is *hilaskesthai*. This verb has three meanings. (i) When it is used with a man as the subject, it means *to placate*, or *to pacify* someone who has been injured or offended or insulted, and especially to placate a god. It is to bring a sacrifice, or to perform a ritual, whereby a god, offended by sin, is placated and pacified. (ii) But if the subject of the verb is *God*, then the verb means *to forgive*, for then the meaning is that God Himself provides the means whereby the lost relationship between Him and men is restored. (iii) But it has a third meaning, which is allied with the first meaning. The verb can, and often does mean, to perform some deed, some ritual, by which the taint of guilt is removed. A man sins; he thereby at once acquires the taint of sin. He needs something, which, to use C. H. Dodd's metaphor, will *disinfect* him from that taint, and which will enable him once again to enter into the presence of God. In that sense *hilaskesthai* means, not to propitiate, but to *expiate*. The word means, not so much to pacify and to placate God, as to disinfect man from the taint of sin, and thereby to fit him again to enter into fellowship with God.

Now when John says that Jesus is the *hilasmos* for our sins, he is, we think, bringing all these different senses into one. Jesus is the person through whom guilt for past sin and defilement from present sin are removed. Through what He did the penalty is remitted, the guilt is removed, the defilement is taken away. He brings us forgiveness for the sins which we have committed; and He clothes us with a new purity in which our defilement is taken away. The great basic truth behind this word is that it is through Jesus Christ that man's fellowship with God is first restored, and then maintained.

We note one other thing. As John sees it, this work of Jesus was carried out, not only for us, but for the whole world. There is in the New Testament a strong line of thought in which the universality of the salvation of God is stressed. God so loved *the world* that He sent His Son (*John* 3: 16). Jesus is confident that, if He is lifted up, He will draw *all men* unto Him (*John* 12: 32). God is the God who will have *all men* to be saved (1 *Timothy* 2: 4). He would be a bold man who would set limits to the grace and love of God, or to the effectiveness of the work and sacrifice of Jesus Christ. Truly the love of God is broader

and wider than the measures of man's mind; and in the
New Testament itself there are hints of a salvation whose
arms are as wide as the world.

THE TRUE KNOWLEDGE OF GOD

1 *John* 2: 3-6

> And it is by this that we know that we have come to
> know Him—if we keep His commandments.   He
> who says, " I have come to know Him," and who
> does not keep His commandments is a liar, and the
> truth is not in such a man.   The love of God is truly
> perfected in any man who keeps His word.   This
> is the way in which we know that we are in Him.
> He who claims that he abides in Him ought himself
> to live the same kind of life as He lived.

THIS passage deals in phrases and thoughts which were
very familiar to the ancient world.   The ancient world
talked much about *knowing God*, and about *being in God*.
And it is important that we should see wherein the difference
lay between the pagan world in all its greatness and
Judaism and Christianity.   To know God, to abide in God,
to have fellowship with God has always been the quest
of the human spirit, for Augustine was right when he
said that God had made men for Himself and that they were
restless until they found their rest in Him.   We may say
that in the ancient world there were three lines of thought
in regard to knowing God.

(i) In the great classical age of Greek thought and
literature, in the sixth and fifth centuries, before Christ,
the Greeks were convinced that they could arrive at God
by the sheer process of intellectual reasoning and argument
and thought.   In *The World of the New Testament*, T. R.
Glover has a chapter on *The Greek* in which he brilliantly
and vividly sketches the character of the Greek mind in
its greatest days.   In those days the Greek glorified the
intellect.   " A harder and more precise thinker than Plato
it will be difficult to discover," said Marshall Macgregor.

48

Xenophon tells how Socrates had a conversation with a young man. " How do you know that? " asked Socrates. " Do you know it, or are you guessing? " The young man had to say, " I am guessing." " Very well," answered Socrates, " when we are done with guessing, and when we know, shall we talk about it then? " Guesses were not good enough for the Greek.

To the classical Greek curiosity was not a fault; it was the greatest of the virtues; for curiosity was the mother of philosophy. Glover writes of the outlook of these Greeks: " Everything must be examined; all the world is the proper study of man; there is no question which it is wrong for man to ask; nature in the long run must stand and deliver; God too must explain Himself, for did He not make man so? " So for the Greeks of the great classical age the way to God was by the intellect. Now it has to be noted that an intellectual approach to religion is not necessarily ethical at all. If religion is a series of mental problems, if God is the goal at the end of intense mental activity, then religion becomes something not very unlike the higher mathematics. It becomes intellectual satisfaction, and not moral action. And the plain fact is that many of the great Greek thinkers were not specially good men, for even men so great as Plato and Socrates saw no sin in homosexuality. A man could know God in the intellectual sense, but that did not presuppose that he was a good man.

(ii) The later Greeks, in the immediate background time of the New Testament, sought to find God in emotional experience. The characteristic religious phenomenon of these days was the Mystery Religions. In any view of the history of religion the Mystery Religions are an amazing feature. Their aim was union with the divine. They were all in the form of passion plays. They were all founded on the story of some god who lived, and suffered terribly, and died a cruel death, and rose again. The initiate was given a long course of instruction; he was made to practise asting and ascetic discipline. He was worked up to an ntense pitch of expectation and emotional sensitivity. He was then allowed to come to a passion play in which the story of the suffering, dying, and rising god was played out on the stage. Everything was designed to heighten the emotional atmosphere. There was cunning lighting; sensuous music; perfumed incense; a marvellous liturgy. In this atmosphere the story was played out, and the worshipper identified himself with the experiences of the god until he could cry out: " I am thou, and thou art I "; until he shared the god's suffering and also shared his victory and immortality.

This was not so much *knowing* God as *feeling* God. But this was a highly emotional experience, and, as such, it was necessarily transient. It was a kind of religious drug. It quite definitely found God in an abnormal experience, and its aim was to escape from ordinary life.

(iii) Lastly, there was the Jewish way of knowing God, which is closely allied with the Christian way. To the Jew knowledge of God came by revelation from God. The knowledge of God came, not by man's speculation, not by an exotic experience of emotion; but by God's own revelation to man. Now the God who revealed Himself was a holy God, and His holiness brought the obligation to His worshipper to be holy too. A. E. Brooke says, " John can conceive of no real knowledge of God which does not issue in obedience." Knowledge of God can only be proved by obedience to God; and knowledge of God can only be gained by obedience to God. C. H. Dodd says, " To know God is to experience His love in Christ, and to return that love in obedience."

Here was John's problem. In the Greek world he was faced with people who saw God as an intellectual exercise, and who could say, " I know God," without being conscious of any ethical obligation whatever. In the Greek world he was faced with people who had had an emotional experience and who could say, " I am in God, and God is in me," and who yet did not see God in terms of commandments at all.

John is determined to lay it down quite unmistakably and without compromise that the only way in which we can show that we know God is by obedience to God, and the only way we can show that we have union with Christ is by imitation of Christ. Christianity is the religion which offers the greatest privilege, and which brings with it the greatest obligation.   In Christianity intellectual effort and emotional experience are not neglected—far from it—but they must combine to issue in moral action.

THE COMMANDMENT WHICH IS OLD AND NEW

I *John* 2: 7, 8

> Beloved, it is not a new commandment which I am writing to you, but an old commandment, which you had from the beginning; the old commandment is the word which you heard.   Again, it is a new commandment which I am writing to you, a thing which is true in Him and in you, because the darkness is passing away, and the light is now shining.

Beloved is John's favourite address to his people (cp. 3: 2, 21; 4: 1, 7; 3 *John* 1, 2, 5, 11). The whole accent of John's writing is love.   As Westcott puts it: " St. John, while enforcing the commandment of love, gives expression to it." The supreme motive in John's heart is love. There is something very lovely here. So much of this letter is a warning;   and there are parts of it which are rebuke. When we are warning people, or, when we are rebuking them, it is so easy to become coldly critical; it is so easy to scold; it is so easy to allow the accent of anger to be the accent of our voices; it is even possible to take a cruel pleasure in seeing people wince under the lash of rebuke and the threat of warning.   But, even when he has to say hard things, the accent of John's voice is always love.   John had learned the lesson which every parent,

every preacher, every teacher, every leader must learn;
he had learned to speak the truth in love.

John speaks here about a commandment which is
at one and the same time an old commandment and a new
commandment. What is the commandment of which
John speaks? There are some who would take it as referring
to the commandment in verse 6, the implied commandment that he who abides in Jesus Christ must live the
same kind of life as his Master lived. But almost certainly
John is thinking of the words of Jesus in the Fourth Gospel:
" A new commandment I give unto you, That ye love
one another; as I have loved you, that ye also love one
another " (*John* 13: 34). In what sense was that commandment both old and new?

(i) It was old in the sense that it is already there in
the Old Testament. Did not the Law say, " Thou shalt
love thy neighbour as thyself "? (*Leviticus* 19: 18). The
commandment already stands there in the ancient Law.
It was old in the sense that this was not the first time that
John's hearers had heard it. From the very first day of
their entry into the Christian life they had been taught
that this law of love must be the law of their lives. This
commandment went a long way back in history, and a
long way back in the lives of those to whom John was
speaking.

(ii) But this commandment was new in that it had been
raised to a completely new standard in the life of Jesus—
and it was as Jesus had loved men that men were now to
love each other. It could well be said that men did not
really know what love was until they saw it in Jesus Christ.
In every sphere of life it is perfectly possible for a thing
to be old, in the sense that it has for long existed; and
yet to reach a completely new standard in someone's
performance of it. A game may be a new game to a man
when he has seen some master of it play it. A piece of
music may be a new thing to a man when he has heard
some great orchestra play it under the baton of some

master conductor. Even a dish of food can become a new thing to a man when he tastes it after it has been prepared by a cook with a genius for cooking. An old thing can become a new experience in the hands of a master. And love became new in Jesus Christ. In Jesus love became new in two directions.

(a) In Jesus love became new in *the extent to which it reached*. In Jesus love reached out *to the sinner*. To the orthodox Jewish Rabbi the sinner was a person whom God wished to destroy. " There is joy in heaven," they said, " when one sinner is obliterated from the earth." But Jesus was the friend of outcast men and women, and of sinners, and was sure that there was joy in heaven when one sinner comes home. In Jesus love reached out *to the Gentile*. As the Rabbis saw it: " The Gentiles were created by God to be fuel for the fires of Hell." But in Jesus, God so loved *the world* that He gave His Son. Love became new in Jesus because He widened its boundaries until there were none outside its embrace.

(b) In Jesus love became new in *the lengths to which it would go*. No lack of response, nothing that men could ever do to Him, could turn Jesus' love to hate. He could even pray for the mercy of God on those who were nailing Him to His Cross.

The commandment to love was old in the sense that men had known of it for long; but the commandment to love was new, because in Jesus Christ love reached a standard which it had never reached before, and it was by that standard that men were bidden to love.

THE DEFEAT OF THE DARK

I *John* 2: **7,** 8 *(continued)*

JOHN goes on to say that this commandment, the commandment of love, is true in Jesus Christ, and true in the people to whom he is writing. To John, as we have seen, truth was not something to be grasped only with the mind; truth was something to be done. Truth to John is not only a mental exercise; it is also a practical way of life. What John means is this: the commandment to love one another is the highest truth; in Jesus Christ we can see that commandment in all the glory of its fulness; in Him that commandment is true; and in the Christian we can see that commandment, not in the fulness of its truth, but we can see it coming true. Here, then, we have the great conception that the Christian is a man in whom Christ's commandment of love is daily becoming more and more true. For John, Christianity is progress in love.

John then goes on to say that the light is shining and the darkness is passing away. Clearly this must be read in its present context. There is one interesting thing here. It is clear that for John we are living in the midst of a process. By the time that John wrote, at the end of the first century, men's ideas were changing. In the very early days they had looked for the Second Coming of Jesus as a sudden and shattering event within their own life time. That did not happen. They did not abandon the hope, but out of experience they changed it. And to John the Second Coming of Christ was not one sudden, dramatic event; it was a process in which the darkness was steadily being defeated by the light.

Any process must have a consummation; a process involves and implies a goal; without a goal it cannot be a process at all. For John the end of the process is a world in which the darkness is defeated and the light is triumphant.

But in this passage, and in the succeeding verses 10 and 11, with what are the light and the dark identified? The light is identified with love and the dark is identified with hate. That is to say, the end of this process is a world where love reigns supreme, and where hate is banished for ever. That is to say, the end of the process is a world in which the new commandment of Jesus Christ is the only law. Christ has come in the individual heart, when a man's whole being is ruled by love; and Christ will have come in the world of men, when all men submit to, and obey, Christ's commandment of love. The coming of Jesus and the reign of Jesus Christ are identical with the coming of love and the reign of love.

LOVE AND HATE, AND LIGHT AND DARK

I *John* 2: 9-11

> He who says that he is in the light, and who at the same time hates his brother, is still in the darkness. He who loves his brother abides in the light, and there is nothing in him which makes him stumble. He who hates his brother is in the darkness, and he is walking in darkness, and he does not know where he is going, because the darkness has blinded his eyes.

THE first thing which strikes us about this passage is the way in which John sees personal relationships in terms of black and white. In regard to our brother man, it is a case of either love or hate. There is no halfway stage; as John sees it, there is no such thing as neutrality in personal relationships. As Westcott put it: " Indifference is impossible; there is no twilight in the spiritual world." A man is either walking in the light of love or in the darkness of hatred.

It is further to be noted that what John is speaking about is a man's attitude to his *brother*, that is, to the man next door, to the man beside whom he lives and works, to the man with whom he necessarily comes into contact every day. There is a kind of Christian attitude which enthusiastically preaches love to the heathen, in lands across the sea, but which has never got on to any kind of terms of fellowship with its next door neighbour. There is a kind of person who preaches love for other nations, and who has never succeeded in living at peace within his own family circle. John insists on love for our brother, for the man with whom we are in daily contact all the time. As A. E. Brooke puts it: this is not " vapid philosophy, or a pretentious cosmopolitanism "; it is immediate and practical.

John was perfectly right when he drew his sharp distinction between light and dark, love and hate, without shades and halfway stages. Our brother means something to us; the question is *what*? He cannot be disregarded, because he is part of the landscape: the question is *how* do we regard him? We can regard our fellow-men in various ways.

(i) We may regard our brother man as *negligible*. We can make all our plans without taking him into our calculations at all. We can live on the principle, or the assumption, that his need and his sorrow and his welfare and his salvation have nothing to do with us. A man can be so self-centred—often quite unconsciously—that in his world no one matters except himself.

(ii) We may regard our brother with *contempt*. We may regard him as a fool in comparison with our intellectual attainment, as one whose opinions are to be brushed aside, and who has no right to speak. We may regard him as totally unimportant in comparison with our dignity and our prestige. We may regard him much as the Greeks regarded slaves, as a necessary lesser breed, useful enough for the menial duties of life, but not to be compared with ourselves.

(iii) We may regard our brother man as a *nuisance*. We may feel that unfortunately law and convention have given him a certain claim upon us, but that claim is nothing more than an unfortunate necessity. Thus a man may regard any gift he has to make to charity, any tax he has to pay for social welfare for the less fortunate, as a nuisance. There are those who in their heart of hearts regard those who are in poverty, in sickness, in misfortune, those who are under-privileged, as merely a nuisance.

(iv) We may regard our fellow-man as an *enemy*. If we regard competition as the law and principle of life, that is bound to be so. Every other man in the same profession or trade is a potential competitor, and, therefore, a potential enemy; he is someone who may get into our way, and who must be removed out of our way.

(v) We may regard our brother man as our *brother*. We may regard him with love. His needs are our needs; his interests are our interests; to serve him is why we came into the world at all; and to be in fellowship with him is the true joy of life.

Somewhere into these categories we fit, and that is simply to say that in principle we either love or hate our brother man.

THE EFFECT OF LOVE AND HATE

1 John 2: 9-11 (*continued*)

BUT John has something further to say. As he sees it, our attitude to our brother man has an effect not only on him, but also on ourselves.

(i) If we love our brother, we are walking in the light, and there is nothing in us which causes us to stumble. The Greek could mean that, if we love our brother, there is nothing in us which causes *others* to stumble, and, of course, that would be perfectly true. But it is much more likely that John is saying that, if we love our brother, there is nothing in us which causes *ourselves* to stumble. That is to say, love is the one thing which enables us to make progress in the spiritual life, and hatred is the one thing which makes progress impossible. When we think of it, that is perfectly obvious. If God is love, and if the new commandment of Christ is love, then love is the one thing which brings us nearer to men and nearer to God, and hatred is the one thing which separates us from men and separates us from God. Hatred stunts a man's growth, because it comes between him and God, and him and his fellow-men. We ought always to remember that he who has in his heart hatred, bitterness, resentment, the unforgiving spirit, can never grow up in the spiritual life.

(ii) John goes on to say that he who loves his brother walks in darkness and does not know where he is going, because the darkness has blinded him. That is to say, hatred makes a man blind. Again this is perfectly obvious. When a man has hatred and bitterness in his heart, clearly his powers of judgment are obscured. He cannot take a wise decision; he cannot see any issue clearly. It is no uncommon sight to see in any group of people a man opposing a good and useful proposal, because he dislikes, or has quarrelled with, the man who made it. Again and again progress in some scheme or Church or association is held up because of personal animosities. No man is fit to give a verdict on anything while he has hatred in his heart; and no man can rightly direct his own life when hatred dominates him.

Love enables a man to walk in the light; hatred leaves him in the dark—even if he does not realise that it is so.

REMEMBERING WHO WE ARE

I *John* 2: 12-14

> I am writing to you, little children,
>> Because your sins are forgiven you through His name.
> I am writing to you, fathers,
>> Because you have come to know Him who is from the beginning.
> I am writing to you, young men,
>> Because you have overcome the Evil One.
> I have written to you, little ones,
>> Because you have come to know the Father.
> I have written to you, fathers,
>> Because you have come to know Him who is from the beginning.
> I have written to you, young men,
>> Because you are strong,
>> And the word of God abides in you,
>> And you have overcome the Evil One.

THIS is a very lovely passage, and yet for all its beauty it has its problems of interpretation, if we are to arrive at its meaning. We may begin to study it by noting two things which are certain.

First, as to its form. This passage is not exactly poetry, but it is certainly poetical, and strongly rhythmical; and, therefore, it is to be interpreted as poetry ought to be.

Second, as to its contents John has been warning his people of the perils of the dark and the necessity of walking in the light; and now he says to them that in every case their best defence is to remember what they are and what has been done for them. No matter who they are, their sins have been forgiven; no matter who they are, they know Him who is from the beginning; no matter who they are, they have the strength which can face and overcome the Evil One. The best defence of the Christian against sin is to remember who and what he is, and what God has done for him in Jesus Christ. When Nehemiah was urged to seek a cowardly safety, his answer was: "Should such a man as I flee?" (*Nehemiah* 6: 11). And when the Christian is tempted, his answer may well be: "Should such a man as I stoop to this folly, or stain my hands with this evil?" The man who is a forgiven man, the man who knows God, the man who remembers that he can draw on a strength beyond his own strength, has a great defence against temptation in simply remembering who he is, and what has been done for him.

But we said that in this passage there are problems. The first is a quite simple problem. What is the reason for the change of tense? Why does John say three times *I am writing*, and three times *I have written*? It has been argued that there is no difference at all between the two tenses; the Latin Vulgate translates both by the present tense *scribo*. It has been argued that John varies the tense simply for variation and to avoid the monotony that six successive present tenses would bring. Or it is argued that the past tenses are what in Greek is called the *epistolary aorist.* Greek letter-writers had a habit of using the past instead of the present tense in letters, because they put themselves in the position of the reader of the letter. To the *writer* of a letter a thing may be *present*, because at the moment he is doing it; but to the *reader* of the letter it will be *past*, because by that time it has been done. To take a simple instance, a Greek letter-writer might equally well say, "I am going to town today," and, "I went to town today." That is the Greek idiom which is known as the *epistolary*, or the *letter-writer's aorist*, or past tense. If that is the case there is no difference at all between John's *I am writing* and *I have written*. More likely the explanation is this. When John says *I am writing* he is thinking of the passage he is at the moment writing, and of what he still has to say; and when he says *I have written* he is thinking of the part of the letter which goes before, and which has already been written, and which his readers have already read. The sense would then be that the whole letter, the part which is already written, the part which he is writing, and the part which is still to come, is all designed to remind Christians of who and whose they are, and of what has been done for them.

For John it was of supreme importance that the Christian should remember the status and the benefits he has in Jesus Christ, for these would be his defence against error and against sin.

AT EVERY STAGE

I John 2: 12-14 (*continued*)

THE second problem which confronts us is more difficult, and also more important. John uses three words of the people to whom he is writing. He calls them *little children*; in this case the word varies; in verse 12 it is *teknia*, and in verse 13 it is *paidia*; *teknia* thinks of a child as young in age, and *paidia* thinks of a child as young in experience, and, therefore, in need of training and of discipline. He calls them *fathers*, And He calls them *young men*. The question then is: To whom is John writing? To that question three answers have been given.

(i) It is suggested that we are to take these words as representing three age groups in the Church—children, fathers, and young men. The *children* have the sweet innocence of childhood and of forgiveness. Of such is the Kingdom of Heaven. The *fathers* have the mature wisdom which Christian experience can bring. They have spent the years thinking of Him who is from the beginning and learning more about Him. The *young* men have the strength which is the prerogative of youth, the strength which enables them to fight and to win their personal battle with the Evil One. That is most attractive; but there are three reasons which make us hesitate to adopt it as the only meaning of the passage.

(*a*) *Little children* is one of John's favourite expressions. He uses it in 2: 1, 12, 28; 3: 7, 8; 4: 4; 5: 21; and it is clear in the other cases that he is certainly not thinking of *little children* in terms of age, but he is thinking of Christians whose spiritual father he is, and whom he has begotten in the faith. By this time he must have been very nearly a hundred years old; all the members of his Churches were of a far younger generation; to him they were all little children, as a teacher or professor still speaks of his *boys*, when the boys have long since become men. (*b*) The fact that the passage is kin to poetry would make us think twice before we insisted that so literal a meaning must be given to the words, and so cut and dried a classification be regarded as intended. Literalism and poetry do not go comfortably hand in hand. (*c*) But perhaps the greatest difficulty is that the blessings of which John speaks are not the exclusive possession of any one age group. Forgiveness does not belong to the child alone;

a Christian may be young in the faith, and yet have a wonderful maturity; strength to overcome the tempter does not—thank God—belong to youth alone. These blessings are not the blessings of any one age, but of the Christian life.

We do not say that there is no thought of age groups in this. There almost certainly is; but John has a way of saying things which can be taken in two ways, a narrower way and a wider way; and, while the narrower meaning is here, we must go beyond it to find the full meaning.

(ii) It is suggested that we are to find two groups here. The argument is that *little children* describes *Christians in general*. *All* Christians are little children; and that then Christians in general are divided into two groups, the fathers and the young men, that is, the young and the old, the mature and the as yet immature. That is perfectly possible, because any of John's people must have become so used to hearing him call them *my little children* that they would not connect the words with age at all, but would always include themselves in that address.

(iii) It is suggested that in every case the words include *all* Christians, and that no classification is intended, that, in fact, there is but one universal group. *All* Christians are like little children, for all can regain their innocence by the forgiveness of Jesus Christ. *All* Christians are like fathers, like full-grown, responsible men, who can think and learn their way deeper and deeper into the knowledge of Jesus Christ. *All* Christians are young men, with a glorious and vigorous strength to fight and win their battles against the tempter and his power. It seems to us that indeed this is John's wider meaning. When we read his words we may begin by taking them as a classification of Christians into three age groups; and maybe we will stop there; but as we go on to think of them we come to see that the blessings of each group are the blessings of all the groups, and that each one of us finds himself included in each and in all of them.

GOD'S GIFTS IN CHRIST

I John 2: 12-14 (*continued*)

THIS passage finely sets out God's gifts to all men in Jesus Christ.

(i) There is the gift of *forgiveness through Jesus Christ*. This was the essential message of the gospel. This was the essential message of the early preachers. They were sent out to preach repentance and remission of sins (*Luke* 24: 47). It was Paul's message at Antioch in Pisidia, that to men there was preached, through Jesus Christ, forgiveness of sins (*Acts* 13: 38). To be forgiven is to be at peace with God, at home with God, in fellowship and friendship with God—and that is precisely the gift that Jesus brought to men.

John uses the curious phrase *through His name* (verse 12). Forgiveness comes *through the name* of Jesus Christ. The Jews used this phrase, *the name*, in a very special way. The name is not simply the name by which a person is called; the name stands for the whole character and nature of a person in so far as it has been made known and revealed to men. This use is very common in the Book of Psalms. " They that know Thy name will put their trust in Thee " (*Psalm* 9: 10). This clearly does not mean that those who know that God is called *Jahweh* will put their trust in Him; it means that those who know God's nature, God's character, what God is, in so far as it has been revealed to men, will be ready and eager to put their trust in Him, because they know what He is like. The Psalmist prays: " For Thy name's sake, O Lord, pardon mine iniquity " (*Psalm* 25: 11), which to all intents and purposes means *for Thy love and mercy's sake*. The grounds of the Psalmist's prayer are the nature and the character of God as he knows them to be. " For Thy name's sake," prays the Psalmist, " lead me, and guide me " (*Psalm* 31: 3). The Psalmist can only bring his request because he knows the name—the nature and

the character—of God. " Some trust in chariots," says
the Psalmist, " and some in horses; but we will remember
the name of the Lord our God " (*Psalm* 20: 7). Some
people put their trust in earthly helps; we will trust God
because we know His name, His nature, His love and
His mercy.

So, then, John means that we are assured of forgiveness
because we know the nature and the character of Jesus
Christ. We know that Jesus is the express image of God,
that in Him we see God. We see in Jesus sacrificial love
and patient mercy; therefore we know that God is like
that; and, therefore, we can be sure that there is forgiveness
for us.

(ii) There is the gift of *increasing knowledge of God.*
John no doubt was thinking of his own experience. He
was an old man now; he was writing about A.D. 100. For
seventy years he had lived with Christ and had thought
about Christ and had come to know Him better every
day. For the Jew knowledge was not merely an intellectual
thing. To know God was not merely to know Him as the
philosopher knows Him; it was to know Him as a friend
knows Him. In Hebrew the word *to know* is used of the
relationship between husband and of wife, and especially
of the sexual act, the most intimate of all relationships
(cp. *Genesis* 4: 1). To know a person was to be intimately
and integrally one with that person. When John spoke
of the increasing knowledge of God, he did not mean that
the Christian would become an ever more and more learned
theologian; he meant that throughout the years the
Christian can become more and more intimate with God as
lover and friend.

(iii) There is the *gift of victorious strength.* It is to be
noted that John looks on the struggle with temptation
as a personal struggle. He does not speak in the abstract
of conquering evil; he speaks of conquering the Evil One.
He sees evil as a personal power which seeks to defeat
us and to seduce us from God. Once Robert Louis Steven-

son, speaking of an experience which he never told in detail, said, " You know the Caledonian Railway Station in Edinburgh? *Once I met Satan there.*" There can be none of us who has not experienced the attack of the tempter, the personal assault on our virtue and on our loyalty. It is in Christ we receive the power to meet and to defeat this attack. To take a very simple human analogy —we all know that there are some people in whose presence it is easy to be bad, and some people in whose presence it is necessary to be good. When we walk with Jesus, always remembering Him, always conscious of His presence with us, we are walking with Him in whose company we can defeat the assaults of the Evil One.

RIVALS FOR THE HUMAN HEART

1 *John* 2: 15-17

> Do not love the world, nor the things in the world. If anyone loves the world, the love of the Father is not in him. For everything that is in the world—the flesh's desire, the eye's desire, life's empty pride— does not come from the Father, but comes from the world. And the world is passing away, and so is its desire; but he who does God's will abides for ever.

IT was characteristic of ancient thought to see the world in terms of two conflicting principles. We see this characteristic very vividly in Zoroastrianism, the religion of the Persians; and that was a religion with which the Jews had been brought into contact, and which had left a mark upon their thinking. Zoroastrianism saw the world as the battle-ground between the opposing forces of the light and the dark. The god of the light was Ahura-Mazda; and the god of the dark was Ahura-Mainyu. Between the two there was an eternal conflict, and the great decision in life was the decision on which side to serve. Every man had to decide to ally himself with the light or with the dark. That was a conception which the Jews knew well.

But for the Christian the cleavage between the world

and the Church for the Christian had another background.
The Jews had for many centuries one basic belief. They
divided time into two ages. There was *this present age*,
which was wholly evil, and wholly abandoned to wickedness; and there was *the age to come*, which was the age of
God, and, therefore, wholly good. Now it was a basic
belief of the Christian that in Christ the age to come had
arrived; the Kingdom of God was here. But the age to
come, the Kingdom of God, had not arrived in and for the
world; it had arrived only in and for the *Church*. Hence
the Christian was bound to draw a contrast. The life
of the Christian within the Church was the life of the age
to come, the life of the Kingdom, the life of God, the life
which was wholly good; on the other hand the world
was still living in this present age, the age which was wholly
abandoned to evil; and, therefore, it follows inevitably
that there is a complete cleavage between the Church and
the world, and that there could be no fellowship, and even
no compromise, between them. This is how John arrives
at his clear-cut distinction between the Church and the
world.

But we must be careful to understand what John means
by the world. The world, as we have already seen, is the
kosmos. The Christian did not hate, and withdraw from
and refuse to use, *the world as such*. The world is God's
creation; and God made all things well. Jesus had loved
the beauty of the world; not even Solomon in all his glory
was arrayed like one of the scarlet anemones which bloomed
for a day and died. Jesus again and again took His parables
and His illustrations from the world, and from nature
and its processes. In that sense the Christian did not hate
the world. The earth was not the devil's; the earth was
the Lord's and the fulness thereof. But this word *kosmos*
acquired a moral sense. It began to mean *the world apart
from God*. C. H. Dodd defines this meaning of *kosmos*:
" Our author means human society in so far as it is organized
on wrong principles, and characterized by base desires,

false values, and egoism." In other words, to put it quite simply and concretely, to John *the world was nothing other than pagan society* with its false values and its false standards and its false gods. The world in this passage does not mean the world in general, for God so loved the world which He had made; it means the world which, in fact, had forsaken the God who had made it.

It so happened that there was a factor in the situation of John's people which made the circumstances even more perilous. It is clear that, although they might be unpopular, they were not undergoing persecution. They were, therefore, under the great and dangerous temptation to compromise with the world, to conform their standards to the world, to adjust Christianity in such a way that the difference between the Church and the world was lessened and minimised. It is always difficult to be different, and it was specially difficult for them.

To this day the Christian cannot escape the obligation to be different from the world. In this passage John sees things as he always sees them; he sees them in terms of black and white. As Westcott has it: " There cannot be a vacuum in the soul." This is a matter in which there is no neutrality; a man either loves the world, or he loves God. Jesus Himself said, " No man can serve two masters " (*Matthew* 6: 24). The ultimate choice remains the same. Are we to accept the world's standards, or are we to accept the standards of God? Are we to obey the world, or to obey God?

THE LIFE IN WHICH THERE IS NO FUTURE

I *John* 2: 15-17 (*continued*)

JOHN has two things to say about the man who loves the world, and who compromises with it.

First, he sets out the sins which are the typical sins of the world. He chooses three.

(i) There is the *flesh's desire*. This means far more

than *sins of the flesh* as we use that expression. To us that expression has to do exclusively with sexual sin. But in the New Testament *the flesh* is that part of our nature, which, when it is without God and without the grace of Jesus Christ, offers a bridgehead to sin. It includes the sins of the flesh, but it also includes all worldly ambitions, all selfish aims. To be subject to the flesh's desire is to judge everything in this world by purely material standards. It is to make a god of the pleasures which are purely worldly pleasures. It is to live a life which is dominated by the senses. It is to be gluttonous in food; effeminate in luxury; slavish in pleasure; lustful and lax in morals; selfish in the use of possessions; regardless of all the spiritual values; extravagant in the gratification of worldly, earthly and material desires. The flesh's desire is forgetful of, blind to, or regardless of the commandments of God, the judgment of God, the standards of God, and the very existence of God. We need not think of this as the sin of the gross and blatant and notorious sinner. Anyone who demands a pleasure which may be the ruin of someone else, anyone who has no respect for the personalities of other people in the gratification of his own desires, anyone who lives in luxury while others live in want, anyone who has made a god of his own comfort, and of his own ambition, in any part of life, is the servant of the flesh's desire.

(ii) There is the *eye's desire*. This, as C. H. Dodd, puts it is " the tendency to be captivated by outward show." It is the spirit which identifies lavish ostentation with real happiness and real prosperity. It is the spirit which can see nothing without wishing to acquire it, and which, having acquired it, flaunts it in the face of men. It is the spirit which believes that happiness is to be found in the things which money can buy and which the eye can see. In its scheme of things it has no values other than material values. It has sold itself to the things which are seen and temporal, and has forgotten the things which are unseen and eternal.

(iii) There is *life's empty pride*. Here John uses a most vivid Greek word, the word *alazoneia*. To the ancient moralists the *alazōn* was the man who laid claims to possessions and to deeds and to achievements which did not belong to him in order to impress others and to exalt himself. The *alazōn* is the braggart; and C. H. Dodd calls *alazoneia pretentious egoism*. Theophrastus, the great Greek master of the character study, has a study of the *Alazōn*, He stands in the harbour and boasts of the ships that he has at sea; he ostentatiously sends a messenger to the bank when he has a shilling to his credit; he talks of his friends among the mighty, and of the letters he receives from the famous. He details at length his charitable benefactions, and his services to the state. All that he occupies is a hired lodging, but he talks of buying a bigger house to match his lavish entertaining. His conversation is a continual boasting about things which he does not possess, and all his life is spent in an attempt to impress everyone he meets with his own non-existent importance.

As John sees him, the man of the world is the man who judges everything by his appetites, the man who is the slave of lavish ostentation, the boastful braggart who tries to make himself out a far bigger man than he is.

And then comes John's second warning. The man who attaches himself to the world's aims and the world's ways is giving his life to things which literally have no future. All these things are passing away; none of them has any permanency in them. They are the very things which are essentially the victims of change and decay. But the man who has taken God as the centre of his life has given his life to the things which last for ever. The man of the world is doomed to disappointment; the man of God is certain of lasting joy. John's argument is that it is obviously the act of a fool to dedicate life to that which, by its nature, cannot do other than pass away; and it is obviously the act of a wise man to dedicate life to that which is sure and certain through all eternity.

THE TIME OF THE LAST HOUR

I *John* 2: 18

> Little children, it is the time of the last hour; and
> now many antichrists have arisen, just as you heard
> that antichrist was to come. That is how we know
> that it is the time of the last hour.

IT is very important that we should understand what
John means when he speaks of the time of the last hour.
The idea of the last days and of the last hour runs all
through the Bible; but it does not always mean the same
thing; there is a most interesting development in the
meaning of the phrase.

(i) The phrase occurs frequently in the very early
books of the Old Testament. Jacob, for instance, before
his death assembles his sons, that he may tell them what
will befall them in the last days (*Genesis* 49: 1; cp. *Numbers*
24: 14). Now at that time the last days were the days
when the people of Israel would enter into the Promised
Land, and would at last enter into full enjoyment of the
promised blessings of God.

(ii) The phrase frequently occurs in the prophets. It
is the dream of Isaiah that in the last days the mountain
of the Lord shall be established in the top of the mountains,
and shall be exalted above the hills, and all nations shall
flow unto it (*Isaiah* 2: 2; *Micah* 4: 1). In the prophets
in the last days God's Holy City will be supreme; and
Israel will render to God the perfect obedience which is
God's due (cp. *Jeremiah* 23: 20; 30: 24; 48: 47). In
the last days there would be the supremacy of God and
the obedience of God's people.

(iii) In the Old Testament itself, and in the times between
the Old and the New Testament, the last days become
associated with the Day of the Lord. This is a conception
which has repeatedly met us, for there is no conception
more deeply interwoven into Scripture. The Jews had
come to believe that all time was divided into two ages.

There is *this present age*, which is wholly evil, and w... abandoned to evil; there is *the age to come*, which is the golden age of the supremacy of God; and in between there was the Day of the Lord, the last days, which would be a time of terror, of cosmic dissolution, and of judgment, the birthpangs of the emergence of the new world and the new age.

Now what we have to see is this; the last days, the last hour, does not mean a time of annihilation; it does not mean a time when everything will cease to exist, and when at the end there will be a great nothingness as there was at the beginning. In biblical thought the last time is the end of one age and the beginning of another. It is not only a time of ending; it is a time of new beginning. It is not only a time of destruction; it is a time of recreation. It is *last* in the sense that things as they are pass away; but it leads not to world obliteration, but to world recreation. In other words, the last hour and the last days lead not to extinction, but to consummation.

Here is the centre of the whole matter. The question then becomes: " Will a man be wiped out in the judgment of the old, or will he enter into the glory of the new?" That is the alternative with which John—and indeed all the biblical writers—are confronting men. Men have the choice of allying themselves with the old world, which is doomed to dissolution, or of allying themselves with Christ, and entering into the new world, which is the very world of God. Here is the urgency for John. If it was a simple matter of utter obliteration, then no one could do anything about it. But it is a matter of recreation, and whether a man will enter into the new world or not depends on whether or not he has given his life to Jesus Christ.

What is the relevance of that for today? In fact John was wrong. It was not the last hour for his people. Eighteen hundred years have gone by, and the world still exists. Is then the whole conception irrelevant, and does it belong to a sphere of thought which must be discarded and left behind? The answer is that in this conception there is an eternal relevance. *Every hour is the last hour.* In the world there is a continual conflict between good and evil, between God and that which is anti-God. And in every moment in life, and in every decision in life, a man is confronted with the choice of allying himself with God or with the evil of the forces which are against God, and of thereby ensuring, or failing to ensure, his own share in eternal life. The conflict between good and evil never stops; therefore, the choice never stops; therefore, in a very real sense every hour is the last hour.

THE ANTICHRIST

I John 2: 18 (*continued*)

IN this verse we meet the conception of *antichrist*. *Antichrist* is a word which occurs only in John's letters in the New Testament (I *John* 2: 22; 4: 3; 2 *John* 7); but it is the expression of an idea which is as old as religion itself.

From its derivation the word *antichrist* can have two meanings. *Anti* is a Greek preposition which can mean either *against* or *in place of*. *Stratēgos* is the Greek word for a *commander*, and *antistratēgos* can mean either *the hostile commander* of the enemy's forces, or the *deputy commander*, who can act in place of the commander. *Antichrist* can therefore mean either the opponent or adversary of Christ, or, the one who seeks to put himself in the place of Christ. In this case the meaning will come to the same thing, but there will be this difference. If we take the meaning to be *the one who is opposed to Christ*, then the opposition is open and clear and plain. If we take the meaning to be *the one who seeks to put himself in the place of Christ*, then antichrist can be one who does not work by open opposition, but who subtly tries to take the place of Christ from within the Church and within the Christian community. The one will be an open opposition;

the other will be a subtle undermining and infiltrat.. We need not choose between these meanings, for in truth antichrist can act in either way.

The simplest way to think of the antichrist idea is this; Christ is the incarnation of God and goodness; antichrist is the incarnation of the devil and evil. Christ stands for God; antichrist stands for everything which is against God, and in opposition to God.

We began by saying that this is an idea which is as old as religion itself; men have always felt that in the universe there is a power which is in opposition to God. One of its earliest forms occurs in the Babylonian legend of creation. According to it there was in the very beginning a primaeval sea monster called Tiamat; this sea monster was subdued by Marduk; but the monster was not killed; it is only asleep; and the final battle is still to come. That legendary, mythical idea of the old primaeval monster occurs in the Old Testament again and again. There the monster is often called Rahab, or the crooked serpent, or leviathan. " Thou hast broken Rahab in pieces," says the Psalmist (*Psalm* 89: 10). " His hand hath formed the crooked serpent," says Job (*Job* 26: 13). Isaiah speaking of the arm of the Lord, says, " Art thou not it that hath cut Rahab, and wounded the dragon? " (*Isaiah* 51: 9). Isaiah writes: " In that day the Lord with His sore and great and strong sword shall punish leviathan the piercing serpent, even leviathan the crooked serpent, and He shall slay the dragon that is in the sea " (*Isaiah* 27: 1). All these are references to the primaeval dragon. This idea is obviously an idea which belongs to the childhood of mankind; but the basic idea is there, the idea that in the universe there is a power which is hostile to God.

Originally this power was conceived of as the old dragon. Inevitably as time went on this power became personalized. Every time there arose a man who was great in evil, and who seemed to be setting himself against God, and who seemed to be bent on the obliteration of God's people, the inevitable tendency was to identify him with this anti-God force, to think of him as the supreme enemy of God. For instance about 168 B.C. there emerged the figure of Antiochus Epiphanes, the King of Syria. He resolved on a quite deliberate attempt to eliminate Judaism from this earth, and to destroy the worship of the Jews. He invaded Jerusalem, and killed thousands of Jews, and sold tens of thousands into slavery. To circumcise a child, or to own a copy of the Law was a crime punishable by instant death. In the Temple courts there was erected a great altar to Zeus. Swine's flesh was offered on it. The Temple chambers were made into public brothels. Here was a deliberate attempt at desecration, a cold-blooded effort to wipe out Jewish religion and to destroy God. It was Antiochus whom Daniel called " The Abomination that maketh desolate " (Daniel 11: 31; 12: 11). Here was the anti-God force incarnate, men thought.

It was this very same phrase that men took in the days of Mark's gospel when they talked of " The Abomination of Desolation "—" The Appalling Horror," as Moffatt translates it—being set up in the Temple itself (Mark 13: 14; Matthew 24: 15). Here the reference is to Caligula, the more than half-mad Roman Emperor, who wished to set up his own image in the Holy of Holies in the Temple. Men felt that that was the act of one who was anti-God incarnate.

In 2 Thessalonians 2: 3, 4, Paul speaks of " the man of sin," the one who exalts himself above all that is called God and all that is worshipped and who sets himself up in the very Temple of God. We do not know whom Paul was expecting, but again there is this expectation of one who was the incarnation of everything which was opposed to God.

In Revelation there is the beast and the dragon (13: 1; 16: 13; 19: 20; 20: 10). Here there is very probably another figure involved. Nero was regarded by all as a human monster. His excesses and his murders disgusted the Romans, and his savage persecution tortured the Christians. In due time Nero died; but he was so great in wickedness that men could not believe that he had died. And so there arose the *Nero Redivivus*, Nero resurrected, legend, which said that Nero was not dead, that he had gone to Parthia, and that he would come with the Parthian hordes and descend upon men. He is the beast, the antichrist, the incarnation of devilish and Satanic evil.

All down history there have been these identifications of human figures with antichrist. The Pope, Napoleon, Mussolini, Hitler, have all been in their day and generation identified with antichrist.

But the fact is that antichrist is not so much a person as a principle, the principle which is hostile to, and actively opposed to, God, a principle which may well be thought of as incarnating itself in men who in every generation have seemed to be the open and blatant and wicked opponents of God.

THE BATTLE OF THE MIND

I *John* 2: 18 (*continued*)

BUT John has a view of antichrist which is characteristically his own. To him the sign that antichrist is in the world is the false belief and the dangerous teaching of the evil teachers. The Church had been well forewarned that in the last days false teachers would come. Jesus had said, " Many shall come in my name, saying, I am Christ; and shall deceive many " (*Mark* 13: 6; cp. *Matthew* 24: 5). Before he left them, Paul had warned his Ephesian friends: " After my departure shall grievous wolves enter in among you, not sparing the flock. Also of your own selves shall men arise, speaking perverse things, to draw away disciples after them " (*Acts* 20: 29, 30). The situation which has been foretold had now arisen.

But John had a special view of this whole situation. When we read what he says, we can see that he did not think of antichrist as one single individual figure. He rather thought of antichrist as a power of falsehood speaking in and through the false teachers. Just as there was a Holy Spirit inspiring the true teachers and the true prophets, so there was a false and evil spirit inspiring the false teachers and the false prophets.

Now the great interest, and the great relevance of this, is that for John *the battleground is in the mind*. The spirit of antichrist was struggling with the Spirit of God for the possession of men's minds. What makes this so significant is that we can see exactly this process at work today. Men have brought the indoctrination of men's minds to a science. We have in our own day and generation seen how men can take an idea and repeat it and repeat it and repeat it until it settles into men's minds, and until men begin to accept it as true simply because they have heard it so often. In our generation this is easier than ever it was. There are available today so many means of mass communication—books, newspapers, wireless, television, and the vast resources of modern advertising. And we have seen how a skilled propagandist can take an idea, and by the use of these means of communication, can infiltrate it into men's minds, until, all unaware, they are indoctrinated with it. We do not say that John foresaw all this, but John did see the mind as the field of operations for antichrist. He no longer thinks in terms of a single demonic figure; he thinks in terms of a force of evil deliberately seeking to pervade men's minds; and there is nothing more potent for evil than an evil idea inserted into the minds of many men.

If there is one special task which confronts the Church today, it is to learn the technique of mobilizing the forces and media of mass communication to counteract the poison of the evil ideas with which the minds of men are being deliberately indoctrinated.

THE SIFTING OF THE CHURCH

I *John* 2: 19-21

> They have gone out from among us, but they are
> not of our number. If they had been of our number,
> they would have remained with us. But things have
> happened as they have happened, that it may be
> clearly demonstrated that all of them are not of us.
> But you have received anointing from the Holy
> One, and you all possess knowledge. I have not
> written this letter to you because you do not know
> the truth, but because you do know it, and because
> no lie comes from the truth.

As things have turned out, John sees in the Church a
time of sifting. The false teachers had left the Church;
they had gone out from the Christian fellowship. They
had not been excommunicated; they had voluntarily
gone out; and that very fact had shown that they did not
belong to the body of the Christian Church. They were
aliens and their own conduct had shown it to be so.

The last phrase of verse 19 can have two meanings.

(i) It may mean, as in our translation: " All of them
are not of us," or, as we would rather say in English:
" None of them are from us." That is to say, however
attractive some of them may be, however fine their teaching
sounds, they are all alike alien to the Church. They may
have a superficial charm, but fundamentally they are
hostile to Christ.

(ii) It is just possible that what the phrase means is
that these men have gone out from the Church to make it
clear that " all who are in the Church do not really belong
to the Church." As C. H. Dodd puts it: " Membership
of the Church is no guarantee that a man belongs to Christ
and not to antichrist." As A. E. Brooke puts it—although
he does not agree that it is the meaning of the Greek—
" External membership is no proof of inward union."
It may well be that it is this second meaning that is right.
These false teachers have made it clear by their going
out that all who are within the Church do not belong to

the Church. As Paul had it: " They are not all Israel who are of Israel " (*Romans* 9: 6). And a time such as had come upon John's people had its value, for it sifted the false from the true.

In verse 20, John goes on to remind his people that all of them possessed knowledge. The people who had gone out were Gnostics; they claimed that there had been given to them a secret, special, and advanced knowledge which was not open to the ordinary Christian. Paul reminds his people that in matters of faith the humblest Christian need have no feeling of inferiority to the most learned scholar. There are, of course, matters of technical scholarship, of language, of history, of technical theology, which must be the preserve of the expert; but the essentials of the faith are the possession of every man.

This leads John to his last point in this section. He writes to them, not because they did not know the truth, but because they did know it. Westcott puts it in this way: " The object of the apostle in writing was not to communicate fresh knowledge, but to bring into active and decisive use the knowledge which his readers already possessed." The greatest Christian defence is simply to remember what we know. It is not new truth we need; what we need is that the truth which we already know should be awakened until it becomes active, effective, and operative in our lives. This is an approach which Paul continually uses. He writes to the Thessalonians: " But as touching brotherly love ye need not that I should write unto you; for you yourselves are taught of God to love one another " (*I Thessalonians* 4: 9). What they needed was not new truth, but to put into actual living practice the truth which they already knew. He writes to the Romans: " I myself, also, am persuaded of you, my brethren, that ye also are full of goodness, filled with all knowledge, able also to admonish one another. Nevertheless, brethren, I have written the more boldly unto you in some sort, as *putting you in mind*, because of the grace that is given to me of God " (*Romans* 15: 14, 15). What they needed was not so much to be taught as to be reminded.

It is the simple fact of the Christian life that life would be different at once, if we would only put into practice that which we already know. That is not to say that we never need to learn anything new; but it is to say that, even as we are, we have light enough to walk by, if we use the light we have.

THE MASTER LIE

I *John* 2: 22, 23

> Who is the liar, but the man who denies that Jesus is the Anointed One of God? Antichrist is he who denies the Father and the Son. Anyone who denies the Son does not even have the Father; and everyone who acknowledges the Son has the Father also.

IN this passage the Authorized Version wrongly weakens the force of the first sentence. The Authorized Version has: " Who is *a* liar but he that denieth that Jesus is the Christ? " (verse 22); but the Greek is: " Who is *the* liar but he who denieth that Jesus is the Christ." As someone has put it, to deny that Jesus is the Christ is the master lie; it is the lie *par excellence*; it is the lie of all lies.

John says that he who denies the Son has not the Father either. What lies behind that saying is this. The false teachers made a plea like this. They said, " It may be that we have different ideas from yours about *Jesus*; but you and I do believe the same things about *God*. We may differ about the *Son*; but we do agree about the *Father*." It is John's answer that that is an impossible position, and that no man can deny the Son and still have the Father. How does John arrive at that position?

He arrives at it because no one who accepts New Testament teaching can arrive at any other. It is the consistent teaching of the New Testament, and it is the claim of Jesus Himself, that apart from Jesus no man can know

God. Jesus said quite clearly that no man knows the Father except the Son, and he to whom the Son reveals the knowledge of the Father (*Matthew* 11: 27; *Luke* 10: 22). As John has it in his gospel; Jesus said, " He that believeth on me, believeth not on me, but on Him that sent me. And he that seeth me seeth Him that sent me " (*John* 12: 44, 45). When, towards the end, Philip said that they would be content, if Jesus would only show them the Father, Jesus' answer was: " He that hath seen me hath seen the Father " (*John* 14: 6-9). It is through Jesus that men know God; it is in Jesus that men can approach God. If we deny Jesus' right to speak, if we deny His special knowledge, and His special relationship to God, then we can have no more confidence in what He says. His words are no more than the guesses which any good and great man could make. And, therefore, apart from Him we have no secure knowledge of God. So, then, to deny Jesus is at the same time to lose all grip of God.

Still further, it was Jesus' claim that a man's reaction to Him was, in fact, a reaction to God, and that that reaction settled a man's destiny in time and in eternity. He said, " Whosoever, therefore, shall confess me before men, him will I confess before my Father which is in heaven; but whosoever shall deny me before men, him will I also deny before my Father which is in heaven " (*Matthew* 10: 32, 33). It is impossible to separate Jesus and God. To deny Jesus is to lose all knowledge of God, for He alone can bring that knowledge of God. To deny Jesus is to be separated from God, for on our reaction to Jesus our relationship to God depends.

To deny Jesus is indeed the *master lie*, for to deny Jesus is to lose entirely the faith and the knowledge which He alone makes possible.

We may say that there are three New Testament confessions of Jesus; there is the confession that Jesus is the *Son of God* (*Matthew* 16: 16; *John* 9: 35-38); there is the confession that Jesus is *Lord* (*Philippians* 2: 11); and there is the confession that Jesus is *Messiah* (I *John* 2: 22); and the essence of every one of them is the affirmation that Jesus stands in an absolutely unique relationship to God; and to deny that relationship is to deny the certainty that everything that Jesus said about God is true. The whole Christian faith depends on the unique relationship of Jesus to God. John is, therefore, right; the man who denies the Son has lost the Father too.

THE UNIVERSAL PRIVILEGE

I *John* 2: 24-29

> If that which you have heard from the beginning remains within you, you too will remain in the Son and in the Father. And this is the promise which He made to you—eternal life. I am writing these things to you to warn you about those who are seeking to lead you astray. As for you, if that anointing which you have received from Him remains in you, you have no need for anyone to teach you. But, as His anointing teaches you about all things, and is true, and is no lie, and as He has taught you, remain in Him. And now, little children, remain in Him, so that, if He appears, we may have confidence, and may not shrink in shame away from Him at His coming. If you know that He is righteous, you must be aware that everyone who does righteousness is born of Him.

HERE John is pleading with his people to abide in the things which they have learned, and which they have been taught, for, if they do, they will abide in Christ. The great interest of this passage lies in an expression which John has already used. In verse 20, John has already spoken of the *anointing* which his people had had from the Holy One, and through which all of them were equipped with knowledge. And here he speaks of the anointing which they have received, and the anointing which teaches them all things. What is the thought behind this word *anointing*? What is John thinking of, and what does he mean? We shall have to go back some distance in Hebrew thought to find the idea behind this passage.

In Hebrew thought and practice anointing was connected with three kinds of people. (i) *Priests* were anointed The ritual regulation runs: " Thou shalt take the anointing oil, and pour it upon his (the priest's) head and anoint him" (*Exodus* 29: 7; cp. 40: 13; *Leviticus* 16: 32). (ii) *Kings* were anointed. Samuel anointed Saul as king of the nation (I *Samuel* 9: 16; 10: 1). Later, Samuel anointed David as king (I *Samuel* 16: 3, 12). Elijah was bidden to anoint Hazael and Jehu (I *Kings* 19: 15, 16). Anointing was the symbol of coronation, as it still is. (iii) *Prophets* were anointed. Elijah was bidden to anoint Elisha as his successor (I *Kings* 19: 16). The Lord had anointed the prophet Isaiah to bring good tidings to the nation (*Isaiah* 60: 1).

Here, then, is the first significant thing. In the old days anointing had been the privilege of the chosen few, the priests, the prophets and the kings; but now anointing is something which is the privilege of every Christian, however humble he may be. First, then, the anointing stands for the privilege of the Christian in Jesus Christ.

Now the High Priest was called *The Anointed*; but the supreme *Anointed One* was the *Messiah*, for that word means in Hebrew *The Anointed One*, and *Christos* means the same in Greek. So Jesus was supremely *The Anointed One*. The question then arises: When was Jesus anointed? The answer which the Church always gave to that question was that, *at His baptism*, Jesus was anointed with the Holy Spirit (*Acts* 10: 38).

To this we have to add that the Greek world also knew of anointing. Anointing was one of the ceremonies of initiation into the Mystery Religions in which a man was supposed to gain special knowledge of, and special contact with, God. We also know that some at least of the false teachers claimed a special anointing, a special initiation, which brought them a special knowledge of God. Hippolytus tells us how these false teachers said, " We alone of all men are Christians, who complete the mystery at the third portal, and who are anointed there with speechless anointing." The false teachers must have been claiming that they had a special anointing which gave them a special knowledge of God. John's answer is that it is the ordinary Christian who has the only true anointing, the anointing which Jesus gives.

But when did that anointing come to the Christian, and of what does it consist, and what does it give?

The first question is easy to answer. There was only one ceremony that all Christians passed through, and that ceremony was *baptism*; it was indeed in later days the standard practice at baptism literally to anoint Christians with holy oil, as Tertullian tells us.

The second question is not so easy to answer. There are indeed two equally possible answers.

(i) It may be that the anointing means the coming of the Spirit upon the Christian in baptism. In the early Church that happened in the most visible way (*Acts* 8: 17). If in this passage we were to substitute the phrase the *Holy Spirit* for the word anointing we would get excellent sense. It would be the Holy Spirit whom they have received who remains in them. It would be the Holy Spirit, given by Christ, who teaches them all things.

(ii) But there is another possibility. Verses 24 and 27 are almost exactly parallel in expression. In verse 24 we read: " Let that therefore abide in you which you have heard from the beginning." And in verse 27 we read: " But the anointing which ye have received of Him abideth in you." *That which you have received from the beginning* and *the anointing* are exactly parallel. Therefore, it may well be that the anointing which the Christian receives is the instruction in the Christian faith which he receives when he enters the Church. The Christian is anointed with the true knowledge of the Christian faith and the Christian way.

Now it may well be that we do not need to choose between these two interpretations, but that they are both present. This would mean something very valuable. It would mean that we have two tests by which to judge any new teaching which is offered to us. (i) Is it in accordance with the Christian tradition which we have been taught, and which must abide in our minds and in our hearts? (ii) Is it in accordance with the witness of the Holy Spirit speaking within?

Here are the Christian criteria of truth. There is an *external* test. All teaching must be in accordance with the teaching and the tradition which have been handed down to us in Scripture and in the Church. We have an *internal* test. All teaching must undergo the test of the Holy Spirit witnessing within our hearts.

It is John's teaching that if a man abides in the truth he has been taught, and if he brings the test of the Holy Spirit to all truth, he will then be enabled to accept only the truth, and to reject every lie, and so for ever to abide in Christ.

ABIDING IN CHRIST

I *John* 2: 24-29 (*continued*)

BEFORE we leave this passage we must note two great and practical things in it.

(i) In verse 28, John urges his people to abide continually in Christ so that, when He does come back in power and glory, they may not shrink from Him in shame. Here is a great and practical truth. By far the best way to be ready for the Coming of Christ is to live with Him every day. If we do that, His Coming will be no shock to us; it will simply be the entry into the nearer presence of one with whom we have lived for long. The best way to prepare for the Coming of Christ is never to forget the presence of Christ.

Even if we have doubts and difficulties and questions about the actual physical Second Coming of Christ, this still remains true. For every man life will some day come to an end; God's summons comes to all to rise and to bid this world farewell. If we have never thought of God, and if Jesus has been but a dim and distant memory, seldom in our minds, that summons will be a summons to go out to meet a stranger and to voyage into the frightening unknown. But if all our days we have lived consciously in the presence of Christ, if day by day we have lived and talked and walked with God, then that summons will be a summons to come home, and an entry into the nearer presence of God with the veil of sense and time for ever removed and taken away. It is the simple and the obvious truth that a man's emotions at the end of life will depend entirely on how he lived life, for he will be going either to God who is a stranger or to a God who is a friend.

(ii) In verse 29, John comes back again to a thought which is never far from his mind. The only way in which a man can prove that he is abiding in Christ, the only way in which he can prove that he really has had a new birth is by the righteousness of his life. The profession of a man's lips will always be proved or disproved by the practice of his life.

REMEMBER THE PRIVILEGES OF THE CHRISTIAN LIFE

I *John* 3: 1, 2

> See what kind of love the Father has given to us, that we should be called the children of God—and such we indeed are. The reason why the world does not recognize us is that it did not recognize Him. Beloved, even as things are we are children of God, and it has not yet been made clear what we shall be. We know that, if it shall be made clear, we shall be like Him, because we shall see Him as He is.

It may well be that the best illumination of this passage is the Scottish Paraphrase of it:

> Behold the amazing gift of love
>   the Father hath bestow'd
> On us, the sinful sons of men,
>   to call us sons of God!
>
> Conceal'd as yet this honour lies,
>   by this dark world unknown,
> A world that knew not when he came,
>   ev'n God's eternal Son.
>
> High is the rank we now possess;
>   but higher we shall rise;
> Though what we shall hereafter be
>   is hid from mortal eyes.
>
> Our souls, we know, when he appears,
>   shall bear his image bright;
> For all his glory, full disclos'd,
>   shall open to our sight.
>
> A hope so great, and so divine,
>   may trials well endure;
> And purge the soul from sense and sin,
>   as Christ Himself is pure.

In that Paraphrase the meaning of this passage is finely crystallized.

John begins by demanding that his people should remember their privileges. It is their privilege that they are called *the children of God*. There is something even in a name. Chrysostom, in his sermon on how to bring up children, advises parents to give their boy some great scriptural name, to teach him repeatedly the story of the original bearer of the name, and thus to give him a standard to live up to, and an inspiration for living, when he grows to manhood. So the Christian has the privilege of being called the child of God. Just as to belong to a great school, a great regiment, a great Church, a great household is an inspiration to fine living, so, even more, to bear the name of the family of God is something to keep a man's feet on the right way, and to set him climbing.

But, as John points out, we are not merely *called* the children of God; we *are* the children of God. Not only the name is ours; the reality is also ours.

There is something here which we may well note. It is by the gift of God that a man becomes a child of God. By nature man is the *creature* of God, because God is his Creator, but it is by grace that man *becomes* the child of God. There are two English words which are closely connected, but whose meanings are widely different. There is the word *paternity* and the word *fatherhood*. *Paternity* describes a relationship in which a father is responsible for the physical existence of a son; but, as far as paternity goes, it can be, and it not infrequently happens, that the father has never even set eyes on the son, and would not even recognize him, if in later years he met him. *Fatherhood* describes an intimate, loving, continuous relationship in which father and son grow closer to each other every day. In the sense of *paternity* all men are children of God; but in the sense of *fatherhood* men are only children of God, when God makes His gracious approach to them, and when they respond.

There are two pictures, one from the Old Testament and one from the New Testament, which aptly and vividly set out this relationship. In the Old Testament there is the *covenant idea*. Israel was the covenant people of God. That is to say, God on His own initiative had made a ρecial approach to Israel; He was to be uniquely their God, and they were to be uniquely His people. As an integral part of the covenant God gave to Israel His law, and it was on the keeping of that law, and the maintenance of the law, that the covenant relationship depended. All nations belonged to God and were His sons, but Israel was His son in a special sense because God had called them and they had responded in a special way.

In the New Testament there is the idea of adoption (*Romans* 8: 14-17; I *Corinthians* 1: 9; *Galatians* 3: 26, 27; 4: 6, 7). Here is the idea that by a deliberate act of adoption on the part of God the Christian enters into the family of God. His entry into that family is an act and a gift of God.

We do well to remember that, while all men are children of God in the sense that they owe their lives to Him, they only become children of God in the intimate and loving sense of the term by an act of God's initiating grace, and the response of their own hearts.

Immediately the question arises: If men have that great honour when they become Christians, why are they so downtrodden and despised and unrecognized by the world? The answer is that they are only experiencing what Jesus Christ has already experienced. When He came into the world He was not recognized as the Son of God. He came with standards which turned the world's standards upside down; if His life was the godlike life, then even the best of men stood condemned. The world preferred its own ideas, and rejected the ideas of Jesus Christ. Therefore, the same is bound to happen to any man who chooses to embark on the same way as Jesus Christ did.

REMEMBER THE POSSIBILITIES OF THE CHRISTIAN LIFE

1 *John* 3: 1, 2 (*continued*)

JOHN, then, begins by reminding his people of the privileges of the Christian life. Then he goes on to set before them what is in many ways a still more tremendous truth. He sets before them the great fact that *this life is only a beginning*. And here John observes the only true agnosticism, as we might call it. So great is the future and so great is the coming glory that he will not even guess at it, and he will not even try to put it into inevitably inadequate words. But there are certain things he does say about it.

(i) When Christ appears in His glory, we shall be like Him. Surely in John's mind there was the saying of the

old creation story, that man was made in the image and
in the likeness of God (*Genesis* I: 26). That was God's
intention; and that was man's destiny. We have only
to look into any mirror to see how far man has fallen short
of that destiny. But John believes that in Christ a man
will finally attain that destiny; that in Christ a man
will be like Christ; and that, therefore, in Christ a man
will at last bear the image and the likeness of God. It is
John's belief that only through the work of Christ in
his soul can a man reach true manhood, the manhood
God meant Him to reach, likeness to God Himself.

(ii) When Christ appears, we shall see Him and .be like
Him. The great goal of all the great souls has been the
vision of God. The end of all devotion is to see God. But
the great distinguishing point is that that vision of God
is not even primarily for the sake of intellectual satisfaction; it is in order that we may become like Him.
There is a paradox here. We cannot become like God
unless we see Him; and we cannot see Him unless we are
pure in heart, for only the pure in heart shall see God
(*Matthew* 5: 8). In order to see God, we need the purity
which only God can give. We are not to think of this
vision of God as something which only the great spiritual
mystics can enjoy. There is somewhere the story of a poor
and simple man who would often go into a cathedral
to pray; and he would always pray kneeling before the
crucifix, the statue of the crucified Lord. Someone noticed
that, though he knelt in the attitude of prayer, his lips
never moved and he never seemed to say anything. This
person asked the man what he was doing kneeling like
that; and the simple man answered quite simply: " I
look at Him; and He looks at me." That is prayer, and
that is the vision of God in Christ that the simplest soul
can have; and he who looks long enough at Jesus Christ
must ultimately become like Him.

One thing we must still note. John is here thinking
in terms of the Second Coming of Christ. It may be that

we can think in the same terms; it may be that we cannot
think so literally of a coming of Christ in glory. Be that
as it may, there comes for every one of us the day when
we shall see Christ, and behold His glory. At present
we see through a glass darkly, but then face to face. Here
there is always the veil of sense and time, but the day
comes when that veil too shall be rent in twain.

> When death these mortal eyes shall seal,
>   And still this throbbing heart,
> The rending veil shall Thee reveal
>   All glorious as Thou art.

Therein is the Christian hope, and the vast possibility of
the Christian life.

THE OBLIGATION OF PURITY

I *John* 3: 3-8

> Anyone who rests this hope on Him purifies himself as
> He is pure. Anyone who commits sin commits law-
> lessness, and sin is lawlessness. And you know that
> He appeared that He might take away our sins, and
> there is no sin in Him. Anyone who abides in Him
> does not sin. Anyone who sins has not seen Him, and
> does not know Him. Little children, let no one deceive
> you. He who does righteousness is righteous, even as
> He is righteous. He who does sin is of the devil,
> because the devil is a sinner from the beginning. The
> purpose for which the Son of God appeared was that
> He might destroy the works of the devil.

JOHN has just said that the end and the goal of the Christian
life is the vision of God. The Christian is on the way
to seeing God, and to being like God. There is nothing
like a great aim and goal for keeping a man in purity and
for helping him to resist temptation. A novelist draws
the picture of a young man who always refused to share
in the lower pleasures to which his comrades often invited
and even urged him. His explanation was that, " He knew
that some day something fine was going to come to him,
and he must keep himself ready for it." The man who

knows that God is at the end of the road will make all
life a preparation to meet his God.

In its immediate aim this passage is directed against the
Gnostic false teachers. As we have seen the Gnostics
produced more than one reason to justify sin. They said
that the body is in any event evil, and that, therefore,
there is no harm in sating its lusts and glutting it with its
pleasures, because the body is of no importance, and what
happens to it is of no importance. They said that the truly
spiritual man is so armoured with the Spirit that he can
sin to his heart's content, and take no harm from it. They
even said that the true Gnostic, the man with true knowledge, must know both the heights of virtue and the depths
of sin. He is under obligation both to scale the heights
and to plumb the depths, so that he may be truly said to
know all things. Behind John's answer there is a kind of
complete analysis of sin.

He begins by insisting that there is no one who is superior
to the moral law. There is no one who can say that it is
quite safe for him to allow himself certain things, although
they may be dangerous for others. As A. E. Brooke puts
it: " The test of progress is obedience." Progress does
not confer the privilege to sin; the further on a man is
the purer and the more disciplined a character he will be.
John then goes on to say and to imply certain basic truths
about sin.

(i) He tells us *what sin is.* Sin is lawlessness. Sin is
the deliberate breaking of a law which a man well knows.
Sin is putting one's own desires in the place of the law
of God; to sin is to obey oneself rather than to obey God.

(ii) He tells us *what sin does.* Sin undoes the work of
Christ. Christ is the Lamb of God who takes away the
sins of the world (*John* I: 29). Therefore, to sin is to
undo the work of Jesus Christ. It is to bring back and to
multiply that sin which He came into the world to destroy.

(iii) He tells us *why sin is.* Sin comes from the failure to
abide in Christ. Sin comes from imperfect union with

Jesus Christ. We may put this quite simply. We need not think that this is a truth only for advanced mystics. It simply means this—so long as we remember the continual presence of Jesus, so long as we deliberately walk with Him, we will not sin. It is when we forget Christ, that we do in fact sin. To remember the presence of Jesus Christ for ever with us is to make sin always difficult, and sometimes even impossible.

(iv) He tells us *whence sin comes*. Sin comes from the devil; and the devil is he who sins, as it were, on principle. That very probably is the meaning of the phrase *from the beginning* (verse 8). We sin for the things and the pleasure that we think the forbidden things will bring to us; the devil sins as a matter of principle; sin is the self-chosen principle of his life. The New Testament does not try to explain the devil and his origin; but the New Testament is quite convinced—and it is a fact of universal experience—that in the world there is a principle and a power which is hostile to God, and to sin is to obey that power instead of God.

(v) He tells us how *sin is conquered*. Sin is conquered because Jesus Christ destroyed the works of the devil. The New Testament often dwells on the victorious Christ, the Christ who faced and conquered and subjected for ever the powers of evil (*Matthew* 12: 25-29; *Luke* 10: 18; *Colossians* 2: 15; I *Peter* 3: 22; *John* 12: 31). Jesus Christ, by His victory, broke the power of the forces of evil, and by His help that same victory can be ours.

THE MAN WHO IS BORN OF GOD

I *John* 3: 9

> Anyone who has been born of God does not commit sin, because His seed abides in him; and he cannot be a consistent and deliberate sinner, because he has been born of God.

THIS is a verse which bristles with difficulties, and yet it is obviously of the first importance for life to find out what it means.

First, what does John mean by the phrase: " *Because His seed abides in him* " ? There are three possibilities.

(i) Frequently the Bible uses the word *seed* to mean a man's family and descendants. Abraham and his *seed* are to keep the covenant of God (*Genesis* 17: 9). God made His promise to Abraham and to his *seed* for ever (*Luke* 1: 55). The Jews claim to be Abraham's *seed* (*John* 8: 33, 37). In *Galatians* 3, Paul speaks about Abraham's *seed*, meaning Abraham's descendants (*Galatians* 3: 16, 29). If we take the word *seed* in that sense here, we will need to spell *Him* with a capital H, and then we will get very good sense. " Anyone who has been born of God does not sin, because God's family constantly abides in Him." The man who is born of God is clearly a member of God's family; God's family are those who abide in God, those who never forget God, those who are constantly aware of God, those who live so near to God that they may be said to abide in God. The man who lives like that will have a strong defence and antiseptic against sin. There is no doubt that that gives excellent sense.

(ii) It is human seed which produces human life. It is the father's seed which produces the child, and the child may be said to have his father's seed in him. Now the Christian is reborn through God, and, therefore, has God's seed in him. This was an idea with which the people of John's age were very familiar. The Gnostics said that God had sowed seeds into this world, and through the action of these seeds the world was being perfected; and they claimed that it was the true Gnostics who had received these seeds. There were some Gnostics who said that man's body is a material and an evil thing, made by the hostile creating god; but into some of these bodies Wisdom secretly sowed seeds, and the truly spiritual men have these seeds of God for souls. This is quite closely connected with the Stoic belief that God is fiery spirit, and a man's soul, that which gives him life and reason, is a spark (*scintilla*) of that divine fire which has come from God to reside in a man's body.

If we take John's words this way, it will mean that every reborn man has the seed of God in him, that every man reborn of God has nothing less than this spark of God in him; and that, therefore, he cannot sin. There is no doubt that John's hearers and readers would know this idea and would recognize it.

(iii) There is a much simpler idea which may well be the idea which is here. Twice at least in the New Testament *the word of God* is that which is said to bring rebirth and recreating to men. James has it: " Of His own will begat He us with the word of truth, that we should be a kind of first-fruits of His creatures " (*James* 1: 18). The word of God is like the seed of God which produces new life. Peter has this idea even more clearly, when he speaks of the Christian, " being born again, not of corruptible seed, but of incorruptible, by the word of God, which liveth and abideth for ever " (1 *Peter* 1: 23). There *the word of God* is definitely identified with *the incorruptible seed of God*. If we take it this way, John will mean that the man who is born of God cannot sin, because he has the strength and the power and the guidance of the word of God, which is the seed of God, within him. This third way is simplest, and, on the whole best. It will mean quite simply that the Christian is preserved from sin by the indwelling power of the word of God.

THE MAN WHO CANNOT SIN

1 *John* 3: 9 (*continued*)

SECOND, this verse presents us with the problem of relating it with certain other things which John has already said

about sin. Let us set the verse down, as it is in the Authorized Version:

> Whosoever is born of God doth not commit sin; for
> His seed remaineth in him; and he cannot sin because
> he is born of God.

Taken at its face value that verse means that it is impossible
for the man who is born of God to sin. Now John has
already said most plainly that, " if we say we have no
sin, we deceive ourselves, and the truth is not in us ";
he says that, " if we say that we have not sinned, we make
God a liar "; and he urges us to confess our sins (I *John*
I: 8-10). Then he goes on to say that, " if we do sin, we
have an advocate with the Father in the person of Jesus
Christ." On the face of it there is contradiction here.
In the one place John is saying that man cannot be anything other than a sinner, and that, when he sins, there
is an atonement for his sin. In the other place he is saying
at least equally definitely that the man who is born of
God cannot sin. Wherein lies the explanation?

(i) John thinks in Jewish categories and in Jewish
pictures, because he could do no other. We have already
seen that John knew and accepted the Jewish picture of
the two ages. There was *this present age*, which is wholly
bad and wholly abandoned to evil; and there was *the
age to come*, which is the golden age of God. We have
also seen that it was John's belief that, whatever the world
was like, Christians by virtue of the work of Christ have
already entered into the new age, and are already living
in it. Now it was exactly one of the characteristics of the
new age that those who lived in it would be free from sin.
In *Enoch* we read: " Then too will wisdom be bestowed
on the elect, and they will all live and *never again sin*,
either through heedlessness or through pride " (*Enoch* 5: 8).
If that is true of the new age, it ought to be true of Christians who are living in it. But, in point of fact, it is still
not true, because Christians have not even yet escaped
from the power of sin. We might then say that in this

passage John is setting down the *ideal* of what should be, and in the other two passages John is facing the *actuality* of what is. We might say that he knows the ideal and confronts men with it; but that he faces the facts and sees the cure in Christ for them.

(ii) It may well be so, but there is more to it than that. In the Greek there is a subtle difference in tenses which makes a very wide difference in meaning. In I *John* 2: I it is John's injunction *that ye sin not*. Now in that verse the verb *to sin* is in the *aorist* tense, and the aorist indicates a particular and definite act. So in that verse what John is saying is quite clearly that Christians must not commit individual acts of sin; but if, through temptation, they do lapse into acts of sin, they have in Christ an advocate to plead their cause, and a sacrifice to atone. On the other hand, in our present passage, I *John* 3: 9, in both cases the verb *to sin* is in the *present* tense, and indicates continuous and constant and habitual action. So what John is saying may be put down in four stages. (*a*) The ideal is that in the new age sin is gone for ever. (*b*) Christians must try to make that true, and, with the help of Christ, they must struggle to avoid individual acts of sin, occasional lapses into that which is wrong, temporary departures from goodness. (*c*) In point of fact all men do have these lapses, and, when they have them, they must humbly confess them to God, who will always forgive the penitent and the contrite heart. (*d*) But, in spite of that, no Christian can possibly be a deliberate and a consistent sinner; no Christian can make sin the policy of his life; no Christian can live a life in which sin is dominant and decisive in all his actions. He may have lapses, but he cannot live in sin as the very atmosphere of his life.

John is not setting before us here a terrifying perfectionism, in which he is demanding a life which is totally and absolutely without sin; but he is demanding a life which is ever on the watch against sin, a life which ever fights the battle of goodness, a life which has never surrendered to sin, a life in which sin is not the permanent state, but only the temporary aberration, a life in which sin is not the normal accepted way, but the abnormal moment of defeat. John is not saying that the man who abides in God cannot sin; but he is saying that the man who abides in God cannot continue to be a consistent and deliberate sinner.

THE MARKS OF THE CHILDREN OF GOD

I *John* 3: 10-18

> In this the children of God and the children of the devil are made plain; anyone who does not do right-eousness is not of God, and neither is he who does not love his brother, because the message that we have heard from the beginning is the message that we should love one another, that we should not be like Cain, who was of the Evil One, and slew his brother. And why did he slay him? Because his works were evil, and his brother's works were just. Do not be surprised, brothers, if the world hates you. We know that we have passed from death to life, because we love the brothers. He who does not love remains in death. Anyone who hates his brother is a murderer. He does not possess eternal life abiding within him. In this we recognize His love, that He laid down His life for us; and we ought to lay down our life for the brothers. Whoever possesses enough for his liveli-hood in this world, and sees his brother in need, and shuts his heart against him, how does the love of God abide in him? My dear children, do not make love a matter of talking and of the tongue, but love in deed and in truth.

THIS is a closely wrought passage with a closely wrought argument, with a kind of parenthesis in the middle of it.

As Westcott has it: " Life reveals the children of God." There is no way of telling what a tree is other than by its fruits, and there is no way of telling what a man is other than by his conduct. So John lays it down that any one who does not do righteousness is thereby demonstrated to be not of God. At present we shall omit the parenthesis and go straight on with the argument.

Although John is a mystic, he has a very practical mind; and, therefore, he will not leave righteousness vague and undefined. Someone might say, " Very well, I accept the fact that the only thing which proves that a man belongs to God is the righteousness of his life. But what is righteousness? " John's answer is clear and unequivocal. *To be righteous is to love our brother men.* That, says John, is a duty and a commandment about which we should never be in any doubt. And he goes on to adduce various reasons why that commandment is so central and so binding.

(i) It is a duty which has been inculcated into the Christian from the very first moment that he entered into the Church. The Christian ethic can be summed up in one word, that word is love. From the moment that a man pledges himself to Christ, and undertakes membership of the Church, he has pledged himself to make love the mainspring of his life.

(ii) For that very reason the fact that a man does love his brother men is the final proof that he has passed from death to life. As A. E. Brooke puts it: " Life is a chance of learning how to love." Life without love is death. To love is to be in the light; to hate is to remain in the dark. We need no further proof of that than to look at the face of a man who is in love and the face of a man who is in hate. The very face of the man will show the glory or the blackness in his heart.

(iii) But, further, not to love is to become a murderer. There can be no doubt that John is thinking of the words of Jesus in the Sermon on the Mount (*Matthew* 5: 21, 22). Jesus said that the old law forbade murder, but the new law declared that anger and bitterness and contempt were just as serious sins. Hatred in the heart must precede the outward act of murder. Whenever there is hatred in the heart a man becomes a potential murderer. To allow hatred to settle in the heart is to break a definite and positive commandment of Jesus Himself. Therefore, the man who loves is a follower of Christ, and the man who hates is no follower of His.

(iv) There follows still another step in this closely-wrought argument. A man may say, " I admit this obligation of love; and I will try to fulfil it; but I do not know what it involves. What is this love which I must show, and in which I must live? " John's answer (verse 16) is: " If you want to see what this love is, look at Jesus Christ. In His death for men on the Cross there is fully displayed the meaning of love." John's answer is that, once a man has seen Christ, he knows the meaning of love. In other words, the Christian life is the imitation of Christ. " Let that mind be in you which was also in Christ Jesus " (*Philippians* 2: 5). " He left us an example that we should follow in His steps " (I *Peter* 4: 21). No man can see Christ and then say that he does not know what the Christian life is.

(v) But John meets still one more possible objection. A man may say, " How can I follow in the steps of Christ? How can I show the love that He showed? He laid down His life upon the Cross. You say I ought to lay down my life for the brothers. But opportunities so vast and so dramatic as that do not come into my life. What then? " John's answer is: " True. But when you see your brother in need, and you have enough, to give to him of what you have is to follow Christ. To shut your heart and to refuse to give is to show that that love of God which was in Jesus Christ has no place in you." John insists that we can find plenty opportunities to show forth the love c. Christ in the life of the every day. C. H. Dodd writes finely on this passage: " There were occasions in the life of the early Church, as there are certainly tragic occasions at the present day, for a quite literal obedience to this precept (i.e., to lay down our life for the brothers). But not all life is tragic; and yet the same principle of conduct must apply all through. Thus it may call for the simple expenditure of money we might have spent upon ourselves, to relieve the need of someone poorer. It is, after all, the same principle of action, though at a lower level of intensity: it is the willingness to surrender that which has value for our own life, to enrich the life of another. If such a minimum response to the law of charity, called for by such an everyday situation, is absent, then it is idle to pretend we are within the family of God, the realm in which love is operative as the principle and the token of eternal life."

Fine words will never take the place of fine deeds; and not all the talk of Christian love in the world will take the place of a kindly action to a man in need, made at the expense of some self-denial and some self-sacrifice, for in that action the principle of the Cross is operative again.

THE WORLD'S RESENTMENT OF THE CHRISTIAN WAY

1 *John* 3: 10-18 (*continued*)

WE said that in this passage there is a parenthesis, and we said that we would return to it, and we do so now.

The parenthesis is the passage in verse 11 and the conclusion which is drawn from it in verse 12. The Christian must not be like Cain who murdered his brother. An action like that is the action of man actuated by hatred, that hatred which is of the devil.

John then goes on to ask why Cain murdered his brother; and his answer is that Cain slew his brother because his works were evil and his brother's works were good. And then John drops the remark: " Do not be surprised, brothers, if the world hates you."

In life an evil man will always instinctively hate a good man. Righteousness always provokes hostility in the minds of those whose actions are basically evil. The reason is that the good man is a walking rebuke to the evil man, even if he never speaks a word to him, and even if there is no direct contact between them. The life of a good man always passes a silent judgment on the life of an evil man. That was the attitude of the wild and loose-living and reckless Alcibiades to Socrates. Socrates was the good man *par excellence*; Alcibiades was brilliant but erratic and often debauched. He used to say to Socrates: " Socrates, I hate you, because every time I meet you, you show me what I am."

The *Wisdom of Solomon* has a grim passage (2: 10-20). In it the evil man is made to speak and to express his attitude to the good man: " Let us lie in wait for the righteous; because he is not for our turn, and he is clean contrary to our doings. . . . He was made to reprove our thoughts. He is grievous unto us even to behold: for his life is not like other men's, his ways are of another fashion. We are esteemed of him as counterfeits: he abstaineth from our ways as from filthiness." The very sight of the good man made the evil man hate him.

Wherever the Christian is, even though he speak no word, he acts as the conscience of society; and for that very reason the world will often hate him.

In ancient Athens the noble Aristides was unjustly condemned to death; and when one of the jurymen was asked how he could have cast his vote against such a man his answer was that he was tired of hearing Aristides called " The Just." The hatred of the world for the Christian is still an ever-present phenomenon, and it is due to the fact that the worldly man sees in the Christian the condemnation of himself; he sees in the Christian that which he is not, and that which in his heart of hearts he knows he ought to be; and, because he will not change, he seeks to eliminate the man who reminds him of the lost goodness.

THE ONLY TEST

I *John* 3: 19-24a

> By this we know that we are of the truth, and by this
> we will reassure our heart before Him, when our
> heart condemns us in anything, for God is greater
> than our hearts, and knows all things. Beloved, if
> our heart does not condemn us, we can come confidently
> to God, and receive from Him whatever we ask,
> because we keep His commandments, and do the
> things which are well pleasing to Him. And this
> is His commandment, that we should believe in the
> name of His Son Jesus Christ, and that we should
> love one another, even as He gave us His command-
> ment. And he who keeps His commandment abides
> in Him, and He in him.

INTO the human heart there are bound to come doubts.
Any man with a sensitive mind and heart must sometimes
wonder, if he really is in any way a Christian at all. John's
test is quite simple and very far-reaching. His test is love.
If we feel love for our fellow-men welling up within our
hearts, then we can be sure that the heart of Christ is in us.
We may be conscious of many sins, but if we are conscious
of love, then we are not far from Christ. John would
have said that a so-called heretic, whose heart was over-
flowing with love, and whose life was beautiful with service,
is far nearer Christ than someone who is impeccably
orthodox, yet coldly correct, and remote from the needs
of men.

Then John goes on to say something which, as far as the
Greek of it goes, can mean two things. He says that that
feeling of love can reassure us in the presence of God.
Our hearts may condemn us, but God is greater than our
hearts. The question is: What is the meaning of that last
phrase?

(i) It could mean: Our hearts condemn us; and God is
infinitely greater than our hearts. How much more,
therefore, must God, the all-holy and the all-knowing
and the all-pure, condemn us? If we take it that way, it

leaves us with nothing but the fear of God, and nothing but the inevitable condemnation of God, and nothing to say but: " God be merciful to me, a sinner." That no doubt is a possible translation, and equally no doubt it is true; but it is not what John is saying in this context, for here he is thinking of our confidence in God, and not our dread of God.

(ii) The passage must therefore mean this: Our hearts condemn us—that is inevitable. But God is greater than our hearts; He knows all things. Not only does He know our sins; He also knows our love, our longings, the nobility that never fully works itself out, our penitence and our dreams; and the greatness of His knowledge gives Him the sympathy which can understand, which can accept not only what we have done, but also what we meant to do, which can forgive.

It is this very knowledge of God which gives us our hope. " Man," as Thomas à Kempis said, " sees the deed, but God knows the intention." Men can only judge us by our actions, but God can judge us by the longings which never became deeds, and the dreams which never came true. When Solomon was dedicating the Temple, he spoke of how David had wished to build a house for God, and how that privilege had been denied to him. " It was in the heart of David, my father, to build an house for the name of the Lord God of Israel. And the Lord said unto David, my father, ' Whereas it was in thy heart to build an house unto my name, thou didst well that it was in thine heart ' " (I *Kings* 8: 17, 18). The French proverb says, " To know all is to forgive all." Men judge us by our deeds; they cannot do otherwise. But God judges us by the deep emotions of our hearts; and, if in our heart there is love, then, however dim and feeble and imperfect and helpless that love may be, we can with confidence enter into His presence. The perfect knowledge which belongs to God, and to God alone, is not our terror, but our hope.

THE INSEPARABLE COMMANDS

I *John* 3: 19-24a (*continued*)

JOHN goes on to speak of the two things which are well-pleasing in God's sight, the two commandments on obedience to which our relationship to God depends.

(i) We must believe in the name of His Son Jesus Christ. Here we have that use of the word *name* which is peculiar to the biblical writers. Again and again, as the biblical writers use it, the word *name* does not mean simply the name by which a person is called; it means the whole nature and character of that person as far as it is known and revealed to us. The Psalmist writes: " Our help is in the name of the Lord " (*Psalm* 124: 8). Clearly that does not mean that our help lies in the fact that God is called Jehovah; it means that our help is in the love, the mercy, the power, the compassion which have been revealed to us as the nature and the character of God. So, then, to believe in the *name* of God's Son, Jesus Christ, means to believe in the nature and the character of Jesus Christ. It means to believe that He is the Son of God, that He does stand in relation to God in a way in which no other person in the universe ever stood or ever can stand, that He can perfectly reveal God to men, and that He is the Saviour of our souls. To believe in the name of Jesus Christ is to accept Jesus Christ for what He really is.

(ii) We must love one another, even as He gave us His commandment. The commandment is in *John* 13: 34; it is the commandment that we should love one another as He has loved us. We must love each other with that same selfless, sacrificial, forgiving love with which Jesus Christ loved us.

When we put these two commandments together we find the great truth that the Christian life depends on right belief and right conduct combined. We cannot have the one without the other. There can be no such thing as a Christian theology without a Christian ethic; and equally

there can be no such thing as a Christian ethic without a Christian theology. The one depends on the other. Our belief is not real belief unless it issues in action; and our action has neither sanction nor dynamic unless it is based on belief.

We cannot begin the Christian life until we accept Jesus Christ for what He is and for who He is; and we have not accepted Him in any real sense of the term util our attitude to men is the same as His own attitude of love.

THE PERILS OF THE SURGING LIFE OF THE SPIRIT

I *John* 3: 24b—4: I

> This is how we know that He abides in us, by the Spirit which He gave to us. Beloved, do not believe every spirit, but test the spirits to see if their source is God, because many false prophets have gone out into the world.

BEHIND this warning there is a situation of which we in the modern Church know little or nothing. In the early Church there was a surging life of the Spirit which brought its own perils. These perils came from the very fact that the early Church was so vividly and vitally alive. In the Church there were so many and such diverse spiritual manifestations that some kind of criterion and test and touchstone was necessary. First of all, let us try to think ourselves back into that electric atmosphere.

(i) Even in Old Testament times men realized the perils of false prophets who were men of spiritual power. *Deuteronomy* 13: 1-5 demands that the false prophet, who sought to lure men away from the true God, should be put to death. But that very passage frankly and freely admits that the false prophet may offer and promise signs and wonders, and may perform them. The spiritual power is there, but it is an evil and a misdirected power.

(ii) We must always remember that in the early Church the spiritual world was very near and close. All the world believed in a universe, not only peopled, but thronged with demons and spirits and spiritual powers. Every rock and tree and river and grove and lake and mountain had its demon, its spiritual power; and these spiritual powers were always seeking an entry into men's bodies and men's minds. In the time of the early Church all men lived in a haunted world. There never was a time when men were so conscious of being surrounded by spiritual powers.

(iii) That ancient world was very conscious of a personal power of evil. It saw the whole universe as a battleground between the forces of the light and the forces of the dark. It did not speculate about the source of that personal power of evil, but it was sure that that power was there, and that that power was seeking for men who might be its agents and its instruments. It therefore follows that not only the universe, but also the minds of men, were the battleground on which the power of the light and the power of the dark fought out the issue.

(iv) It must be remembered that in the early Church the coming of the Spirit was a much more visible phenomenon than it is nowadays. The coming of the Spirit was usually connected with baptism; and when the Spirit came things happened that anyone could see. The man who received the Spirit was visibly and obviously affected; he was physically moved. When the apostles came down to Samaria, after the preaching of Philip, and conferred the gift of the Spirit on the new converts, the results and effects were so obvious and startling that the local magician, Simon Magus, wished to buy the power to produce the same effect (Acts 8: 17, 18). The coming of the Spirit on Cornelius and his people was something which anyone could see (Acts 10: 44, 45). In the early Church there was an ecstatic element in the coming of the Spirit the effects of which were violent and obvious.

(v) This had its effect in the congregational life of the early Church. The best commentary on this passage of John is, in fact, I *Corinthians* 14. Because of the power of the Spirit men spoke with tongues. That is to say, they poured out a flood of Spirit-given sounds in no known language, and which no one could understand, unless there was someone present who had the equally Spirit-given power to interpret. So violent and extraordinary was this phenomenon that Paul does not hesitate to say that, if a stranger came into a congregation in which it was in action, he would think that he had arrived in an assembly of madmen (I *Corinthians* 14: 2, 23, 27). Even the prophets, who delivered their message in plain language, were a problem. They were so moved by the Spirit that they could not wait for each other to finish, and each would leap to his feet determined to shout out his Spirit-given message (I *Corinthians* 14: 26, 27, 33). A service in an early Christian congregation was very different from the placidity of a modern Church service. So diverse and varied were the manifestations of the Spirit that Paul numbers the *discerning of spirits* among the spiritual gifts which a Christian might possess (I *Corinthians* 12: 10). We can see what might happen in such a case when Paul speaks of the possibility of a man saying in a Spirit that Christ is accursed (I *Corinthians* 12: 3).

When we come further down in Christian history we find the problem still more acute. The *Didache*, or *The Teaching of the Twelve Apostles*, is the first service order book, and dates to somewhere not long after A.D. 100. It has regulations on how to deal with the wandering apostles and prophets who came and went amongst the Christian congregations. " Not every one who speaks in a spirit is a prophet; he is only a prophet if he walks in the ways of the Lord " (*Didache* 11 and 12). The matter reached its peak and *ne plus ultra* when, in the third century, Montanus burst upon the Church with the claim that he was nothing less than the promised Paraclete, and that he proposed to tell the Church the things which Christ had said that His apostles could not at the moment bear.

The early Church was full of this surging life of the Spirit. The ministry was not professionalized; the exuberance of life had not been organized out of the Church; men lived in a Spirit-filled world. Clearly that was a great age; but its very exuberance had its dangers. If there was a personal power of evil, men could be used by that power. If there were evil spirits as well as the Holy Spirit, men could be occupied by these spirits. Men could be swept away by a kind of self-hypnotism into what looked like possession by the Spirit. Men could delude themselves into a quite subjective experience in which they thought—quite honestly—that they had a message from the Spirit.

All that is in John's mind; and it is in face of that surging atmosphere of pulsating spiritual life that he sets out his criteria to judge between the true and the false. We may well feel that, with all its perils, that exuberant vitality of the early Church was a far better thing than the listless, unexcited, apathetic placidity of so much of the life of the modern Church. It was surely better that men should expect the Spirit everywhere, than that they should expect Him nowhere.

· · · · · · ·

A Note on the Translation of I *John* 4: 1-7

There is a recurring Greek phrase in this passage which is by no means easy to translate. It is the phrase which the Authorized Version consistently renders *of God.* Its occurrences are as follows:

Verse 1: Try the spirits whether they are *of God.*

Verse 2: Every spirit that confesseth that Jesus Christ is come in the flesh is *of God.*

Verse 3: Every spirit that confesseth not that Jesus Christ is come in the flesh is not *of God.*

Verse 4: Ye are *of God,* little children.

Verse 6: We are *of God.* . . . He that is not *of God* heareth not us.

Verse 7: Love is *of God*.

The difficulty in the translation of this phrase can be seen in the expedients to which various translators are driven.

The American Revised Standard Version retains the Authorized Version translation in all cases.

Moffatt, in verses 1, 2 and 3, translates *comes from God*; and in verses 4, 6 and 7 *belongs to God*.

Weymouth, in verses 1, 2 and 3, translates *is from God*. In verse 4 he translates: *You are God's children*. In verse 6 he translates: We are *God's children. . . .* He who is not *a child of God* does not listen to us. In verse 7 he has: Love *has its origin in God*.

In every case, except verse 7, Kingsley Williams translates *from God*; in verse 7 he has *of God*.

The difficulty is easy to see; and yet it is of the first importance to be able to attach a precise meaning to this phrase. The phrase in Greek is *ek tou theou*. *Ho theos* means *God*, and *tou theou* is the genitive case after the preposition *ek*. *Ek* is one of the commonest Greek prepositions and means *out of* or *from*. To say that a man came *ek tēs poleōs* would mean that he came either *out of* or *from* the city. What then does it mean that a person, or a spirit, or a quality is *ek tou theou*? The simplest translation is simply *from God*. But what does the word *from* mean in that phrase? Quite certainly it means that the person, the spirit, or the quality *has its source and origin in God*. It comes from God in the sense that it takes its source and origin in Him, and its life from Him. So John, for instance, bids his people to test the spirits to see whether they really have their source and origin in God. Love, he says, has its source and origin in God. This is the translation we have used, and this is the explanation of how it has been arrived at.

THE ULTIMATE HERESY

I *John* 4: 2, 3

> This is how you recognize the spirit whose source is God. Every spirit which openly acknowledges that Jesus has come in the flesh and is Christ has its origin in God. And every spirit which is such that it does **not** make this confession about Jesus has not its

source in God; and this is the spirit of antichrist, about which you heard that it was to come, and which is now here present in the world.

AMID all the exuberance of spiritual activity of that world of the early Church, John lays down one final test. For John, Christian belief could be summed up in one great sentence: " The Word became flesh, and dwelt among us " (*John* I: I4). Any spirit which denied the reality of the Incarnation was not of God. John lays down two tests of belief.

(i) To be of God a spirit must acknowledge that Jesus is the Christ, the Messiah. As John saw it, to deny that truth is to deny three things about Jesus. (*a*) It is to deny that He is the centre of history; the one for whom all history was a preparation; the one for whose coming God had chosen the man Abraham and the nation Israel; the one for whom all history had been a preparation, and who came in the fulness of time. (*b*) It is to deny that He is the fulfilment of the promises of God. All through their struggles and their defeats, all through the agonies of their history, the Jews had clung to the promises of God. To deny that Jesus is the promised Messiah is to deny that these promises were true. (*c*) It is to deny His Kingship. Jesus Christ came, not only to sacrifice, but to reign. He came, not only to accept a Cross, but also to found a Kingdom; and to deny His Messiahship is to leave out the essential kingliness of Christ.

(ii) To be of God a spirit must acknowledge that Jesus has come in the flesh. It was precisely this that the Gnostics could never accept. Their view was that matter was altogether evil; that, therefore, the body is evil; and that, therefore, a real incarnation is an impossibility, for God could never take flesh upon Himself. Augustine was later to say that in the pagan philosophers he could find parallels for everything in the New Testament except for one saying—" The Word became flesh." As John saw it, to deny the complete reality of the incarnation, to deny the complete manhood of Jesus Christ, was to strike at the very roots of the Christian faith. To deny the complete reality of the incarnation has certain quite definite consequences.

(i) It is to deny that Jesus can ever be our pattern or example. If He was not in any real sense a man, living under the same conditions as men, then He cannot show men how to live, for life for Him was a completely different thing from life as it is for us.

(ii) It is to deny that Jesus can be the High Priest who opens the way for us to God. The true High Priest, as the writer to the Hebrews saw, must be like men in all things; he must know our infirmities and our temptations (*Hebrews* 4: 14, 15). To lead men to God the High Priest must be a man, or else he will be pointing them to a road which it is impossible for them to take.

(iii) It is to deny that Jesus can in any real sense be Saviour. To save men He had to be one with men; He had to know human experience; He had to identify Himself with the men whom He came to save.

(iv) It is to deny the possibility of the salvation of the body. On one thing Christian teaching is quite clear— salvation is the salvation of the whole man. The body as well as the soul is saved and consecrated. To deny the incarnation is to deny the possibility that the body can ever be consecrated and dedicated to God, and that the body can ever become the temple of the Holy Spirit.

(v) But by far the most serious and terrible thing is that to deny the incarnation is to deny that there can ever be any real union between the human and the divine, between God and man. If spirit is altogether good, and if the body is altogether evil, then God and man can never meet, so long as man is man. God and man might meet, when man had sloughed off the body, and had become, literally, a *disembodied* spirit. But the great truth of the incarnation is that here and now, in this world of sense and time, there can be real communion between God and man. To deny the incarnation and the possibility of that incarnation is to deny that great and precious truth.

Nothing in Christianity is more central than the reality of the incarnation, the manhood of Jesus Christ.

THE CLEAVAGE BETWEEN THE WORLD AND GOD

I *John* 4: 4-6

> You have your source and origin in God, dear children, and you have won the victory over them, because that power which is in you is greater than the power which is in the world. This is why the source of their speaking is the world, and is the reason why the world listens to them. Our source and origin is God. He who knows God listens to us. He who has not his source in God does not listen to us. This is how we know the spirit of truth and the spirit of error.

HERE John lays down one great truth, and faces one great problem.

(i) The Christian need not fear the heretic. In Christ the victory over all the powers of evil was won. The powers of evil did their worst to Him, even to killing Him on a Cross, and in the end He emerged victorious. That victory belongs to the Christian. Whatever things look like the powers of evil and of falsehood are fighting a losing battle. As the Latin proverb has it: " Great is the truth, and in the end it will prevail." All that the Christian has to do is to remember the truth which he already knows, and to cling to it. The truth is that by which men live; error is ultimately that by which men die.

(ii) That is so; but the problem remains that the false teachers will neither listen to, nor accept, the truth which the true Christian offers. How is that to be explained? Here John returns to his favourite antithesis, the opposition between the world, the *kosmos* and God. The world, as we have seen before, is human nature apart from, and in opposition to, God. The man whose source and origin is

God will welcome the truth; the man whose source and origin is the world will reject the truth.

When we come to think of it, that is an obvious truth. How can a man whose watchword is competition even begin to understand an ethic whose key-note is service? How can a man whose aim is the exaltation of the self, who believes in the survival of the fittest, and who holds that the weakest must go to the wall, even begin to understand a teaching whose principle for living is love? How can a man who believes that this is the only world, and that, therefore, material things are the only things which matter, even begin to understand a life which is lived in the light of eternity, and where it is the unseen things which are the greatest values in life? A man can hear only what he has fitted himself to hear, and, therefore, he can unfit himself to hear the Christian message at all.

That is what John is saying. We have seen again and again that it is characteristic of John to see things in terms of black and white. His thinking does not deal in shades. On the one side there is the man whose source and origin is God, the man who can hear the truth; on the other side there is the man whose source and origin is the world, and who is incapable of hearing the truth. There emerges a problem, which very likely John at the moment did not even think of. Are there then people to whom all preaching and all missionary work is quite useless? Are there people whose defences can never be penetrated, whose deafness can never hear, and whose minds are for ever shut to the invitation and command of Jesus Christ? As we have said, that question was not at the moment on John's horizon at all; he was simply stating things in terms of the blackest black and the whitest white.

The answer must be that there are no limits to the grace of God, and that there is such a person as the Holy Spirit. It is the lesson of life that the love of God can break every barrier down. It is true that a man can resist; it is, maybe, true that a man can resist even to the end. But what is also true is that Christ is always knocking at the door of every heart, and it is possible for every man to hear the voice of Christ, even above the many voices of the dominant world.

LOVE HUMAN AND DIVINE

I *John* 4: 7-21

> Beloved, let us love one another, because love has its source in God, and everyone who loves has God as the source of his birth, and knows God. He who does not love has not come to know God. In this God's love is displayed within us, that God sent His only Son into the world that through Him we might live. In this is love, not that we love God, but that He loved us, and sent His Son to be an atoning sacrifice for our sins. Brothers, if God so loved us, we too ought to love each other. No one has ever seen God. If we love each other God dwells in us, and His love is perfected in us. It is by this that we know that we dwell in Him, and He in us, because He has given us a share of His Spirit. We have seen and we testify that the Father sent the Son as the Saviour of the world. Whoever openly acknowledges that Jesus is the Son of God, God dwells in him, and he in God. We have come to know and to put our trust in the love which God has within us. God is love, and he who dwells in love dwells in God, and God dwells in him. With us love finds its peak in this, that we should have confidence in the day of judgment, because, even as He is, so also are we in this world. There is no fear in love; but perfect love casts out fear, for fear is connected with punishment, and he who fears has not reached love's perfect state. We love because He first loved us. If any one says, " I love God," and hates his brother, he is a liar; for he who does not love his brother, whom he has seen, cannot love God whom he has not seen. It is this command that we have from Him, that he who loves God, loves his brother also.

THIS passage is so closely interwoven that we are better first to read it as a whole, and then bit by bit to draw its teaching from it. First of all, then, let us look at its teaching on love.

(i) Love has its origin in God (verse 7). It is from the God who is love that all love takes its source. As A. E. Brooke puts it: " Human love is a reflection of something in the divine nature itself." We are never nearer to God than when we love. Clement of Alexandria said in a startling phrase that the true Gnostic, the real Christian, " practises being God." When we love we are bearing on us the reflection of God, and we are living the very life of God. Love makes us kin to God. He who dwells in love dwells in God (verse 16). Man is made in the image and the likeness of God (*Genesis* 1: 26). God is love, and, therefore, to be like God, to be what he was meant to be, man must also love.

(ii) Love has a double relationship to God. It is only by knowing God that we learn to love, and it is only by loving that we learn to know God (verses 7 and 8). It is when God dwells within our heart that we learn to love; and, when we love, we come closer and closer to God. Love comes from God, and love leads to God.

(iii) It is by love that God is known (verse 12). We cannot see God, because God is spirit; what we can see is the effect of God. We cannot see the wind, but we can see what the wind can do. We cannot see electricity, but we can see the effect that electricity produces. Now the effect of God is love. It is when God comes into a man that a man is clothed with the love of God and the love of men. God is known by His effect on that man. As it has been said, " A saint is a man in whom Christ lives again," and the best demonstration of God comes not from argument, but from a life of love. In such a life God is seen as He is seen nowhere else.

(iv) God's love is demonstrated to us in Jesus Christ (verse 9). It is in Jesus that we see fully displayed the love of God. When we look at Jesus we see two things about the love of God. (*a*) It is the love which holds nothing back. God sent for men His only Son; God was prepared to give His dearest one, to make a sacrifice beyond which no sacrifice can possibly go, in His love for men. (b) It is a totally undeserved love. It would be no wonder if we loved God, when we remember all the gifts He has given to us, even apart from Jesus Christ; the wonder is that God loves poor and disobedient creatures like us.

> How Thou canst think so well of us,
>   And be the God Thou art,
> Is darkness to my intellect,
>   But sunshine to my heart.

(v) Human love is a response to divine love (verse 19). We love because God loved us. It is the sight of the love of God which must waken in us the desire to love God as He first loved us, and to love our fellow-men as He loves them. Human love is not a product of the human heart; it is not something which a man could create for himself; it is the response to the divine love of God.

(vi) When love comes, fear goes (verses 17 and 18). Fear is the characteristic emotion of someone who expects to be punished. So long as we regard God as the Judge, the King, the Law-giver, there can be nothing in our heart but a dominant emotion of fear, for in face of such a God we could expect nothing but punishment, and even annihilation. But once we know that God is love, fear is swallowed up in love. It is true that in its place there is left a different kind of fear, the fear of grieving the love which so loved us.

(vii) Love of God and love of man are indissolubly connected (verses 7, 11, 20, 21). As C. H. Dodd finely puts it: " The energy of love discharges itself along lines which form a triangle, whose points are God, self, and neighbour." If God loves us, we are bound to love each other, because it is our destiny and our highest aim to reproduce the life of God in humanity, and the life of eternity in time. John says, with an almost crude bluntness, that a man who claims to love God, and who hates his brother, is nothing other than a liar. The only way to prove that we love God is to love the men whom God loves. The only way to prove that God is within our hearts is constantly to show the love of men within our lives.

GOD IS LOVE

I *John* 4: 7-21 *(continued)*

It is in this passage that there occurs what is probably the greatest single statement about God in the whole Bible, the statement that *God is love*. It is amazing how many doors that single statement unlocks, and to see to how many questions it is the answer. Let us see some of the things of which the fact that God is love is the explanation.

(i) It is the explanation of *creation*. Sometimes we are bound to wonder why God created this world. To God the world has been a heartbreak. The disobedience, the rebelliousness, the lack of response in men is a continual grief to God. Why should God create a world which was to bring Him nothing but trouble? The answer is that God created the world because creation is essential to the very nature of God. If God is love, it means that God cannot exist in lonely isolation. Love, to be love, must have someone to love, and someone to love it. God's act of creation was a necessity of His divine nature, because, being love, it was necessary for God to have someone whom He might love, and who might love Him.

(ii) It is the explanation of *free-will*. Unless love is a free response it is not love. There can be no love which is not spontaneous love. Had God been only law He could have created a world in which men moved like automata, constantly obedient to the laws of the universe and of God because they had no more choice than a machine has. But, if God had made men like that, there would have been no possibility of a personal relationship between God and man. Love is of necessity the free choice and the free response of the heart; and, therefore, before men could love God in any real sense of the term, their wills had to be free; and, therefore, God, by a deliberate act of self-limitation, had to endow men with free will that the very purpose of creation might be fulfilled.

(iii) It is the explanation of *providence*. Had God been simply mind and order and law, He might, so to speak, have created the universe, wound it up, set it going, and left it. He might have used it as a man uses a machine, never paying any regard to it unless something goes wrong. There are, indeed articles and machines which we are urged to buy because we can fit them and forget them. Their most attractive quality is that they can be left alone to run themselves. But, because God is love, His creating act is followed by His constant care. He not only created the world, His love for ever sustains, upholds and broods over the world of His love.

(iv) It is the explanation of *redemption*. If God were only law and justice, He would simply leave men to the consequences of their sin. The moral law would operate; the soul that sinned would die; and the eternal justice would inexorably hand out its rewards and punishments. But the very fact that God is love means that God must seek and save that which is lost. He must find a remedy for sin, and a cure for the sickness of the soul. It is impossible totally to kill the love of a parent for a child, and God is the Father of men.

(v) It is the explanation of the *life beyond*. If God were simply creator, then men might live their brief span and die for ever. The life which ended too soon would be only another flower which the frost of death had withered too soon. But the very fact that God is love makes it certain that the chances and the changes of life have not the last word, but that there is a love of God which will readjust the balance of this life.

SON OF GOD AND SAVIOUR OF MEN

I John 4: 7-21 (*continued*)

BEFORE we leave this passage we must note that it has also great things to say about Jesus Christ.

(i) It tells us that Jesus is *the bringer of life*. God sent Him, that through Him we might have life (verse 9). There is a world of difference between existence and life. All men have existence, but all do not have life. The very eagerness with which men seek pleasure shows that there is something missing in their lives. A famous doctor once said that men would find a cure for cancer more quickly than they would find a cure for boredom. Jesus gives a man an object for which to live; He gives him strength by which to live; and He gives Him peace in which to live. With Jesus there comes into life the thrill of a great adventure; the strength to master life's frustrations; and a background of serenity and content. Living with Christ turns mere existence into fulness of life.

(ii) It tells us that Jesus is *the restorer of the lost relationship with God*. God sent Him to be the atoning sacrifice for sin (verse 10). Nowadays we do not move in a world of thought in which animal sacrifice is in any sense a reality. But we can fully understand what sacrifice meant. When a man sinned, his relationship with God was broken; and sacrifice was an expression of penitence, designed to restore the lost relationship with God. Jesus, by His life and death, made it possible for man to enter into a new relationship of intimacy and peace and friendship and fellowship with God. He broke the barriers down, and bridged the awful gulf between man and God.

(iii) It tells us that Jesus is *the Saviour of the world* (verse 14). When Jesus came into the world, men were conscious of nothing so much as their own weakness and helplessness. Men, said Seneca, were looking *ad salutem*; they were searching for salvation. They were desperately conscious of " their weakness in necessary things." They wanted " a hand let down to lift them up." It would be quite inadequate to think of salvation as salvation from the penalties and the punishment of hell. Men need to be saved from themselves; they need to be saved from the habits which have become their fetters; they need to be saved from their temptations; they need to be saved from their fears and their anxieties; they need to be saved from their own follies and their own mistakes. In every case Jesus brings men salvation. He brings that which enables men to face time and to meet eternity.

(iv) It tells us that Jesus is *the Son of God* (verse 15). Whatever that may mean, it certainly means this—that Jesus Christ is in a relationship to God in which no other person ever stood, or ever will stand. He alone can show men what God is like; He alone can bring to men the grace, the love, the forgiveness and the strength of God. Through Him alone men can perfectly find and perfectly know and perfectly love God.

One other thing emerges in this passage. It has taught us of God, and it has taught us of Jesus, and it teaches us of the Spirit. In verse 13, John says it is because we have a share of the Spirit that we know that we dwell in God. It is the work of the Spirit which in the beginning makes us seek God at all; it is the work of the Spirit which makes us aware of the presence of God; and it is the work of the Spirit which gives us the certainty that we are truly at peace with God. It is the Spirit in our hearts which makes us dare to address God as Father (*Romans* 8: 15, 16). The Spirit is the inner witness, who, as C. H. Dodd puts it, gives us the "immediate, spontaneous, unanalysable awareness of a divine presence in our lives."

> " And His that gentle voice we hear,
>   Soft as the breath of even,
> That checks each fault, that calms each fear,
>   And speaks of heaven.
>
> And every virtue we possess,
>   And every victory won,
> And every thought of holiness,
>   Are His alone."

LOVE WITHIN THE DIVINE FAMILY

I *John* 5: 1, 2

> Everyone who believes that Jesus is the Christ has experienced the birth which comes from God; and everyone who loves the father loves the child. This is how we know that we must be loving the children of God, whenever we love God and keep His commandments.

As John wrote this passage, there were two things in the background of his mind.

(i) There was the great fact which is the basis of all his thinking, the fact that love of God and love of man are inseparable parts of the same experience. In answer to the questioning scribe Jesus had said that there were two great commandments. The first laid it down that we must love God with all our heart and soul and mind and strength; and the second laid it down that we must love our neighbour as ourselves. Than these commandments there are none greater (*Mark* 12: 28-31). In John's mind there was this word of his Lord.

(ii) But also in his mind there was a natural human law of human life. Family love is a part of nature. The child naturally and instinctively loves his parents; and he just as naturally loves the brothers and sisters whom his father begat. The second part of verse 1 literally runs: " Everyone who loves him who begat loves him who was begotten of him." Put much more simply that means: " If we love a father, we also love his child." So John is thinking of the love which naturally binds a man to the father who begat him, and to the other children whom the father has begotten.

John transfers this to the realm of Christian thought and experience. Christianity is a rebirth; the Christian undergoes the experience of being reborn. In this case the father who begets him is no human father; the father is God; and the Christian is bound to love God for all that God has done for his soul. But birth is always into a family; and the Christian is reborn into the family of God. As it was for Jesus, so it is for him—those who do the will of God, as he himself does, become his mother, his sisters and his brothers (*Mark* 3: 35). If, then, the Christian loves God the Father who begat him, he must also love the other children whom God has begotten. His love of God, and his love of his Christian brothers and sisters, must be parts of the same love, and they must be so closely interlocked that they can never be separated.

As it has been put: " Man is not only born *to love*, he is also born *to be loved*. As A. E. Brooke put it: " Everyone who has been born of God must love those who have been similarly ennobled."

Long before this the Psalmist had said that, " God setteth the solitary in families " (*Psalm* 68: 6). The Christian, by virtue of his rebirth is set within the family of God, and as he loves the Father, so must he also love the children who are of the same family as he is. To love God and to keep His commandments is to love the brothers.

THE NECESSARY OBEDIENCE

I *John* 5: 3, 4a

> For this is the love of God, that we should keep His commandments; and His commandments are not heavy, because everything that is born of God conquers the world.

ONCE again John reverts to an idea which is never far from the surface of his mind and the centre of his thinking. *Obedience is the only proof of love.* We cannot prove our love to anyone in any other way than by seeking to please him and to bring him joy. Love can be exemplified only in obedience.

Then John quite suddenly says a most surprising thing. God's commandments, he says, are not heavy. We must note two general things here. By that he certainly does not mean that obedience to God's commandments is easy to achieve. Christian love is no easy matter. It is never an easy thing to love the people whom we do not like, the people who sometimes hurt our feelings, the people who sometimes insult or injure us. It is never an easy thing to solve the problem of living together; and when that problem becomes the problem of living together on the Christian standard of life, it indeed becomes a task of immense difficulty. Further, there is in this saying an implied contrast. Jesus spoke of the Scribes and Pharisees as " binding heavy burdens and grievous to be borne, and laying them on men's shoulders " (*Matthew* 23: 4). The Scribal and Pharisaic mass of rules and regulations could be an intolerable burden on the shoulders of any man. There is no doubt that John is remembering that Jesus said, " My yoke is easy and my burden is light " (*Matthew* 11: 30). How then is this to be explained? How can it be said that the tremendous commands and demands of Jesus are not a heavy burden on any man? There are three answers to that question.

(i) It is the way of God never to lay a commandment on any man without also giving him the strength to carry it out. With the vision comes the power. With the need for it there comes the strength. God does not give us His commandments and then go away and leave us to ourselves. He is there always by our side and within our hearts to enable us to carry out what He has commanded. God's duty always carries with it God's inspiration. What is impossible for us becomes possible with God, for with God's help all things are possible. It is one of the facts of human experience that we never know what we can do until we try. The impossible is always becoming the possible for the man who will try—with God.

(ii) But there is another great truth here. Our whole response to God must be the response of love; and for love no duty is too hard and no task is too great. That which we would never do for a stranger we will willingly attempt for a loved one. That which we would never give to a stranger we will gladly give to a loved one. That which would be an impossible sacrifice, if a stranger demanded it, becomes a willing gift when love needs it. There is an old and often-retold story which is a kind of parable of this. Someone once met a lad going to school long before the days when transport was provided. The lad was carrying a smaller boy on his back, and the smaller boy was clearly lame and unable to walk and so had to be carried. The stranger said to the lad, " Do you carry him to school every day? " " Yes," said the boy. " That's a heavy burden for you to carry," said the stranger. " He's no' a burden," said the boy. " He's my brother." Love turned the burden into no burden at all. It must be so with us and Christ. His commandments are not a burden, they are a privilege; for to have to carry them is an opportunity to show our love.

Difficult the commandments of Christ are; burdensome they are not; for Christ never laid a commandment on a man without giving him the strength to carry it; and every commandment that is laid upon us provides another chance to show our love.

We must leave the third answer to our next section.

THE CONQUEST OF THE WORLD

1 *John* 5: 4b, 5

> And this is the conquest which has conquered the world, our faith. Who is he who conquers the world but he who believes that Jesus is the Son of God?

(iii) We have seen that the commandments of Jesus Christ are not grievous and heavy, because with the commandment there comes the power, and because we accept them in love. To obey them is to receive an opportunity to demonstrate our love, and is, therefore, a privilege, and not a burden. But there is still another great truth. There is something in the Christian which makes him able to conquer the world. The world, the *kosmos*, is the world apart from God, the world in opposition to God, the world which tries to make us forget God, and to abandon the standards of God. That which enables us to conquer the world is *faith*.

What, then, is this conquering faith? John himself defines it. It is the belief that Jesus is the Son of God. That is to say, the conquering faith is belief in the Incarnation. Why should that be so important and so victory-giving? If we believe in the incarnation, it means that we believe that in Jesus Christ God entered the world and took our human life upon Himself. If God did that, it means that God *cared* enough for men to lay aside His glory and to take upon Himself the limitations of humanity, which is an unimaginable sacrifice and the act of a love which passes human understanding. If God did that, it means that God *shares* in all the manifold activities of human life, and knows the many and varied trials and temptations and sorrows of this life and of this world. It means that God is involved in the human situation. It means that everything that happens to us is fully understood by God; it means that God is in this business of living along with us. Faith in the incarnation is the conviction that God shares and God cares. Once we possess that faith certain things follow.

(i) We have a defence to resist the infections of the world. On all sides there is the pressure of worldly standards and motives. On all sides there are the fascinations of the wrong things. From within and without there come the temptations which are part of the human situation in a world and a society which is not interested in, and which is sometimes hostile to, God. But once we are certain of, and always aware of, the presence of God in Jesus Christ for ever with us, we have a strong prophylactic against the infections of the world. It is the fact of experience that goodness is easier in the company of good people. And if we believe in the incarnation, we have the continual presence of God in Jesus Christ.

(ii) We have a strength to endure the attacks of the world. The human situation is full of things which seek to take our faith away. There are the sorrows of life, the things which happen to us, which are beyond all understanding. There are the disappointments of life, the things which seek to rob us of our dreams. There are for most of us the constant failures of life, which seek to make us feel that it is useless to try, and that we may as well abandon the struggle. But if we believe in the incarnation, we believe in a God who Himself went through all this, even to the Cross, and who can help others who are going through it, because He went through it Himself.

(iii) We have the indestructible hope of final victory. The world did its worst to Jesus. It hunted Him and hounded Him and slandered Him. It branded Him heretic and sinner and friend of sinners. It judged Him and tried Him and crucified Him and buried Him. It did everything humanly possible to break Him and to eliminate Him— *and it failed.* After the Cross there came the Resurrection, and after the shame there came the glory. That is the Jesus who is with us. We have with us One who saw life at its grimmest, One to whom life did its worst, One who died and who could not be holden of death, and One who offers us a share in that victory which was His. If we believe in the incarnation, in the life, the death, and the resurrection of Jesus Christ, then we have with us for ever Christ the Victor to give us the victory.

THE WATER AND THE BLOOD

I John 5: 6-8

> This is He who came through water and blood— Jesus Christ. It was not only by water that He came, but by water and by blood. And it is the Spirit which testifies to this, because the Spirit is truth; because there are three who testify, the Spirit, and the water, and the blood, and the three agree in one.

PLUMMER, in beginning to comment on this passage says: " This is the most perplexing passage in the Epistle, and one of the most perplexing in the New Testament." No doubt, if we knew the circumstances in which John was writing, if we had full knowledge of the heresies against which he was defending his people, if we could reconstruct the whole background of thought, the meaning would become clear, but, as it is, we can only guess. We do, however, know enough of the background to be fairly sure that we can come at the meaning of John's words.

We may first note two general facts. First, it is clear that the words *water* and *blood* in connection with Jesus had for John a very special mystical and symbolic meaning. In John's story of the cross there is a curious pair of verses:

> One of the soldiers with a spear pierced Jesus' side, and forthwith came there out blood and water. And he that saw it bare record and the record is true; and he knoweth that he saith true, that he might believe (*John* 19: 34, 35).

Clearly John attaches very particular importance to that incident, and he guarantees it with a very special certificate of evidence. To John the words *water* and *blood* in connection with Jesus conveyed an essential part of the meaning of the gospel.

The first verse of the passage is obscurely expressed— " This is He who came through water and blood—Jesus Christ." The meaning is that this is He who entered into His Messiahship, or, who was shown to be the Christ, through water and blood.

In connection with Jesus *water* and *blood* can refer only to two events of His life. The *water* must refer to His *baptism*; the *blood* must refer to His *Cross*. So, then, John is saying, that *both* the baptism and the Cross of Jesus are essential parts of His Messiahship. John goes on to say that it was not by water only that He came, but by water *and* by blood. It is, then, clear that there were some who were saying that Jesus did come by water, but not by blood; that is to say, that His baptism was an essential part of His Messiahship, but His Cross was not. This is what gives us our clue to what lies behind this passage.

We have seen again and again that behind this letter there lies the heresy of Gnosticism. And we have also seen that Gnosticism believed that Spirit was altogether good and that matter was altogether evil. This belief made the Gnostics reject any full doctrine of the incarnation, and it made them deny that God came in the flesh. They could not involve God in the flesh, and least of all could they involve the serene, remote, spiritual God in the sufferings of the flesh. So they had a belief of which Irenaeus tells us, a belief which was connected with the name of Cerinthus, one of their principal representatives, and an exact contemporary of John. Irenaeus tells us that Cerinthus taught that at the baptism, from that power which is above all things, the divine Christ descended and came into the man Jesus in the form of a dove; Jesus, allied as it were with the Christ who had descended upon Him, brought to men the message of the God who had hitherto been unknown, and lived in perfect virtue; then at the end the Christ departed from the man Jesus and returned to glory, and that it was only the man Jesus who was crucified on Calvary and who was afterwards resurrected. We might put it more simply by saying that Cerinthus taught that Jesus became divine at the baptism, that divinity left Him before the Cross, and that He died simply a man.

It is clear that all such teaching robs the life and death of Jesus of all value for us. By seeking to protect God from all contact with human pain and the human situation, it removes God from the act of redemption and empties the Cross of its value.

What John is saying is that the Cross is an essential part of the meaning of Jesus, and that God was in the death of Jesus every bit as much as He was in His life.

John is saying that in Jesus, the man Jesus, God really
and truly lived and suffered for men.

THE TRIPLE WITNESS

I John 5: 6-8 (continued)

JOHN goes on to speak of the triple witness.

There is the witness of *the Spirit*. In this John is thinking
of three things. (i) The New Testament story is clear that
at His baptism the Spirit did descend upon Jesus in the
most special way (*Mark* 1: 9-11; *Matthew* 3: 16, 17;
Luke 3: 21, 22; *Acts* 10: 38; *John* 1: 32-34). At the
baptism there was a coming of the Spirit upon Jesus in
an unparalleled fullness and permanency. (ii) The New
Testament is also clear, that, while John came to baptize
men with water, Jesus came to baptize men with the Spirit
(*Mark* 1: 8; *Matthew* 3: 11; *Luke* 3: 16; *Acts* 1: 5;
2: 33). Jesus came to bring men the Spirit in a completely
new way. He brought the Spirit to men with a plentitude
and a power hitherto quite unknown. (iii) The history
of the early Church is the proof that this was no idle and
empty claim, but something that happened in actual,
visible, demonstrable fact. It began at Pentecost (*Acts*
2: 4), and it repeated itself over and over again in the
history and experience of the Church (*Acts* 8: 17; 10: 44).
Jesus had the Spirit, and Jesus could give the Spirit to
men; and the continuing evidence of the Spirit in the
Church was—and is—an undeniable witness to the reality
and the continuing power of Jesus Christ.

There is the witness of *the water*. At Jesus' own baptism
there was the witness to Him of the Spirit descending
upon Him. It was, in fact, that event which revealed to
John the Baptist who Jesus was. Now it is John's point
that in the early Church that witness was carried on and
maintained in Christian baptism. We must remember

that thus early in the Church's history baptism was adult baptism, the confession of faith, and the reception into the Church of men and women who were coming direct from heathenism, who were making a clean break, and who were beginning an absolutely new way of life. Now in Christian baptism things happened. In it a man plunged below the water and died with Christ; he emerged and was resurrected with Christ to a new life. In Christ he became a new creature; he was reborn into new life. Therefore, Christian baptism was a witness to the continuing power of Jesus Christ. It was the witness that He was still alive, and that He was indeed divine.

There was the witness of *the blood*. The blood was the life. In any sacrifice the blood was sacred to God and to God alone. The death of Christ was the perfect sacrifice to God. In the Cross His blood was poured out to God. It was the experience of men that that sacrifice was availing, that it did redeem men, and it did reconcile them to God, and give them peace with God. Now continuously in the Church the Lord's Supper, the Eucharist, was and is observed. In it the sacrifice of Christ is full displayed; in it there is given to men, not only the opportunity to give thanks to Christ for His sacrifice made once for all, but the opportunity to appropriate its benefits and to avail themselves of its healing power. That happened. At the Lord's Table men met the Lord, and experienced His forgiveness, and the peace with God which He brings. Men still have that same experience; and, therefore, that feast is a continuing witness to the atoning power of the sacrifice of Jesus Christ.

The Spirit and the water and the blood all combine to demonstrate the perfect Messiahship, the perfect Sonship, the perfect Saviourhood of this man Jesus, in whom was God. The continued gift of the Spirit, the continued death and resurrection of baptism, the continued availability of the sacrifice of Christ at the Table of Christ are still the witnesses to Jesus Christ.

Note on 1 *John* 5: 7

In the Authorized Version there is a verse which we have altogether omitted. It reads, "For there are three that bear record in heaven, the Father, the Word and the Holy Ghost; and these three are one."

The Revised Version omits this verse, and does not even mention it in the margin, and none of the newer translations include it. It is quite certain that it does not belong to the original text.

The facts are as follows. First, it does not occur in any Greek manuscript earlier than the 14th century. The great manuscripts belong to the 3rd and 4th centuries, and it occurs in none of them. None of the great early fathers of the Church knew it. Jerome's original version of the Vulgate does not include it. The first person to quote it is a Spanish heretic called Priscillian who died in A.D. 385. Thereafter it crept, bit by bit, into the Latin texts of the New Testament, although, as we have seen, it did not gain an entry to the Greek manuscripts.

How then did it get into the text? Originally it must have been a scribal gloss or comment in the margin. Since it seemed to offer good scriptural evidence for the doctrine of the Trinity, bit by bit it came to be accepted by theologians as part of the text, especially in the early days of scholarship before the great manuscripts had been discovered.

But how did it last, and how did it come to be in the Authorized Version? The first Greek testament to be published was published by Erasmus in 1516. Erasmus was a great scholar, and he knew that this verse was not in the original text, and he did not include it in his first edition. By this time theologians used and accepted the text. It had, for instance, been printed in the Latin Vulgate of 1514. Erasmus was therefore criticized for omitting it. His answer was that if anyone could show him a Greek manuscript which did have the words in it, he would print them in his next edition. Someone did produce one of these very late and very bad texts in which the verse did occur in Greek; and Erasmus, true to his word, but very much against his judgment and his will, did print the verse in his 1522 edition.

The next step was that in 1550 Stephanus printed his great edition of the Greek New Testament. This 1550 edition of Stephanus became what was called—he called it by that name himself—The Received Text, and it was the basis of the Authorized Version, and of the Greek printed text for centuries to come. That is how this verse got into the Authorized Version. There is, of course, nothing wrong with it; but modern scholarship has made it quite certain that John did not write it, and that it is a much later commentary on, and addition to, his words; and therefore in all modern translations the verse is omitted.

THE UNDENIABLE WITNESS

1 *John* 5: 9, 10

> If we accept the testimony of men, the testimony of God is greater, for this is the testimony of God, that He has borne testimony about His Son. He who believes in the Son of God has that testimony within himself. He who does not believe God has made God a liar, because he has not believed in the testimony which God bore to His Son.

BEHIND this passage there are two basic ideas.

There is the Old Testament idea of what constitutes an adequate witness. The Old Testament law was quite clear: "One witness shall not rise up against a man for any iniquity, or for any sin, in any sin that he sinneth; at the mouth of two witnesses, or at the mouth of three witnesses, shall the matter be established " (*Deuteronomy* 19: 15; cp. 17: 6). A triple human witness is enough to establish any fact. How much more must a triple divine witness, the witness of the Spirit, the water, and the blood, be regarded as convincing.

Second, the idea of witness is an integral part of John's thought. In the gospel we find different witnesses all converging on Jesus Christ. John the Baptist is a witness to Jesus (*John* 1: 15; 1: 32-34; 5: 33). Jesus' deeds are a witness to Him (*John* 5: 36). The Scriptures are a witness to Him (*John* 5: 39). The Father who sent Him is a witness to Him (*John* 5: 30-32, 37; 8: 18). The Spirit is a witness to Him. " When the Comforter is come . . .

even the Spirit of truth . . . He shall testify of me " (*John* 15: 26). It is John's argument that all these witnesses converge on Jesus Christ.

John goes on to use a phrase which is a favourite phrase of his in his gospel. He speaks of the man who " believes in the Son of God." There is a wide difference between *believing* a man and *believing in* a man. If we *believe* a man, we do no more than accept the fact that whatever statement he may be making at the moment is true. All that we are saying is that in a particular case we believe that he is telling the truth. If we *believe in* a man, we accept the whole man and all that he stands for in complete confidence and trust. We would not only be prepared to trust his spoken word; we would also be prepared to trust ourselves and our life to him. To believe in Jesus Christ is not simply to accept what He says as true; it is to commit all life into His hands and into His direction; it is to place ourselves in His hands in time and in eternity.

When a man does that, the Holy Spirit within him testifies that he is acting aright. It is the Holy Spirit which gives him the conviction of the ultimate worth and value of Jesus Christ, and which assures him that he is right to make this act of commitment to Him. The man who refuses to do that is refusing the promptings of the Holy Spirit within his heart. He is refusing to listen to the messenger of God.

Now if a man refuses to accept this witness, if he refuses to accept the evidence of men who have experienced what Christ can do, the evidence of the deeds of Christ, the evidence of the Scriptures, the evidence of God's Holy Spirit, the evidence of God Himself, then in effect what he is doing is that he is calling God a liar; he is placing no belief in the witness of God. It is John's claim that the man who rejects the evidence with which life and God confront him is treating God as a liar—and that is a blasphemy beyond which blasphemy can hardly go.

THE LETTERS OF JOHN

THE ESSENCE OF THE FAITH

I *John* 5: 11-13

> And this is the testimony, that God gave us eternal
> life, and that that life is in His Son. He who has the
> Son has life; he who has not the Son has not life.
> I have written these things to you, to you who believe
> in the name of the Son of God, that you may know
> that you have eternal life.

WITH this paragraph the letter proper comes to an end,
and what follows is in the nature of a postscript or addition.
And the letter ends with a statement of the very essence
of the Christian life. The essence of the Christian life is
eternal life. What, then, is eternal life, and what are its
gifts and characteristics?

The word for eternal is *aiōnios*. It means far more than
simply *lasting for ever*. A life which lasted for ever might
well be a curse and not a blessing, an intolerable burden
and not a shining gift. There is only one person to whom
the word *aiōnios* may properly be applied, and that one
person is God. In the real sense of the term it is God alone
who possesses and who inhabits eternity. *Eternal life*
is, therefore, nothing other than *the life of God Himself*.
What we are promised is that here and now there can be
given to us a share in the very life of God.

In God there is *peace*, and, therefore, *eternal life* means
serenity. It means a life liberated from the fears which
haunt the human situation. In God there is *power*, and,
therefore, *eternal life* means *the defeat of frustration*. It
means a life filled with the power which is the power of
God, and which is, therefore, a life victorious over circumstance. In God there is *holiness*, and, therefore, *eternal life*
means *the defeat of sin*. It means a life clad with the purity
which is the purity of God, and armed with a defence
against the soiling infections of the world. In God there
is *love*, and, therefore, *eternal life* means *the end of bitterness
and hatred*. It means a life which has the love of God
in its heart, and the undefeatable love of man in all its

feelings and in all its action. In God there is *life*, and, therefore *eternal life* means *the defeat of death*. It means a life which is indestructible, because it has in it the indestructible life of God Himself.

It is John's conviction that such a life comes through Jesus Christ and in no other way. Why should that be? If eternal life is the life of God, it means that we can only possess that life when we know God, and when we are enabled to approach God, and to rest in Him. We can only do these two things in Jesus Christ. The Son alone fully knows the Father, and, therefore, only Jesus Christ can fully reveal to us what God is like. As John had it in his gospel: " No man hath seen God at any time; the only begotten Son, who is in the bosom of the Father, He hath declared Him " (*John* 1: 18). And Jesus Christ alone can bring us into the presence of God. It is in Him that there is open to us the new and living way into the presence of God (*Hebrews* 10: 19-23). We may take a simple analogy. If we wish to meet someone whom we do not know, and who moves in a completely different circle from the circle in which we ourselves move, we can only achieve that meeting by finding someone who knows that person, and who is willing to introduce us to him. That is what Jesus does for us in regard to God. Eternal life is the life of God; and we can only find that life through Jesus Christ.

THE BASIS AND THE PRINCIPLE OF PRAYER

1 *John* 5: 14, 15

> And this is the confidence that we have towards Him, that, if we ask anything which is in accordance with His will, He hears us; and, if we know that He hears anything that we ask, we know that we possess the requests that we have made from Him.

HERE there are set down both the basis and the principle of prayer.

(i) The *basis of prayer* is the simple fact that God listens to our prayers. The word which John uses for *confidence* is an interesting word. It is the word *parrēsia*. Originally *parrēsia* meant *freedom of speech*, that freedom to speak boldly which exists in a true and a great democracy. Later it came to denote any kind of confidence and boldness. With God we have freedom of speech. God is always listening. He is more ready to hear than we are to pray. God is always waiting. We never need to force our way into the presence of God, or to compel God to pay attention to us. He is waiting for us to come. To use a very human analogy. We know how we have often waited for the knock of the postman, or the ring of the telephone bell, to bring us a message from someone whom we love. In all reverence we can say that God is like that with us.

(ii) But here also is the *principle* of prayer. Prayer to be answered must be *in accordance with the will of God*. Four times in his writings John lays down what might be called the conditions of prayer. (*a*) He says that *obedience* is the condition of prayer. We receive whatever we ask, because we keep His commandments (I *John* 3: 22). (*b*) He says that *remaining in Christ* is the condition of prayer. If we abide in Him, and His words abide in us, we will ask what we will, and it will be done for us (*John* 15: 7). The closer we live to Christ, the more we shall pray aright; and the more we pray aright, the greater the answer to prayer. (*c*) He says that to pray *in His name* is the condition of prayer. If we ask anything in His name, He will do it (*John* 14: 14). One of the supreme tests of any desire is, *Can* we take it to Jesus in prayer? The ultimate test of any request is, *Can* we say to Jesus, " Give me this for *your* sake, and in *your* name "? A prayer of which we can honestly say that will be granted.

(*d*) And here we have the great principle of prayer. Prayer must be *in accordance with the will of God*. Jesus teaches us to pray: " Thy will be done," not, " Thy will be changed." Jesus Himself, in the moment of His greatest

struggle and agony and crisis, prayed, " Not as I will, but
as Thou wilt. . . . Thy will be done " (*Matthew* 26: 39, 42).
Here is the very essence of prayer.   C. H. Dodd writes:
" Prayer rightly considered is not a device for employing
the resources of omnipotence to fulfil our own desires, but
a means by which our desires may be redirected according
to the mind of God, and made into channels for the forces
of His will."   A. E. Brooke suggests that John thought of
prayer as " including only requests for knowledge of, and
acquiescence in, the will of God."   Even the great pagans
saw this.   Epictetus wrote: " Have courage to look up to
God and say, Deal with me as Thou wilt from now on.
I am as one with Thee; I am Thine; I flinch from nothing
so long as Thou dost think that it is good.   Lead me where
Thou wilt; put on me what raiment Thou wilt.   Wouldst
Thou have me hold office or eschew it, stay or flee, be
rich or poor?   For all this I will defend Thee before men."

Here, indeed, is something on which to ponder.   We are
so apt to think that prayer is asking God for what we
want, whereas true prayer is asking God for what He
wants.   We are so apt to think of prayer as talking to
God—as indeed it is—whereas it is even more listening
to God.

In the last analysis the only true prayer is the prayer
which says: " Thy will be done," and whose only request
is for grace to accept that will and strength to do it.

PRAYING FOR THE BROTHER WHO SINS

I *John* 5: 16, 17

> If anyone sees his brother sinning a sin which is not a
> sin whose end is death, he will ask life for him, and
> he will give it to him, that is, to those whose sin is
> not a sin, whose end is death.   There is a sin whose
> end is death.   It is not about that that I mean he
> should ask.   All wrongdoing is sin; but there is a
> sin whose end is not death.

THERE is no doubt that this is a most difficult and a most disturbing passage. Before we approach its problems, let us look at its certainties.

John has just been speaking about the Christian privilege of prayer; and now he goes on to single out for special attention the prayer of intercession for the brother who needs praying for. It is very significant that, when John speaks about one kind of prayer, it is not prayer for ourselves; it is prayer for others. Prayer must never be selfish; it must never be concentrated entirely upon our ownselves, and our own problems, and our own needs. Prayer must be an outgoing activity; prayer must be prayer for others. As Westcott put it: " The end of prayer is the perfection of the whole Christian body."

Again and again the New Testament writers stress the need of this prayer of intercession. Paul writes to the Thessalonians: " Brothers, pray for us " (I *Thessalonians* 5: 25). The writer to the Hebrews says: " Pray for us " (*Hebrews* 13: 18, 19). James says that, if a man is sick, he ought to call the elders, and the elders should pray over him (*James* 5: 14). It is the advice to Timothy that prayer must be made for all men (I *Timothy* 2: 1). The Christian has the tremendous privilege of bearing his brother man to the throne of grace. There are three things to be said about this.

(i) We naturally pray for those who are ill, and we should just as naturally pray for those who are straying away from God. It is just as natural a thing to pray for the cure of the soul as it is to pray for the cure of the body. It may be that there is nothing greater that we can do for the man who is straying away, and who is in peril of making shipwreck of life, than to commit him to the grace of God.

(ii) But it must be remembered that, when we have prayed for such a man, our duty is not yet done. In this, as in all other things, our first duty is to seek to make our own prayers come true. It will often be our duty to speak to the man himself. We must not only speak to God about the man, we must also speak to the man about himself. God needs a channel through which His grace can come; He needs an instrument and agent through whom He can act; and it may well be that we are to be the voice of God to speak to the man who is endangering his soul.

(iii) We have previously thought about the basis of prayer and about the principle of prayer; but here we come on another fact, for here we meet the limitation of prayer. It may well be that God wishes to answer our prayer; it may well be that we ourselves pray with heartfelt sincerity; but that aim of God and that prayer of ours can be frustrated by the man for whom we pray. If we pray for a sick person and that sick person disobeys his doctors, and acts recklessly and foolishly, our prayer is frustrated. It may be that we do not remember enough that it is one of the tragedies of life that even the most fervent prayer can be frustrated by the stubborn foolishness and disobedience of the one for whom we pray. God will urge, God will plead, God will warn, God will offer, but not even God can violate the inviolable freedom of choice which He Himself has given to us. It is often the folly of man which frustrates our prayers and cancels the grace of God.

SIN WHOSE END IS DEATH

I *John* 5: 16, 17 *(continued)*

THIS passage speaks of the sin whose end is death, and the sin whose end is not death.

There have been many suggestions in regard to the sin which the Authorized Version describes as being *unto death.*

The Jews themselves distinguished two kinds of sins. There were the sins which a man committed unwittingly, or at least, not deliberately. These were sins which a man might commit in ignorance, or when he was swept away by some overmastering impulse, or in some moment of strong emotion when his passions were too strong for the leash of the will to hold. On the other hand, there were the sins of the high hand and the haughty heart, the sins which a man deliberately committed, the sins in which he was well aware that he was sinning, the sins in which he proudly and defiantly took his own way in spite of the known will of God for him. It was for the first kind of sin which sacrifice atoned; but for the sins of the haughty heart and the high hand no sacrifice could atone.

Plummer lists three suggestions. (i) Sins unto death, it is suggested, are sins which are *punishable* by death. But it is quite clear that this means more than that. This passage is not thinking of sins which are a breach of man-made laws, however serious. (ii) It is suggested that sins unto death are sins which God visits with death where the punishment of God is death. Paul writes to the Corinthians that, because of their unworthy conduct at the table of the Lord, many among them are weak, and many are asleep, that is, many have died (I *Corinthians* 11: 30); and the suggestion is that the reference is to sins which are so serious that God visits the sinner with death. (iii) It is suggested that sins unto death are sins punishable with excommunication from the Church. When Paul is writing to the Corinthians about the notorious sinner with whom they have not adequately dealt, he demands that he should be " delivered unto Satan." That was the phrase for excommunication. But Paul goes on to say that, serious as this punishment is, and sore as its bodily consequence may be, it is designed to save the man's soul in the Day of the Lord Jesus (I *Corinthians* 5: 5). It is a punishment which is not unto death. None of these explanations will do.

There are three further suggestions as to the identification of this sin which is the sin " unto death."

(*a*) There is a line of thought in the New Testament which points to the fact that some held that there was no forgiveness for post-baptismal sin. There were those who believed that baptism cleansed from all previous sins, but that after baptism there was no forgiveness for sin. There is an echo of that line of thought in *Hebrews*: "It is impossible for those who were once enlightened, and have tasted of the heavenly gift, and were made partakers of the Holy Ghost, and have tasted the good word of God, and the powers of the world to come, if they shall fall away, to renew them again unto repentance" (*Hebrews* 6: 4-6). In early Christian terminology *to be enlightened* was often a technical term for *to be baptised*. It is indeed that belief which made many postpone baptism until the last possible moment of life. But the real essence of that statement in *Hebrews* is that restoration becomes impossible when penitence has become impossible. The connection is not so much with baptism as it is with penitence.

(b) Later on in the early Church there was a strong line of thought which declared that apostasy could never be forgiven. In the days of the great persecutions there were those who said that those who in fear or in torture had denied their faith could never have forgiveness; for had not Jesus said, "Whosoever shall deny me before men, him will I also deny before my Father which is in heaven" (*Matthew* 10: 33; cp. *Mark* 8: 38; *Luke* 9: 26). But it must always be remembered that the New Testament itself tells of the terrible denial of Peter, and of the gracious restoration of Peter. In later days there were those in the Church who wished to excommunicate for ever the man who in the stress of persecution had denied his faith; but we must remember that Jesus Himself gave Peter another chance to redeem himself. As so often happens, Jesus was gentler and more sympathetic and understanding than His own Church was.

(c) It could be argued from this very letter of John that the most deadly of all sins is to deny that Jesus really came in the flesh, for that sin is nothing less than the mark of antichrist (1 *John* 4: 3). And if the sin which is unto death is to be identified with any one sin that surely must be it. But we think that there is something more to it than even that.

THE ESSENCE OF SIN

I *John* 5: 16, 17 (*continued*)

FIRST of all, let us try to fix more closely the meaning of this phrase, *the sin unto death*. In the Greek it is the sin which is *pros thanaton*. That does not mean the *deadly sin*; it means *the sin which is going towards death*, the sin whose goal and end is death, the sin, which, if continued in, must finish in death. The terrible thing about the sin which is *pros thanaton* is not so much what it is in itself, as where it will end, if a man persists in it.

Now in life it is a fact of experience that there are two kinds of sinners. There is the man who may be said to sin against his will; he sins because he is swept away by a passion or a desire, which at the moment is too strong for him; his sin is not so much a matter of choice as it is of a compulsion which he is not able to resist. On the other hand there is the man who sins completely deliberately, in cold blood, with his eyes wide-open, of set purpose taking his own way, even when he is well aware that it is wrong. There is the man who hates his own sin; in the moment of temptation he falls to sin, but afterwards he hates his sin, and he hates himself. On the other hand there is the man who rejoices in his sin, the man who never even thinks of temptation as an evil thing at all, and who, when he has sinned, has no regrets whatever. There is the man who is ashamed of his sin, and whose one desire is to hide it; he has never any doubt that he has done the wrong thing. On the other hand there is the man who glories in his sin, and who boasts of it, and who has no sense of shame; he is proud that he knows how to sin, and how, as he thinks, to get away with it. There is the man who is fundamentally sorry for his sin; and the man who fundamentally delights in his sin.

Now the fundamental point of life and experience is that these two men began by being the same man. It is the experience of every man that the first time that he does a wrong thing, he does it with shrinking and with fear; it is an effort to make himself do it; and, after he has done it, he experiences grief and remorse and regret and revulsion. But, if he allows himself again and again to flirt with temptation, and again and again to fall to temptation, on each occasion the sin becomes easier; and, if he escapes, as he thinks, the consequences, on each occasion the self-disgust and the remorse and the regret become less and less; until in the end he can reach a state when he can sin without a tremor, and can congratulate himself on being able to get what he wants and to escape the consequences. It is precisely that which is the sin which is leading to death. So long as a man in his heart of hearts hates sin and hates himself for sinning, so long as he *knows* that he is sinning, he is never beyond repentance, and, therefore, never beyond forgiveness; but once a man begins to revel in sin, and to make sin the deliberate policy of his life, and loses all sense of the terror and the awfulness of sin and also the feeling of self-disgust, he is on the way to death, for he is on the way to a state where the idea of repentance will not, and cannot, enter his head.

The sin unto death is the state of the man who has listened to sin so often, and refused to listen to God so often, that he has come to a state when he loves his sin, and when he regards sin as the most profitable thing in the world.

THE THREEFOLD CERTAINTY

I *John* 5: 18-20

> We know that he who has received his birth from God does not sin, but He whose birth was from God keeps him, and the Evil One does not touch him.

> We know that it is from God that we draw our being, and the whole world lies in the power of the Evil One.
>
> We know that the Son of God has come, and that He has given us discernment to come to know the Real One; and we are in the Real One, even through His Son Jesus Christ. This is the real God, and this is eternal life.

JOHN draws to the end of his letter with a statement of the threefold Christian certainty.

(i) The Christian is emancipated from the power of sin. We must be careful to see what this means. It does not mean that the Christian never sins in actual fact; but it does mean that he is not the helpless slave and victim of sin. As Plummer put it: " A child of God may sin, but his normal condition is resistance to evil." The difference lies in this. The pagan world was conscious of nothing so much as moral defeat. The pagan world knew its own evil, and felt that there was no possible escape. Seneca spoke of " our weakness in necessary things." He said that men " hate their sins but cannot leave them." Persius, the Roman satirist, in a famous picture, spoke of " filthy Natta, a man deadened by vice, . . . who has no sense of sin, no knowledge of what he is losing, and is sunk so deep that he sends up no bubble to the surface." The pagan world was utterly defeated by sin. But the Christian is the man who has never lost, and never can lose, the battle. Because he is a man, he will sin; but he never can be conscious of the utter moral defeatedness of the pagan. F. W. H. Myers makes Paul speak of the battle with the flesh:

> " Well, let me sin, but not with my consenting,
>   Well, let me die, but willing to be whole:
> Never, O Christ—so stay me from relenting—
>   Shall there be truce betwixt my flesh and soul."

The reason of the Christian's ultimate undefeatedness is that *He who has His birth from God* keeps him. That is to say, Jesus keeps him. As Wescott has it: " The Christian

has an active enemy, but he has also a watchful guardian."
The heathen is the man who has been defeated by sin,
and who has accepted defeat. The Christian is the man
who may sin, but who never accepts the fact of defeat.
" A saint," as someone has said, " is not a man who never
falls; he is a man who gets up and goes on every time he
falls."

(ii) The Christian is on the side of God against the world.
The source of our being is God, but the world lies in the
power of the Evil One. In the early days the cleavage
between the Church and the world was much clearer
than it is now. Nowadays, at least in the Western world,
we live in a civilization which is permeated by Christian
principles. Even if men do not practise them, they accept
the ideals of chastity, mercy, service, love. But the ancient
world knew nothing of chastity, and little of mercy, and of
service, and of love. John says that the Christian knows
that he is with God, while the world is in the grip of the
Evil One. No matter how the situation may have changed,
there remains the necessity of a clear-cut choice. The
choice still confronts men whether they will align themselves with God, or with the forces which are against God.
As Myers makes Paul say:

> " Whoso hath felt the Spirit of the Highest,
>   Cannot confound nor doubt him nor deny:
> Yea with one voice, O World, tho' thou deniest,
>   Stand thou on that side, for on this am I."

(iii) The Christian is conscious that he has entered
into that reality which is God. Life is full of illusions and
impermanencies; by himself man can but guess and grope;
but in Christ he enters into the knowledge of reality.
Xenophon tells of the discussion between Socrates and
the young man. " How do you know that? " says Socrates.
" Do you know it, or are you guessing? " " I am guessing,"
is the answer. " Very well," says Socrates, " when we
are done with guessing and when we know, shall we talk
about it then? " Who am I? What is life? What is God?

Whence did I come? Whither do I go? What is truth
and where is duty? These are the questions to which
men can only reply in guesses apart from Jesus Christ.
But in Christ we reach the reality, which is God. The
time of guessing is gone, and the time of knowing has come.

THE CONSTANT PERIL

I *John* 5: 21

My dear children, guard yourselves from idols.

WITH this sudden, sharp injunction John brings his
letter to an end. Short as it is there is a world of meaning
in this phrase.

(i) In Greek the word *idol* has in it the sense of unreality.
Plato used it for the illusions of this world as opposed to
the unchangeable realities of eternity. When the prophets
spoke of the idols of the heathen, they meant that the
idols were unreal, counterfeit gods, as opposed to the one
true and real God. This may well mean, as Westcott has
it, " Keep yourselves from all objects of false devotion."

(ii) An idol is anything in this life which men worship
instead of God, and which men allow to take the place of
God. A man may make an idol of his money, of his career,
of his safety, of his pleasure. Again to quote Westcott:
" An idol is anything which occupies the place due to
God." Every man must have a care lest he erect an idol
in his life, and worship it instead of God.

(iii) But it is likely that John means something more
definite than either of these two things. It was in Ephesus
that John was writing, and it was of conditions in Ephesus
that he was thinking. It is likely that he means simply and
directly, " Keep yourselves from the pollutions of heathen
worship." No town in the world had so many connections
with the stories of the ancient gods; and no town was
more proud of them. Tacitus writes of Ephesus: " The
Ephesians claimed that Diana and Apollo were not born
at Delos, as was commonly supposed; they possessed

the Cenchrean stream and the Ortygian grove where Latona, in travail, had reposed against an olive tree, which is still in existence, and had given birth to these deities. . . . It was there that Apollo himself, after slaying the Cyclops, and escaped the wrath of Jupiter: and again that father Bacchus in his victory had spared the suppliant Amazons who had occupied his shrine." The stories of the ancient gods gathered thick around Ephesus, and were the pride of the Ephesians.

Further, in Ephesus there stood the great Temple of Diana, which was one of the wonders of the ancient world. There were at least three things about that Temple which would justify John's stern injunction to have nothing to do with heathen worship.

(a) The Temple was the centre of immoral rites. The priests were called the *Megabyzi*. They were eunuchs. It was said by some that the goddess was so fastidious that she could not bear a real male near her; it was said by others that the goddess was so lascivious that it was unsafe for any real male to come near her. Heraclitus, the great philosopher, was a native of Ephesus. He was called the weeping philosopher, for he had never been known to smile. He said that the darkness to the approach of the altar of the Temple was the darkness of vileness; that the morals of the Temple were worse than the morals of beasts; that the inhabitants of Ephesus were fit only to be drowned, and that the reason that he could never smile was that he lived in the midst of such terrible uncleanness. For a Christian to have any contact with that was to touch infection.

(b) The Temple had the right of asylum. Any criminal, if he could reach the Temple of Diana, was safe. The result was that the Temple was the haunt of criminals. Tacitus accused Ephesus of protecting the crimes of men and calling it the worship of the gods. To have anything to do with the Temple of Diana was to be associated with the very dregs of society.

(c) The Temple of Diana was the centre of the sale of Ephesian letters. These were charms, worn as amulets, which were supposed to be effective in bringing about the wishes of those who wore them. Ephesus, as it has been said, was " pre-eminently the city of astrology, sorcery, incantations, amulets, exorcisms, and every form of magical imposture." To have anything to do with the Temple at Ephesus was to be brought into contact with commercialized superstitition, and the black arts.

It is hard for us to imagine how much Ephesus was dominated by the Temple of Diana. It would not be easy for a Christian to keep himself from idols in a city like Ephesus. But John demands that it must be done. The Christian must never be lost in the illusions of pagan religion; the Christian must never erect in his heart an idol which will take the place of God; the Christian must keep himself from the infections of all false faiths; and he can do so only when he walks with Christ.

THE LETTERS OF JOHN

INTRODUCTION TO SECOND AND THIRD JOHN

THE very shortness of these two little letters is the best
guarantee of their genuineness. They are so brief, and
they are so comparatively unimportant that no one would
have gone to the trouble of inventing them, and of attaching
them to the name of John. A standard papyrus sheet
measured ten by eight inches, and their length is to be
explained that they would each take up almost exactly
one sheet.

The Elder

Each of them is said to come from " The Elder." *2 John*
begins: " The Elder unto the elect lady and her children."
3 John begins: " The Elder unto the well-beloved Gaius."
It is in the last degree unlikely that the title *The Elder*
is an official or ecclesiastical title. Elders were officials
who were attached to one congregation, and whose juris-
diction certainly did not extend outside the congregation
of which they were elders, whereas the writer of these
letters certainly assumes that he has the right to speak,
and that his word will carry weight in congregations in
which he is not actually present in person. He speaks
as one whose authority goes out to the Church at large.
The word is *presbuteros*, which originally meant *an older
man*, and *elder man*, not in the official, but in the natural
sense of the term. We would be better to translate it
The Ancient, or *The Aged*, for it is not from an ecclesiastical
position but from his age and his personal qualities that
the writer of these letters draws his authority.

In point of fact we know that in Ephesus there was an
aged John who held a very special and unique position.
In the days of the early Church there was a churchman
called Papias who lived from A.D. 70 to 146. He had a
passion for collecting all the information he could lay
hands on about the early days of the Church. He was not a

great scholar; Eusebius dismisses him as " a man of very limited intelligence," but he does transmit to us some most interesting information. He became Bishop of Hierapolis, but he had a close connection with Ephesus, and he tells us of his own methods of acquiring information. He frequently uses this word *elder* in this sense of *one of the fathers of the Church*, and he mentions a particularly distinguished *elder* whose name was John. " I shall not hesitate," he writes, " to put down for you, along with my own interpretations, whatsoever things I have at any time learned carefully from the *elders*, and carefully remembered, guaranteeing their truth. For I did not, like the multitude, take pleasure in those that speak much, but in those that teach the truth; not in those who relate strange commandments, but in those who deliver the commandments given by the Lord to faith, and springing from the truth itself. If, then, anyone came who had been a follower of the *elders*, I questioned him in regard to the words of the *elders*—what Andrew, or what Peter, had said, or what was said by Philip, or by Thomas, or by James, or by John, or by Matthew, or by any other of the disciples of the Lord; and what things Aristion, or the *Elder John* say. For I did not think that what was to be gotten from books would profit me as much as what came from the living and abiding voice." Clearly the *Elder John*, John the aged, was a notable figure in Ephesus, although he is clearly distinguished from John the apostle.

It must be this John who wrote these two little letters. By this time he is an old man, John the aged. He is one of the last surviving links with Jesus and His disciples. He was a man who had the authority of a bishop in Ephesus and in the places around Ephesus; and when he saw that a Church was threatened with trouble and heresy, he wrote with gracious and loving correction to his people. Here are the letters of an aged saint, one of the last of the first generation of Christians, a man whom all men loved, and whom all men respected.

Common Authorship

That the two letters are from the one hand there is
no doubt. Short as they are, they have much in common.
2 *John* begins: " The Elder unto the elect lady and her
children, whom I love in the truth." 3 *John* begins: " The
Elder unto the well-beloved Gaius, whom I love in the
truth." 2 *John* goes on: " I rejoiced greatly that I found
some of thy children walking in the truth " (verse 4); and
3 *John* goes on: " I have no greater joy than to hear
that my children walk in truth." 2 *John* comes to an
end: " Having many things to write unto you, I would
not write with paper and ink; but I trust to come unto
you, and to speak face to face, that our joy may be full "
(verse 12). 3 *John* comes to an end: " I had many things
to write, but I will not write with ink and pen unto thee;
but I trust I shall shortly see thee, and we shall speak
face to face " (verses 13, 14). There is the closest possible
similarity between the two letters.

There is further the closest possible connection between
the situation of these letters and the situation in I *John*.
In I *John* 4: 3 we read: " Every spirit that confesseth
not that Jesus Christ is come in the flesh is not of God;
and this is that spirit of antichrist, whereof ye have heard
that it should come, and even now already is it in the
world." In 2 *John* 7 we read: " Many deceivers are entered
into the world, who confess not that Jesus Christ is come
in the flesh. This is a deceiver and an antichrist."

It is clear that 2 and 3 *John* are closely connected with
each other; and that both are closely connected with I *John*.
They are dealing with the same situation, the same dangers,
and the same people.

The Problem of the Second Letter

These two little letters confront us with few serious
problems. The only real problem is to decide whether
the Second Letter was sent to an individual or to a Church.
The Authorized Version begins the Second Letter: " The

Elder unto the elect lady and her children." The problem centres on this phrase *the elect lady*. The Greek is *eklektē kuria*. There are three possible ways of taking this.

(i) It is just barely possible, though it cannot be said to be really likely, that *Eklektē* is a proper name; and that *kuria* is a quite usual affectionate address. The word *kurios* (the masculine form) has many meanings. It very commonly means *sir*; it means *master* of slaves and *owner* of possessions; on a much higher level it means *lord*, and is the word which is so often used as a title for Jesus. In letters this word *kurios* has a special use. It is practically the equivalent of the English phrase *My Dear*. So a soldier writes home saying, *Kurie mou patēr*, My Dear Father, as we would say in English. In letters *kurios* is an address combining affection and respect. So it is just possible that this letter is addressed to *My Dear Eklektē*. Rendel Harris, indeed, went the length of saying that 2 *John* is nothing other than a Christian love letter. This is unlikely, as we shall see, for more than one reason. But one thing is decisive against it. 2 *John* ends, as the Authorized Version has it: " The children of the elect sister greet thee." Now the word is in Greek again *eklektē*; and, if it is a proper name at the beginning of the letter, it must also be a proper name at the end. If that is so, we would have to believe that there were two sisters, both called by the very unusual name of *Eklektē*, which is not possible.

(ii) In the phrase *eklektē kuria*, it would be possible to take *Kuria* as a proper name, for there are examples of people called by this name. We would then take *eklektē* in its normal New Testament sense; and the letter would be written to the *elect Kuria*. The objections against that are threefold. (*a*) It seems unlikely that any single individual could be spoken of as loved by all those who have known the truth (verse I). (*b*) Verse 4 says that John rejoiced when he found some of her children walking in the truth; the implication is that others were not so walking. And this seems to imply a number greater than one woman's family. (c) But the decisive objection is that throughout the letter the *eklektē kuria*, the elect lady, is addressed sometimes in the singular and sometimes in the plural. The singular occurs in verses 4, 5 and 13; and the plural occurs in verses 6, 8, 10, 12. It would be almost impossible that an individual would be so addressed.

(iii) So, then, we must come to the conclusion that the phrase *the elect lady* means *a Church*. There is, in fact, good evidence that the expression was so used. I *Peter*, in the Authorized Version, ends with greetings from " the Church that is at Babylon elected together with you " (I *Peter* 5: 13). It will be noticed that in the Authorized Version the words *church that is* are in italics; that, of course, means that they are not in the Greek, and that they have been supplied in translation to fill out the sense. The Greek literally reads: " The Elect One at Babylon," and *The Elect One* is feminine. There are few who have ever doubted that the phrase means *The Church which is at Babylon*, and so we must take it in John's letter also. No doubt the phrase, The Elect Lady, when used of the Church, goes back to the idea of the Church as the Bride of Christ. We can be certain that 2 *John* is written, not to an individual, but to a Church.

The Problem in the Early Church

2 and 3 *John* are letters which are very important and very interesting because they throw a vivid light on a problem which sooner or later had to arise within the organization of the early Church. Let us see if we can reconstruct the situation which lies behind them. It is clear that John the aged regards himself as having a right to act as guide and counsellor, and to administer warning and rebuke, in the Churches whose members are his children. In 2 *John* he writes of those who are doing well (verse 4), and by implication infers that there are others who are not so satisfactory. He further makes it

clear that there are itinerant teachers in the district, some of whom are preaching false and dangerous doctrine, and he gives orders that such teachers are not to be accepted and are not to be given hospitality (verses 7-11). Here, then, John is exercising what is to him an unquestioned right to issue orders to his Churches, and he is seeking to guard against a situation in which itinerant teachers of falsehood may arrive at any moment.

The situation behind 3 *John* is somewhat more complicated. The letter is written to one called Gaius, whose character and whose actions John most thoroughly approves (verses 3-5). Wandering missionaries have come to the Church, men who are fellow-helpers of the truth, and Gaius has given them true Christian hospitality (verses 6-8). In the same Church there is another man called Diotrephes, who loves to have the pre-eminence (verse 9). Diotrephes is depicted as a dictatorial character who will brook no rival to his authority. Diotrephes has refused to receive the wandering teachers of the truth, and has actually tried to drive out of the Church those who did receive them. He will have nothing to do with wandering teachers, even when these teachers are true preachers of the word (verse 10). Then into the picture there comes a man called Demetrius, to whom John gives a personal testimonial as a good man, and a man to be hospitably welcomed and received (verse 12). The simplest explanation of Demetrius is that he must be the leader of a wandering band of teachers who are on their way to the Church to which John is writing. Diotrephes will certainly refuse to have anything to do with them, and he will certainly try to eject those who do receive them; and John is writing to urge Gaius to receive the wandering teachers, and not to be intimidated by the domineering Diotrephes, whom he (John) will deal with when he visits the Church in question (verse 10). The whole situation turns on the reception of the wandering teachers. Gaius has received such teachers before, and John urges him to receive them, and their leader Demetrius, again. Diotrephes has refused to receive them, and has shut the door on them, and has defied the authority of John the aged.

The Threefold Ministry

All this looks like a very unhappy situation, and indeed it was. None the less, it was a situation which was bound to arise. In the nature of things a problem of ministry was bound to emerge within the Church. In its earliest days the Church had three different kinds of ministries. (i) Unique, and above all others, stood the *apostles*, those who had companied with Jesus, and who had been witnesses of the resurrection. They were the undisputed leaders of the Church. Their ministry and their authority were not confined to any one place; their writ ran throughout the whole Church; in any country and in any congregation their ministry was supreme. (ii) There were the *prophets*. The prophets were not attached to any one congregation. They were wandering preachers, going where the Spirit moved them, and giving to men the message which the Spirit of God gave to them. They had given up home and occupation, and the comfort and security of settled life, to be the wandering messengers of God. They, too, had a very special place in the Church. *The Didachē*, or, to give it its English name, *The Teaching of the Twelve Apostles*, is the earliest book of Church order. In it the unique position of the prophets is made clear. The order of service for the Eucharist is laid down, and the prayers are given; the service ends with the prayer of thanksgiving which is given in full; and then there comes the sentence: " But suffer the prophets to give thanks as much as they will " (*Didachē* 10: 7). The prophets were not to be brought under the rules and regulations which governed ordinary people. So, then, the Church had two sets of people whose authority was not confined to any one congregation, and who had the right of entry to any and to every congregation. (iii) The third kind of ministry was the ministry of the *elders*. During their first missionary journey part of the work of Paul and Barnabas was to ordain elders in all the local Churches which they had founded (*Acts* 14: 23). The elders were the officials of the settled community; their work was within their congregation, and they did not move outside it. They were not wandering and itinerant; they were settled permanently in the one place; and, therefore, it is clear that they were the backbone of the organization of the early Church. On them the routine work and the solidity of the individual congregations depended.

The Problem of the Wandering Preachers

The position of the apostles presented no real problem; they were unique, and their position could never really be disputed. But the wandering prophets and preachers did present a problem. Their position was one which was singularly liable to abuse. They had an enormous prestige; and it was possible for the most undesirable characters to enter into a way of life in which they moved from place to place, living in very considerable comfort at the expense of the local congregations. A clever rogue could make a very comfortable living as an itinerant prophet. Even the pagan satirists saw this. Lucian, the Greek writer, in his work called the *Peregrinus*, draws the picture of a man who had found the easiest possible way of making a living without working. He was an itinerant charlatan who lived on the fat of the land by travelling round the various communities of the Christians, and settling down wherever he liked, and living luxuriously at their expense. This was an abuse which even the pagans saw. *The Didachē* clearly saw this danger and laid down quite definite regulations to meet it. The regulations are long, but, so vivid a light do they throw on the life of the early Church, that they are worth quoting in full (*Didachē* 11 and 12).

Whosoever, therefore, shall come and teach you all these things aforesaid, receive him. But if the teacher himself turn and teach another doctrine to pervert, hear him not. But unto the increase of righteousness and knowledge of the Lord, receive him as the Lord. And as touching the apostles and prophets, according to the decree of the gospel, so do ye. But let every apostle that cometh unto you be received as the Lord. And he shall stay one day, and, if need be, the next also, but, if he stay three, he is a false prophet. And, when the apostle goeth forth, let him take nothing save bread, till he reach his lodging, but, if he ask money, he is a false prophet. And every prophet that speaketh in the Spirit ye shall not try nor judge: for every sin shall be forgiven, but this sin shall not be forgiven. But not everyone that speaketh in the Spirit is a prophet, but if he has the manners of the Lord. By their manners, therefore, shall the prophet and the false prophet be known. And no prophet who ordereth a table in the Spirit shall eat of it, else he is a false prophet. And every prophet that teacheth the truth, if he doeth not what he teacheth, is a false prophet. . . . Whosoever shall say in the Spirit: Give me money, or any other thing, ye shall not hearken to him: but, if he bid you give for others who are in need, let no man judge him.

Let everyone that cometh in the name of the Lord be received, and then, when ye have proved him, ye shall know, for ye shall have understanding to distinguish between the right hand and the left. If he that cometh is a passer-by, succour him as far as ye can; but he shall not stay with you longer than two or three days, unless there be necessity. But, if he be minded to settle among you, and be a craftsman, let him work and eat. But, if he hath no trade, according to your understanding, provide that he shall not live idle among you, being a Christian. But, if he will not do this, he is a Christmonger: of such men beware.

The Didachē even invents the word Christmonger, trafficker in Christ, Christemporos, to describe this kind of person.

The whole passage from The Didachē vividly shows the very real problem of the wandering teacher. John was entirely justified in warning his people that the wrong kind of wandering prophets might come claiming hospitality; and he was perfectly justified in saying that they must on no account be received. There is no doubt that in the early Church these wandering prophets became a problem. Some of them were heretical teachers, even if they were sincerely convinced of their own teaching. Some were nothing better than clever and plausible rogues who had found an easy way to make a comfortable living. That is the picture which lies behind 2 *John.*

The Clash of Ministries

But the situation behind 3 *John* is in some ways even more serious. The problem figure in it is Diotrephes. He is the man who will have nothing to do with wandering teachers, who shuts the door against them, and who seeks to eject anyone who dares to give them a welcome. He is the man who will not accept the authority of John, and whom John brands as a domineering character. There is much more behind this than meets the eye. This was no storm in a tea-cup. This was a fundamental cleavage. It was the clash between the local and the itinerant ministry. Obviously the whole structure of the Church depended on a strong settled ministry. That is to say, the very existence of the Church depended on a strong and authoritative eldership. Now as time went on the settled ministry was bound to chafe under the remote control of even one so famous as John the aged; and it was bound to resent the quite possibly disturbing and upsetting invasions of wandering prophets and itinerant evangelists. It was by no means impossible that, however well-intentioned they were, these itinerant prophets and evangelists, could do far more harm than good. Here is the situation behind 3 *John.* John represents the old apostolic remote control; Demetrius and his band of missionaries represent the wandering prophets and preachers; Diotrephes represents the settled ministry and the local elders, who wish to run their own congregation, and who regard the wandering preachers as possibly dangerous intruders; Gaius represents the good, well-meaning man who is torn in two and who cannot make up his mind.

What happened in this case, we do not know. But the end of the matter in the Church was that the wandering preachers faded from the scene, and the apostles in the nature of things passed from this earth, and the settled ministry became the ministry of the Church. In a sense even in the modern Church the problem of the clash between the itinerant evangelist and the settled ministry is not fully solved; but these two little letters are of the most fascinating interest because they show the organisation of the Church in a transition stage, when the clash between the itinerant and the settled ministry is beginning to arise—and —who knows?—Diotrephes may not have been as bad as he is painted, and may not have been altogether wrong.

THE LETTERS OF JOHN

THE ELECT LADY

2 John 1-3

> The Elder to the Elect Lady and to her children,
> whom I love in truth (it is not only I who love you
> and them, but so do all who love the truth) because
> of the truth which abides in us, and which will be
> with us for ever. Grace, mercy and peace will be with
> you from God the Father, and from Jesus Christ
> the Son of the Father, in truth and love.

THE writer of this letter designates himself simply by the
title of The Elder. The word *Elder* can have three different
meanings. (i) It can mean simply *an older man*, one who
by reason of his years and experience is deserving of
affection and of respect. There will be something of that
meaning here. The letter is from an aged servant of Christ
and the Church, a servant who is full of years and honour.
(ii) In the New Testament the elders are the *officials of
the local Churches*. They were the first of all the Church
officials, and Paul set apart and ordained elders in his
Churches on his missionary journeys, as soon as it was
possible to do so (*Acts* 14: 21-23). The word cannot be
used in that sense here, because these elders were local
officials, whose authority and duties were confined to the
congregation in which they held office, whereas The Elder
of this letter clearly has an authority which extends over
a much wider area. He claims the right to advise and
admonish and exhort congregations in places where he
himself is not a resident. (iii) Almost certainly this letter
was written in Ephesus in the province of Asia. In Asia
in the Church there the word *Elder* was used in a special
sense, which seems to have been characteristic of that
district as it was not of any other. The elders were men
who had been direct disciples of the Apostles; it is from
these men that both Papias and Irenaeus, who both lived
and worked and wrote in Asia, tell us that they got their
information and drew their facts. The elders were the
direct links between the second generation of Christians

and the first followers of Christ in the flesh. It was therein that their authority lay. It is undoubtedly in that sense that the word is used here. The writer of the letter is one of the last direct links with Jesus Christ; and therein lies his right to speak.

As we have already said in the introduction to these letters, the phrase *The Elect Lady* is something of a problem. There are two suggestions.

(i) There are those who hold that this letter is written to *an individual person*. In Greek the phrase is *Eklektē Kuria*. *Kurios* (the masculine form of the adjective) is a common form of respectful address, and *Eklektē* could just possibly—though not probably—be a proper name, in which case the letter would be written to *My Dear Eklektē*. *Kuria*, besides being a title of respectful address, can quite definitely be a proper name, in which case *eklektē* would be an adjective, and the letter would be to *The Elect Kuria*. Just possibly *both* words are proper names, in which case the letter would be to a lady called *Eklektē Kuria*. But, if this letter is written to an individual at all, it is much more likely that *neither* word is a proper name, and the Authorized Version is correct in translating the phrase *The Elect Lady*. As was only to be expected, there has been much speculation as to who The Elect Lady might be. We may mention only two of the suggestions. (a) It has been suggested that *The Elect Lady* is none other than Mary the mother of our Lord. She was to be a mother to John, and he was to be a son to her (*John* 19: 26, 27), and a personal letter from John might well be a letter to her. (b) *Kurios* means *Master*; and *Kuria* as a proper name would mean *Mistress*. In Latin, *Domina* is the same name; and in Aramaic, *Martha* is the same name; both words also mean *Mistress* or *Lady*; so, it has been suggested that the letter was written to none other than Martha of Bethany.

(ii) It is much more likely that the letter is written to a *Church*. It is far more likely that it is a Church which all men love who know the truth (verse 1). Verse 4 says that some of the children are walking in the truth. In verses 4, 8, 10, 12 the word *you* is in the plural, which much more probably suggests a Church. Finally, Peter uses almost exactly the same phrase when he sends greetings from The Elect One (the form is feminine) which is at Babylon (1 *Peter* 5: 13).

It may well be that this difficulty is deliberate. It may well be that the address is deliberately unindentifiable. The letter was written at a time when persecution was a real possibility. If the letter were to fall into the wrong hands, there might well be trouble. And it may well be that the letter is addressed in such a way that to the insider its destination is quite clear, while to the outsider it would look like a personal letter from one friend to another. The address may in fact be a skilful attempt to baffle any hostile person into whose hands the letter might come; and, if that is so, our difficulty in identifying the person or Church to whom the letter is addressed is nothing other than a tribute to the skill of John.

LOVE AND TRUTH

2 John 1-3 (*continued*)

IT is of great interest to note how in this passage *love* and *truth* are inseparably connected. It is *in the truth* that The Elder loves The Elect Lady. It is *because of the truth* that he loves and writes to the Church. In Christianity we learn two things about love; it is only in the truth of Christianity that we can love as we ought.

(i) Christian truth tells us the way in which we ought to love. We must always remember that *agapē* is the Christian word for Christian love. *Agapē* is not passion with its ebb and flow, its flicker and its flame; nor is *agapē* an easy-going an indulgent sentimentalism; nor is *agapē* an easy thing to acquire or a light thing to exercise. *Agapē* is undefeatable goodwill; it is the attitude towards others which, no matter what others do, will never feel bitterness, and which will always seek their highest good. There is a love which seeks to possess; there is a love which softens and enervates; there is a love which withdraws a man from the battle; there is a love which shuts its eyes to faults and failings and to ways which end in ruin. But Christian love is that which will always seek the highest good of others, and which accepts all the difficulties, all the problems, and all the toil which that search involves. It is of significance that John writes in love, that John writes to warn.

(ii) Christian truth tells us the reason for the obligation of Christian love. In his First Letter, John clearly lays down that obligation. He has talked of the suffering, sacrificing, incredibly generous love of God; and then he says, " Beloved, if God so loved us, we ought also to love one another " (I *John* 4: II). *The Christian must love because he is loved.* The Christian cannot accept the love of God without showing love to the men whom God loves. The divine love lays on men the inescapable obligation of human love. Because God loves us, we must love others with the same generous and sacrificial love.

Before we leave this passage we must note one other thing. John begins this letter with a greeting, but it is a very unusual greeting. He says, " Grace, mercy and peace will be with you all." In every other New Testament letter the greeting is in the form of a wish or a prayer. Paul usually says, " Grace be to you and peace." Peter says, " Grace unto you and peace be multiplied " (I *Peter* I: 2). Jude says, " Mercy unto you, and peace, and love, be multiplied " (*Jude* 2). In every case the greeting is a wish or a prayer. But in the case of John the greeting is not a wish or a prayer; it is a *statement*: " Grace, mercy and peace *will be* with you all." John is so sure of the gifts of the grace of God in Jesus Christ that he does not pray that his friends should receive them; rather, he assures them without question that they will receive them. Here

is the faith which never doubts the promises of God in
Jesus Christ.

TROUBLE AND CURE

2 John 4-6

> It gave me great joy to find some of your children
> walking in the truth, as we have received command-
> ment from the Father. And now, Lady, not as if I
> were writing a new commandment to you, but a
> commandment which we have had from the beginning,
> I beg you that we should love one another. And this
> is love, that we should walk according to His com-
> mandments; and this is the commandment, as you
> have heard from the beginning, that we should walk
> in it.

IN the Church to which he is writing there are things to
make John's heart glad, and there are things to make it
sad. It brings him joy to know that some of its members
are walking in the truth; but that very statement implies
that some are not. That is to say, within the Church
there is division, for there are those who have chosen to
walk different roads. For all things John has but one
remedy, and that remedy is love. That is no new remedy,
and no new commandment; it is the word of Jesus Himself:
" A new commandment give I unto you, that ye love one
another; as I have loved you, that ye also love one another.
By this shall all men know that ye are my disciples, if ye
have love one to another " (*John* 13: 34, 35). Only love
can mend a situation in which personal relationships are
broken and interrupted. Rebuke and criticism are liable
to awaken only resentment and hostility; argument and
controversy are liable only to widen the breach; love is
the one thing to mend the breach and to restore the lost
relationship.

But it is possible that those who, as John sees it, have
gone out on the wrong way might say, " We do indeed
love God." Immediately John's thoughts went to another

saying of Jesus: " If ye love me, keep my commandments "
(*John* 14: 15). Jesus' actual commandment was to love
one another, and, therefore, anyone who does not keep
this commandment does not really love God, however
much he may claim to do so. The only proof of our love
of God is our love for the brethren. This is the commandment, says John, which we have heard from the beginning,
and in which we must walk.

As we go on we shall see that there is another side to
this, and that there is no soft sentimentality in John's
attitude towards those who were seducing men from the
truth; but it is significant to note that his first cure for
all the troubles of the Church is love.

THE THREATENING PERIL

2 *John* 7-9

> There is all the more reason to speak like this because
> there have gone out into the world many deceivers,
> men who do not confess that Jesus is Christ, and
> His coming in the flesh. Such a man is the deceiver
> and the antichrist. Look to yourselves that you do
> not ruin that which we have wrought, but see to it
> that you receive a full reward. Everyone who advances
> too far, and who does not abide in the teaching of
> Christ, does not possess God; it is he who abides in
> that teaching who has both the Father and the Son.

ALREADY, in I *John* 4: 2, John has dealt with the heretics
who deny the reality of the incarnation. There is one
difficulty here in the Greek. In I *John* 4: 2 the Greek is
that Jesus *has* come in the flesh. The idea is expressed in a
participle and the participle is in the past tense. It is the
fact that the incarnation has happened which is stressed.
Strangely enough here there is a change, and the participle
is in the present tense; and the literal translation would
be that Jesus *comes*, or, *is coming* in the flesh. As far as
the language goes this could mean either of two things.
(i) It could mean that Jesus is always coming in the flesh,

that there is a kind of permanence about the incarnation, that the incarnation was not one act which finished in thirty years during which Jesus was in Palestine, but that the incarnation is a permanent reality, that in fact the incarnation is timeless. That would indeed be a great thought, and it would mean that now and always Jesus Christ, and God through Him, is entering into the human situation, and into human life. (ii) It could be a reference to the *Second Coming*; and it could mean that Jesus is *coming again* in the flesh. It may well be that there was a belief in the early Church that that was the case, that there was to be a second coming of Jesus in the flesh, a kind of incarnation in glory to follow the incarnation of humiliation. That, too, would be a great thought. But it may well be that C. H. Dodd is right when he says that in a late Greek writer like John, who did not know Greek as one of the great classical writers knew it, we cannot lay all this stress on tenses; and that we are better to take it that John means the same as he meant in I *John* 4: 2, and that these deceivers are denying the reality of the incarnation, and are therefore denying that God can fully enter into the life of man.

It is intensely significant to note how the great thinkers held on with both hands to the reality of the incarnation. In the second century, again and again, Ignatius insists that Jesus was *truly* born, that He *truly* became man, that He *truly* suffered, and that He *truly* died, as if in every case the word *truly* was written in italics and in red ink and underlined. Dr. Vincent Taylor, in his book on *The Person of Christ*, reminds us of two great statements of the incarnation. Martin Luther said of Jesus: " He ate, drank, slept, waked; was weary, sorrowful, rejoicing; He wept and He laughed; He knew hunger and thirst and sweat; He talked, He toiled, He prayed . . . so that there was no difference between *Him* and other men, save only this, that He was *God*, and had no sin." Emil Brunner cites that passage, and then goes on to say, " The Son of

God in whom we are able to believe must be such a One that it is possible to mistake Him for an ordinary man."

If God could only enter into life as a disembodied phantom, then the body stands for ever despised; then there can be no real and ultimate communion between the divine and the human; then there can be no real salvation, for He had to become what we are to make us what He is.

In verses 8 and 9 we hear beneath the words of John the claims of the false teachers.

It is their claim that they are *developing* Christianity, that they are expressing it in new and better terms, that they are discovering more truly what it means. It is John's insistence that they are destroying Christianity, and wrecking the foundation which has been laid, and on which everything must be built.

Verse 9 is an interesting and significant verse. We have translated the first phrase of it *everyone who goes too far.* The Greek word is *proagōn.* The verb means *to go on ahead,* or *to go out in advance.* The false teachers claimed that they were the progressives, that they were the advanced thinkers, that they were the men of the open and the adventurous mind. John himself was one of the most adventurous thinkers in the New Testament. But he insists that, however far a man may advance, he must abide in the teaching of Jesus Christ, or he loses touch with God. Here, then, is the great truth. John is not condemning advanced thinking; he is not saying that Christian doctrine must be a static thing in which there is no advance; but he is saying that Jesus Christ must be the touchstone of all thinking, and that which is out of touch with Christ can never be right. John would say, " Think—but let your thinking be led by Jesus Christ. Think—but when you have thought, take your thinking to the touchstone of Jesus Christ, and to the New Testament picture of Him." Christianity is not a nebulous, undefined, uncontrolled theosophy; it is anchored for ever to the historical figure of Jesus Christ.

NO COMPROMISE

2 John 10-13

> If anyone comes to you, and does not bring this teaching, do not receive him into your house, and do not greet him on the street; for he who greets him becomes a partner in his evil deeds.
>
> Although I have many things to write to you, I do not wish to do so with paper and ink, but I hope to come to see you, and to speak to you face to face, that our joy may be completed.
>
> The children of your Elect Sister send their greetings to you.

HERE we see very clearly the danger which John saw in these false teachers. They are to be given no hospitality; the door is to be shut in their faces; and the refusal of hospitality would be the most effective way of effectively stopping the work of these wandering teachers. John goes further; they are not even to be given a greeting on the street. To greet them is to indicate that to some extent you have sympathy with them; it must be made quite clear to the world that the Church has no dealings with, and no tolerance for, those whose teaching destroys the faith. This is a passage which seems on the face of it to run counter to all Christian love and charity. But C. H. Dodd has certain very wise things to say about it.

It is by no means without parallel. When the saintly Polycarp met the heretic Marcion, Marcion said: " Do you recognize me? " " I recognize Satan's firstborn," answered Polycarp. It was John himself who fled from the public baths when Cerinthus, the heretic, entered them. " Let us hurry away lest the building collapse on us," he said, " because Cerinthus, the enemy of truth, is here."

We have to remember the situation. There was a time when it was touch and go whether the Christian faith would be swamped and destroyed by the speculations of those pseudo-philosophic heretics. The actual existence of the faith was in peril. There was a situation of peril which has no parallel in western civilization. The Church dared not even seem to compromise with this destructive corrosion of the faith.

This, then, as C. H. Dodd wisely points out, is an emergency regulation, and " emergency regulations make bad law." We may recognize the necessity of this way of action in the situation in which John and his people found themselves without in the least holding that we must treat mistaken thinkers in the same way. And yet, to return to C. H. Dodd, a good-humoured tolerance can never be enough. " The problem is to find a way of living with those whose convictions differ from our own upon the most fundamental matters, without either breaking charity or being disloyal to the truth." It is there that love must find a way. The best way to destroy our enemies, as Abraham Lincoln said, is to make them our friends. We can never compromise with mistaken teachers, but we are never freed from the obligation of seeking to lead them into the truth.

So John comes to an end. He will not write any more for he hopes to come to see his friends, and to speak to them face to face. Both Greek and Hebrew say, not *face to face*, but *mouth to mouth*. In the Old Testament God says of Moses: " With him I will speak mouth to mouth " (*Numbers* 12: 8). John was wise and John knew that letters can often only bedevil a situation, and that five minutes heart to heart talk can do what a whole file of letters is powerless to achieve. In many and many a Church, and in many and many a personal relationship, letters have merely succeeded in exacerbating a situation, for the most carefully written letter can be misunderstood and misinterpreted, when a little speech together would have mended matters. Cromwell never understood John Fox, the Quaker, and much disliked him. Then he met him, and after he had spoken to him he said, " If you and I had but an hour together, we would be better friends than we are." Church courts and Christian people would do well to make a resolution never to write when they can speak.

So the letter closes with greetings from John's Church to the friends to whom he writes, greetings, as it were, from one sister's children to another's, for all Christians are members of one family in the faith.

THE LETTERS OF JOHN

THE TEACHER'S JOY

3 John 1-4

> The Elder to Gaius, the beloved, whom I love in truth.
> Beloved, I pray that everything is going well with you, and that you are in good health of body, as it goes well with your soul. It gave me great joy when certain brothers came and testified of the truth of your life, as indeed you do walk in the truth. No news brings me greater joy than to hear that my children are walking in the truth.

3 John is a short letter, and there is no New Testament letter which better shows that the Christian letters were exactly on the model which all letter-writers used in the time of the early Church. There is a papyrus letter from Irenaeus, a ship's captain, to his brother Apolinarius:

> Irenaeus to Apolinarius his brother, my greetings. Continually I pray that you may be in health, even as I myself am in health. I wish you to know that I arrived at land on the 6th of the month Epeiph, and I finished unloading my ship on the 18th of the same month, and went up to Rome on the 25th of the same month, and the place welcomed us, as God willed. Daily we are waiting for our discharge, so that up till today no one of us in the corn service has been allowed to go. I greet your wife much, and Serenus, and all who love you, by name. Goodbye.

The form of Irenaeus' letter is exactly the same as the form of John's letter. There is first the greeting. There is next the prayer for good health. There is then the main body of the letter with its news and its information. There are the final greetings, in which even John's instruction to greet his friends *by name* recurs. The early Christian letters were not something remote and distant and religious and ecclesiastical; they were just the kind of letters which people wrote to each other every day in the ancient world.

John writes to a friend called Gaius. In the world of the New Testament Gaius was the commonest of all names.

In the New Testament there are three men called Gaius. There was Gaius, the Macedonian, who, along with Aristarchus, was with Paul at the riot in Ephesus (*Acts* 19: 29). There was Gaius of Derbe, who was the delegate of his Church to convey the collection for the poor to Jerusalem (*Acts* 20: 4). There was the Gaius of Corinth who had been Paul's host, and who was such a hospitable soul that he could be called the host of the whole Church (*Romans* 16: 23), and who was one of the very few people whom Paul had personally baptized (I *Corinthians* 1: 14), and who, according to tradition, became the first Bishop of Thessalonica. As we have said, in the ancient world Gaius was the commonest of all names; and there is no reason to identify our Gaius with any of the other three. According to tradition our Gaius was made the Bishop of Pergamum by John himself. Here he stands before us as a man with an open house and an open heart.

Twice in the first two verses of this little letter John uses the word *beloved*. (The *well-beloved* and the *beloved* of the Authorized Version, in the first two verses, translate the same Greek word, *agapētos*). In this group of letters John uses the word *agapētos* no fewer than ten times. This is a very notable fact. These letters are stern letters; they are letters of warning and rebuke; and yet their accent is the accent of love. It was the advice of a great scholar and preacher: " Never scold your congregation." Even if he has to rebuke, annoyance and irritation never creep into the accent of John. The whole atmosphere of his writing is love.

Verse 2 shows us the comprehensive care of the good and the devoted pastor. John is interested both in the physical and the spiritual health of Gaius. John was like Jesus; he never forgot that men have bodies as well as souls; and that the physical health of men is just as much the concern of the real pastor as the spiritual health of the soul is.

In verse 4 John tells us of the teacher's greatest joy. The teacher's greatest joy is to see his pupils and his disciples walking in the truth. The truth is not something to be simply intellectually assimilated; it is the knowledge which fills a man's mind and the charity which clothes his life. The truth is that which makes a man think like God and act like God.

CHRISTIAN HOSPITALITY

3 John 5-8

> Beloved, whatever service you render to the brothers, strangers as they are, is an act of true faith, and they testify to your love before the Church. It will be a further kindness, if you send them on their way worthily of God. For they have gone out for the sake of the Name, and they take no assistance from pagans. It is a duty to support such men, that we may show ourselves fellow-workers with the truth.

HERE we come to John's main object in writing. A group of travelling missionaries are on their way to the Church of which Gaius is a member, and John is urging Gaius to receive them, and to give them every support, and to send them on their way in a truly Christian manner.

In the ancient world hospitality was a sacred duty. Strangers were under the protection of Zeus Xenios, Zeus the god of strangers (*Xenos* is the Greek for a *stranger*). In the ancient world inns were notoriously unsatisfactory. The Greek had an instinctive dislike of taking money for the giving of hospitality; and, therefore, the profession of innkeeper ranked very low. Inns were notoriously dirty and flea-infested. Innkeepers were notoriously rapacious, so that Plato compared them to pirates who hold their guests to ransom, before they allow them to escape. The ancient world had a system of *guest-friendships* whereby families in different parts of the country undertook to give each other's members hospitality in their part of the country. This connection between families lasted throughout the generations, and, when it was claimed, the claimant brought with him a *sumbolon,* or *token,* which identified him to his hosts. In the larger cities other cities kept an official called the *Proxenos* to whom their citizens, when they were travelling, might appeal for shelter and for help.

If the heathen world accepted the obligation of hospitality it was only to be expected that the Christians would take it even more seriously. It was Peter's injunction: " Use hospitality one to another without grudging " (I *Peter* 4: 9). " Be not forgetful to entertain strangers," says the writer to the Hebrews, and then adds: " For thereby some have entertained angels unawares " (*Hebrews* 13: 2). In the Pastoral Epistles a widow is to be honoured if she has " lodged strangers " (I *Timothy* 5: 9). Paul bids the Romans to be " given to hospitality " (*Romans* 12: 13).

Hospitality was to be specially the characteristic of the leaders of the Church. A bishop must be a man who is given to hospitality (I *Timothy* 3: 2). Titus is told to be " a lover of hospitality " (*Titus* I: 8). When we come down to the time of Justin Martyr (A.D. 170) we find that on the Lord's Day the well-to-do contributed as they would, and it was the duty of the president of the congregation " to succour the orphans and the widows, and those who through sickness or any other cause are in want, and those who are in bonds, and the strangers sojourning amongst us " (Justin Martyr, *First Apology* I: 67).

In the early Church the Christian home was, as it should be now, the place of the open door and the loving welcome. There can be few nobler works than to give a stranger the right of entry to a Christian home. The family circle should always be wide enough to have a place for the stranger, no matter where he comes from, and no matter what his colour may be.

THE CHRISTIAN ADVENTURERS

3 *John* 5-8 (*continued*)

FURTHER, this passage tells us about the wandering missionaries. These are the wandering preachers who have given up home and comfort to carry the word of God wherever they went. In verse 7 Paul says that they have gone forth for the sake of the Name, and they take no assistance from pagans. (It is just barely possible that verse 7 might refer to those who have come out from the Gentiles, taking nothing with them, those who for the sake of their Christianity have left their work and their home and their friends, and who have no means of support). In the ancient world the " begging friar," with his wallet, was well known. There is, for instance, a record of a man who calls himself " the slave of the Syrian goddess," and who went out begging, and who claimed that he never came back with fewer than seventy bags of money for his goddess. But these Christian wandering missionaries would take nothing from the Gentiles, even if the Gentiles would have given it.

John commends those adventurers and wanderers of the faith to the hospitality and the generosity of Gaius. He says that it is a duty to help them that we may show ourselves fellow-workers with the truth (verse 8). Moffatt translates this very vividly: " We are bound to support such men, to prove ourselves allies of the truth."

There is a great Christian thought here. A man's circumstances may be such that he cannot become a missionary or a preacher. Life may have put him in a position where he must get on with a secular job, and where he must stay in the one place, and carry out the routine duties of life and living. But where he cannot go his money and his prayers and his practical support can go; and, if he gives that support, he has made himself an ally of the truth. It is not everyone who can be, so to speak, in the front line; but every man by supporting those who are in the front line can make himself an ally of the truth. By giving our practical support to those who are carrying out the wider work of the Church, without leaving our bench or our desk or our office or our factory or our home town, we can still become an ally of the truth. When we remember that, all giving to such a cause must become, not an obligation, but a privilege, not a duty, but a delight. The Church needs those who will go out with the truth, but the Church also needs those who, although they must stay at home, will be the allies of the truth.

LOVE'S APPEAL

3 John 9-15

I have already written something to the Church, but Diotrephes, who is ambitious for the leadership, does not accept our authority. So, then, when I come, I will bring up the matter of his actions, for he talks nonsensically about us with wicked words; he refuses to receive the brothers, and attempts to stop those who wish to do so, and tries to eject them from the Church.

Beloved do not imitate the evil, but the good. He who does good has the source of his life in God; he who does evil has not seen God.

Everybody testifies to the worth of Demetrius, and so does the truth itself; and so do we testify, and you know that our testimony is true.

I have many things to write to you; but I do not wish to write to you with ink and pen. I hope to see you soon, and we shall talk face to face.

Peace be to you. The friends send their greetings. Greet the friends by name.

HERE we come to the reason why this letter was written. Here we are introduced to two of the main characters in the situation.

There is Diotrephes. In the introduction we have already seen the situation in which John and Diotrephes and Demetrius are all involved. In the early Church there was a double ministry. There were the apostles and the prophets. Their sphere was not confined to any one Church. The authority of the apostles and of the apostolic men extended all over the Church; and the prophets wandered from congregation to congregation preaching the inspired word of God. On the other hand there were the elders; and they were the permanent settled ministry of the local congregations; they were the backbone of the local Churches. In the early days this presented no problem, for the local congregations were still very much infant Churches who had not yet learned to walk by themselves, and to handle their own affairs. But as time went on there was bound to come a tension between the two kinds of ministry. As the local Churches became stronger and more self-conscious of their identity, they would inevitably become less and less willing to submit to remote control and to the invasion of itinerant strangers. They would wish to run their own affairs; and they would resent the interference of wandering strangers, who would often unsettle and disturb the congregation. The problem is still, at least to some extent, with us. There is still the problem of the itinerant evangelist who may well have a theology and work with methods and in an atmosphere which is very different from that of the settled local congregation. In the younger Churches there is still the question of how long the missionaries must remain in control, and of when the time has come for the missionaries to withdraw and to allow the indigenous Churches to govern themselves and to rule their own affairs.

Here in this letter Diotrephes is the representative of the local congregation. He will not accept the authority of John, the apostolic man. He will not receive the itinerant missionaries. He is so determined to see that the local congregation manages its own affairs that he will even eject those who are still prepared to accept the authority of John, and to receive the wandering preachers and teachers. What exactly Diotrephes was we cannot tell. He certainly was not a bishop in anything like the modern sense of the word. He may have been a very strong-minded elder.

Or, he may even have been an aggressive member of the congregation, who by the force of his personality was sweeping all before him. Certainly he emerges as a strong and dominant character.

There is Demetrius. Demetrius is most likely the leader of the wandering preachers, and most probably he is actually the bearer of this letter. John goes out of his way to give Demetrius a testimonial as to character and ability, and it may well have been that there were certain circumstances attaching to Demetrius which gave Diotrephes a handle for his opposition.

Demetrius is by no means an uncommon name. Attempts have been made to identify him with two New Testament characters. He has been identified with Demetrius, the silversmith of Ephesus, and the leader of the opposition to Paul (*Acts* 19: 21ff). It may be that Demetrius afterwards became a Christian, and that his early opposition was still a black mark against him. He has been identified with Demas (which is a shortened form of *Demetrius*), who had once been one of Paul's fellow-labourers, but who had forsaken Paul because he loved this present world (*Colossians* 4: 14; *Philemon* 24; 2 *Timothy* 4: 10). It may be that Demas came back to the faith, and that his desertion of Paul was never forgotten, and was always held against him.

Into this situation there comes John, whose authority is being flouted; and Gaius, who is a kindly soul, but very probably not so strong a character as the aggressive Diotrephes, and whom John is seeking to align with himself, for Gaius, left to himself, might well succumb to the forceful Diotrephes.

There is our situation. We may have a good deal of sympathy with Diotrephes; we may well think that he was taking a stand which sooner or later had to be taken. But for all his strength of character Diotrephes had one fault—he was lacking in charity. As C. H. Dodd has put it: " There is no real religious experience which does not express itself in charity." And that is why for all his powers of leadership, and for all his dominance of character, Diotrephes was not a real Christian, as John saw it. The true Christian leader must always remember that strength and gentleness must go together, that personal ambition must have no place in his demands, that leadership and love must go hand in hand. Diotrephes was like so many leaders in the Church and in the Church's congregations. He may well have been right, but he took the wrong way to the right end, for no amount of strength of mind can take the place of love of heart.

What the issue of all this was we do not know. But John comes to the end in love. Soon he will come and talk, and his presence will do what no letter can ever do; and for the present he sends his greetings and his blessing. And we may well believe that the, " Peace be to you " of the aged Elder brought peace to the troubled Church to whom he wrote.

THE LETTER OF JUDE

THE LETTER OF JUDE

INTRODUCTION

The Difficult and the Neglected Letter

IT may well be said that for the great majority of modern readers to read the little letter of Jude is a bewildering rather than a profitable undertaking. There are two verses of *Jude* which everyone knows—the resounding and magnificent doxology with which it ends:

> Now unto Him who is able to keep you from falling, and to present you faultless before the presence of His glory with exceeding joy, to the only wise God our Saviour, be glory and majesty, dominion and power, both now and for ever. Amen.

But, apart from these two great verses, *Jude* is largely unknown, and seldom read. The reason for the difficulty of *Jude* is that it is written in the language and in the thought of its day. It is written out of a background of thought, against the challenge of a situation, in pictures, and with quotations, which are all quite strange to us. Beyond a doubt it would hit those who read and heard it for the first time like a hammer-blow and like a trumpet call to defend the faith. Moffatt calls *Jude* " a fiery cross to rouse the Churches." But, as J. B. Mayor, one of the greatest editors of *Jude* has said: " To a modern reader it is curious rather than edifying with the exception of the beginning and the end." All this is, in itself, one of the great reasons for addressing ourselves to the study of *Jude;* for, when we understand Jude's thought, and when we disentangle the situation against which he was writing, his letter becomes of the greatest interest for the history and the understanding of the earliest Church, and by no means without relevance for today. There have indeed been times in the history of the Church, and especially in the revivals of the Church, when *Jude* was not far off from being the most relevant book in the New Testament. Let us, then, begin by simply setting down the substance of the letter without at the moment waiting for the explanations and the elucidations which must follow later.

Meeting the Threat

It had been Jude's intention to write a treatise on the faith which all Christians share; but that task had to be laid aside in view of the rise of men whose conduct and whose thought was a threat and a menace to the Christian Church (verse 3). In view of this situation the need was not so much to expound the faith as to rally Christians in defence of the faith. Certain men had insinuated themselves into the Church, and were busily engaged in turning the grace of God into an excuse for blatant and open immorality, and were denying the only true God and Jesus Christ the Lord (verse 4). These men were immoral in life and heretical in belief.

The Warnings

Against these men Jude marshals his warnings. Let them remember the fate of the Israelites. The Israelites had been brought in safety out of Israel, but they had never been permitted to enter the Promised Land because of their unbelief (verse 5). The generation of Israelites who had come out of Egypt were debarred from entry into the Promised Land because of their faithless fears when they reached its borders (*Numbers* 13: 26—14: 29). A man might have received the grace of God, but even then he might still lose his eternal salvation, if he drifted into disobedience and unbelief. The angels had been angels with the glory of heaven as theirs; but they had come to earth and had corrupted mortal women with their lust (*Genesis* 6: 2), and now they were imprisoned in the abyss of darkness, awaiting judgment (verse 6). He who rebels against God must needs look for judgment. The cities of Sodom and Gomorrah had given themselves over to lust and to unnatural vice, and their destruction in flames is a dreadful warning to everyone who gives himself up to lust (verse 7).

The Evil Life

These men are visionaries of evil dreams; they defile their flesh; and they speak evil of the angels (verse 8). No one, not even Michael the archangel, dare speak evil of angels, not even of the evil angels. It had been given to Michael to bury the body of Moses. The devil had tried to stop him, and had tried to claim the body for himself. Michael had spoken no evil against the devil, even in circumstances like that, but had simply said, " The Lord rebuke you! " (verse 9). Angels must be respected, even evil and hostile angels. These evil men condemn everything which they do not understand, and spiritual things are beyond their understanding. They do understand their fleshly instincts, and they allow themselves to be governed by them as the brute beasts do (verse 10).

They are like Cain, the cynical selfish murderer; they are like Balaam, whose one desire was for gain, and who lead the people into sin; they are like Korah, who rebelled against the legitimate authority of Moses, and was swallowed up by the earth for his arrogant disobedience (verse 11).

They are like the hidden rocks on which a ship may founder; they have their own clique in which they consort with people like themselves, and thus destroy Christian fellowship; they deceive others with their promises, like clouds which promise the longed-for rain, and then pass over the sky; they are like fruitless and rootless trees, which have no harvest of good fruit; as the foaming spray of the waves casts the sea-weed and the wreckage on the beaches, they foam out shameless deeds; they are like disobedient stars who refuse to keep their appointed orbit, and who are doomed to the dark (verse 13). Long ago the prophet Enoch had described these men, and had prophesied their divine destruction (verse 15). They murmur against all true authority and discipline as the children of Israel murmured against Moses in the desert; they are discontented with the lot which God has appointed to them; their lusts are their dictators; their speech is arrogant and vaunting and proud; they are toadies and flatterers of the great for sake of gain (verse 16).

Words to the Faithful

Having castigated the evil men with this torrent of invective, Jude turns to the faithful. They could have expected all this to happen, for the apostles of Jesus Christ had foretold the rise of evil men (verses 18, 19). But the duty of the true Christian is to build his life on the foundation of the most holy faith; to learn to pray in the power of the Holy Spirit; to remember the conditions of the covenant into which the love of God has called him; to wait for the mercy of Jesus Christ (verses 20, 21).

As for the false thinkers and the loose livers—some of them may be saved with pity while they are still hesitating on the brink of their evil ways; others have to be snatched like brands from the burning; and, in all his rescue work, the Christian must have that godly fear which will love the sinner but hate the sin, and avoid the pollution of those he seeks to save (verses 22, 23).

And all the time there will be with him the power of that God who can keep him from falling, and who can bring him pure and joyful into His presence (verses 24, 25).

The Heretics

Who were the heretics whom Jude blasts, and what were their beliefs, and what was their way of life? That Jude never tells us. He was not a theologian, but, as Moffatt says, he was " a plain honest leader of the Church." " He denounces rather than describes " the heresies he attacks. He does not seek to argue and to refute, for he writes as one " who knows when round indignation is more telling than argument." So, then, we must make our deductions from the letter itself. From the letter we can deduce three things about these heretics.

(i) They were antinomians. Antinomians have existed in every age of the Church. Antinomians are people who pervert grace. The position of the antinomian is that the law is dead, and that he is under grace. The prescriptions of the law are no longer valid; they may apply to other people, but they no longer apply to him. He can do precisely and absolutely what he likes. Grace is supreme; grace can forgive any sin; the more the sin, the more the opportunities for grace to abound (*Romans* 6). The body is of no importance; what matters is the inward heart of man. All things belong to Christ, and, therefore, all things are his. And, therefore, for him there is nothing forbidden. So these heretics in *Jude* turn the grace of God into an excuse for flagrant and blatant immorality (verse 4); they even practise nameless and shameless unnatural vices, as the people of Sodom did (verse 7). They defile the flesh and think it no sin (verse 8). They allow their brute instincts to rule their lives (verse 10). With their sensual ways, they are like to make shipwreck of the Love Feasts of the Church (verse 12). It is by their own lusts that they direct their lives (verse 16). These were men who argued that, since they were under grace, the law was irrelevant, and its ethical demands no longer obligatory. They argued that they were so spiritual that sin for them had ceased to exist. They argued that, if they loved God with their hearts, they could do what they liked with their bodies.

Modern Examples of the Ancient Heresy

It is a curious and a tragic fact of history that the Church has never been entirely free of this antinomianism, and it is natural that it flourished most in the ages when the wonder of grace was being rediscovered.

It appears in the Ranters of the seventeenth century. The Ranters were pantheists and antinomians. A pantheist believes that God is literally everything. Literally *all things* are Christ's, and Christ is the end of the law. They talked of " Christ within them," and paid no heed to the Church or its ministry, and belittled scripture. One of them called Bottomley wrote: " It is not safe to go to the Bible to see what others have spoken and written of the mind of God as to see what God speaks within me, and to follow the doctrine and leading of it in me." When George Fox rebuked them for their lewd practices, they answered, " We are God." This may sound very fine, but, as John Wesley was to say, it most often resulted in " a gospel of the flesh." It was their argument that " swearing, adultery, drunkenness and theft are not sinful unless the person guilty of them apprehends them to be so." When Fox was a prisoner at Charing Cross they came to see him, and mightily offended him, by calling for drink and tobacco. They swore terribly, and when Fox rebuked them, justified themselves by saying that Scripture tells us that Abraham, Jacob, Joseph, Moses, the priests, and the angel all swore. To which Fox replied that He who was before Abraham commanded, " Swear not at all." Richard Baxter said of them that, " They conjoined a cursed doctrine of libertinism, which brought them to all abominable filthiness of life; they taught . . . that God regardeth not the actions of the outward man, but of the heart; and that to the pure all things are pure (even things forbidden) and so, as allowed by God, they spoke most hideous words of blasphemy, and many of them committed whoredoms commonly. . . . The horrid villainies of this sect did speedily extinguish it." Doubtless many of the Ranters were definitely insane; doubtless some of them were pernicious and deliberate sensualists; but doubtless some of them were earnest, but misguided, men, who had misunderstood the meaning of grace, and what it means to be freed from the law.

Later, John Wesley was to have trouble with the antinomians. He talks of them preaching a gospel of flesh and blood. At Jenninghall he says that " the Antinomians had laboured hard in the Devil's service." At Birmingham he says that " the fierce, unclean, brutish, blasphemous Antinomians " had utterly destroyed the spiritual life of the congregation. He tells of a certain Roger Ball who had insinuated himself into the life of the congregation at

Dublin. At first he had seemed to be so spiritually-minded a man that the congregation had welcomed him as being pre-eminently suited for the service and the ministry of the Church. He showed himself in time to be " full of guile and of the most abominable errors, one of which was that a believer had a right to all women." He would not communicate, for under grace a man must " touch not, taste not, handle not." He would not preach and abandoned the Church services, because, he said, " The dear Lamb is the only preacher."

Wesley, deliberately to show the position of these antinomians, related in his *Journal* a conversation which he had with one of them at Birmingham. It ran as follows. " Do you believe that you have nothing to do with the law of God?" " I have not; I am not under the law; I live by faith." " Have you, as living by faith, a right to everything in the world?" " I have. All is mine, since Christ is mine." " May you then take anything you will anywhere? Suppose out of a shop without the consent or knowledge of the owner?" " I may, if I want, for it is mine. Only I will not give offence." " Have you a right to all the women in the world?" " Yes, if they consent." " And is not that a sin?" " Yes, to him who thinks it is a sin; but not to those whose hearts are free."

Repeatedly Wesley had to meet these people, as George Fox had to meet them. John Bunyan, too, came up against these Ranters who claimed complete freedom from the moral law, and who looked with contempt on the ethics of the stricter Christian. " These would condemn me as legal and dark, pretending that they only had attained perfection that could do what they would and not sin." One of them, whom Bunyan knew, " gave himself up to all manner of filthiness, especially uncleanness . . . and would laugh at all exhortations to sobriety. When I laboured to rebuke his wickedness, he would laugh the more."

Jude's heretics have existed in every Christian generation, and, even if they do not go all the way, there are still many who in their heart of hearts trade upon God's forgiveness, and who make the grace of God an excuse to sin.

The Denial of God and of Jesus Christ

(ii) Of the antinomianism and the blatant immorality of the heretics whom Jude condemns there is no doubt. The other two faults with which he charges them are not so obvious in their meaning. He charges them with, as the Authorized Version has it, " denying the only Lord God, and our Lord Jesus Christ " (verse 4). In the best Greek manuscripts the word *God* does not appear in this phrase; and the translation should most probably be, " denying our only Master and Lord Jesus Christ." The closing doxology is to " the only God." (The word *wise* is not in the best manuscripts). This phrase the *only God* occurs again in *Romans* 16: 27; I *Timothy* 1: 17; I *Timothy* 6: 15. The reiteration of the word *only* is significant. If Jude talks about our *only* Master and Lord, and, if he talks about the *only* God, it is only natural to assume that there must have been those who questioned the uniqueness of Jesus Christ and of God, and who believed in other Masters and Lords and in other gods. Can we then trace any such line of thought in the early Church, and, if so, does it fit in with any other evidence which hints within the letter itself may supply?

As so often in the New Testament, we are here again in contact with that type of thought which came to be known as Gnosticism. The basic idea of Gnosticism is that this is a dualistic universe, a universe with two eternal principles in it. From the beginning of time, the Gnostics held, there has always been spirit and matter. Spirit is essentially and absolutely good; matter is essentially flawed and evil and imperfect. Out of this flawed matter the world was created. Now God is pure spirit, and because of that He could not possibly touch or handle or work with this essentially evil matter; there can be, as the Gnostics saw it, no possible contact between God and matter. How then was creation effected? From Himself God put out aeons or emanations; each of these aeons, in a long series and chain and ladder, was farther away from God. At last at the end of this long chain, distant and remote from God, there was an aeon who was able to touch matter; and it was this aeon, this distant and secondary god, who actually created the world. Nor was this all that was in Gnostic thought. As the aeons in the series grew more and more distant from the true God, they grew more and more ignorant of God; not only did they grow more ignorant of God, they also grew more hostile to God. And the creating aeon, at the end of the series, was at once totally ignorant of, and totally hostile to, God. The world, then, as the Gnostics saw it, was created by a secondary god who was ignorant of, and hostile to, the true God. Having got that length, the Gnostics took another step. They identified the true God with the God of the New Testament, the God whom Jesus Christ came to make known to men; and they identified the secondary, ignorant and hostile god with the God of the Old Testament. They regarded the God of the Old Testament as quite ignorant of, hostile to, and different from, the God of the New Testament. As they saw it, the God of creation is a different God from the God of revelation and redemption. On the other hand, Christianity believes in the *only* God. To Christianity there is only one God in creation, providence and redemption. The Gnostics denied the one God, and introduced two gods hostile to each other.

This was the Gnostic explanation of sin. It is because creation was carried out, in the first place, out of matter, out of stuff which is essentially flawed and evil, and, in the second place, by an ignorant god, that sin and suffering and sorrow and all imperfection exist.

This Gnostic line of thought had one curious, but perfectly logical, result. If the God of the Old Testament is ignorant of, and hostile to, the true God, it must follow that the people whom that ignorant God hurt and punished and afflicted were in fact *good* people. Clearly the ignorant and the hostile God would be hostile to the people who were the true servants of the real and true God. The Gnostics, therefore, so to speak, turned the Old Testament story upside down; and regarded the heroes of the Old Testament as villains, and the villains of the Old Testament as heroes. So there was a sect of these Gnostics called Ophites, because they worshipped the serpent of Eden; there were those of them who regarded Cain and Korah and Balaam as the great heroes of the Old Testament. Now it is these very people whom Jude uses as tragic and terrible examples of sin. So we may take it that the heretics whom Jude attacks are Gnostics who denied the oneness of God, who regarded the God of creation as quite different from the God of redemption, who saw in the Old Testament God an ignorant enemy of the true God, and who, therefore, turned the Old Testament upside down, and who saw the Old Testament sinners as servants of the true God, and the Old Testament saints as servants of the ignorant and the hostile God.

But, not only did these heretics deny the oneness of God, they also denied " our only Master and Lord Jesus Christ." That is to say, they denied the uniqueness of Jesus Christ. How does that fit in with the Gnostic ideas so far as they are known to us? We have seen that, as the Gnostics believed, God put out a series of aeons between Himself and the world. The Gnostics regarded Jesus Christ as one of these aeons. He was only one among many in the chain of being between man and God; He might stand very high in that chain; he might even be nearest of all to God in it; nevertheless He was only one among many; and it might well be that, as time went on, He might be overpassed and a still greater revelation of God might come to men. The Gnostics did not regard Jesus as our *only* Master and Lord; He was only one among many who were links between God and man, although He might be the highest and the closest of all.

There is still one other hint about these heretics in *Jude*, a hint which fits in with what we know about the Gnostics. In verse 19, Jude describes the heretics as, " they who *separate themselves*." The word which Jude uses is a very unusual Greek word, *apodiorizein*. This word has in it the root *horos*, which means a *boundary* or a *limit*; in the best Greek manuscripts there is no word for *themselves*; and the translation ought to be, not, those who *separate themselves*, but, as Moffatt has it, those who *set up divisions and distinctions*. The heretics are those who introduce some kind of class distinctions within the fellowship of the Church. What were these distinctions and divisions and classifications? We have seen that between man and God there stretches an infinite series of aeons or spiritual beings. Now the aim of man must be to achieve fellowship and friendship and contact with God. To reach this contact with God the soul of man must climb this long ladder, and traverse this infinite series of links between God and man. The Gnostics held that, to achieve this, very special and elaborate and recondite and esoteric, knowledge and training and study are required. So deep is this knowledge that only very few can attain to it. The Gnostics, therefore, divided men into two classes, the *pneumatikoi* and the *psuchikoi*. The *pneuma* is the spirit of man, that which makes man kin to God; and the *pneumatikoi* were the *spiritual* people, the people whose spirits were so fine and noble and wise and highly developed and intellectual that they were able to climb the long ladder and to reach God. These *pneumatikoi*, the Gnostics claimed, were so spiritually and intellectually equipped that they could become as good as Jesus— Irenaeus says that some of them believed that the really *pneumatikoi* could become *better* than Jesus and could attain direct union with God. On the other hand, the *psuchē* is simply the principle of physical life. All things which live have *psuchē*; *psuchē* is something which man shares with the animal creation and even the plants which grow. The *psuchikoi* were ordinary people, who had physical life, but whose *pneuma*, spirit, was quite un-developed and who were quite incapable of ever making the intellectual effort and of gaining the intellectual wisdom which would enable them to climb the long road to God. So the Gnostics divided mankind into two classes, the *pneumatikoi*, the spiritual élite, that select few who were able to embark on the long intellectual search for God, and the *psuchikoi*, those who had physical life, but whose spiritual life was quite inadequate ever to attain to the knowledge which was necessary to reach God. The *pneumatikoi* were a very small and select minority; the *psuchikoi* were the vast majority of ordinary people.

It is clear to see that this kind of belief set up a spiritual aristocracy within the Church; it was inevitably pro-ductive of spiritual snobbery and spiritual pride. It introduced into the Church the worst kind of class dis-tinction, and the worst kind of pride.

So, then, the heretics whom Jude attacks were men who denied the oneness of God, and who split God into an ignorant creating God and a truly spiritual God; who denied the uniqueness of Jesus Christ, and who saw Him as only one of the links between God and man; who erected class distinctions within the Church, and who limited fellowship with God to the intellectual few.

The Denial of the Angels

(iii) It is further inferred that these heretics denied and insulted the angels. It is said that " they despise dominion and speak evil of dignities " (verse 8). *Dominion* and *dignities* are both words which describe ranks in the Jewish hierarchy of the angels. Verse 9 is a reference to a story in the *Assumption of Moses*. It is there told that Michael, the archangel, was given the task of the burying of the body of Moses. The devil opposed him and tried to stop him and claimed the body. Michael made no charge against the devil, and said nothing against him. He said only, " The Lord rebuke you ! " If Michael, the archangel, on such an occasion said nothing against an angel, who is the prince of the evil angels, then clearly no man can speak evil of the angels.

The Jewish belief in angels was very elaborate. Every nation had its protecting angel. Every person and every child had his angel. All the forces of nature, the wind and the sea and the fire and all the others, were under the control of angels. It could even be said, " Every blade of grass has its angel." Clearly the heretics attacked the angels. It is likely that they said that the angels were the servants of the creator God, the ignorant and the hostile God, and that a Christian must have nothing to do with angels. We cannot quite be sure what lies behind this, but we do know that to all their other errors the heretics added the despising of the angels; and to Jude this seemed an evil thing.

Jude and the New Testament

We must now examine the questions regarding the date and the authorship of *Jude*.

Jude had some difficulty in getting into the New Testament at all; it is one of these books whose position was always insecure, and which were late in gaining full and final acceptance as part of the New Testament. Let us briefly set out the opinion of the great fathers and scholars of the early Church about *Jude*.

Jude is included in the Muratorian Canon, which dates to about A.D. 170, and which may be regarded as the first semi-official list of the books accepted by the Church at Rome at that time. This is all the more strange when we remember that the Muratorian Canon does not include in its list *Hebrews* and *First Peter*. But thereafter *Jude* is for long spoken of with a doubt. In the middle of the third century Origen knew and used *Jude*, but was well aware that there were many who questioned its right to be Scripture. Eusebius, the great scholar of the middle of the fourth century, made a deliberate examination of the position of the various books which were used, and he classes *Jude* amongst the books which are disputed, which are by many rejected, and which are possibly spurious. Jerome, who produced the Vulgate, had his doubts about *Jude*. And it is in Jerome that we find one of the great reasons for the hesitation which was felt towards *Jude*. The strange thing about *Jude* is the way in which it quotes as authorities books which are *outside* the Old Testament. *Jude* uses as Scripture certain apocryphal books which were written between the Old and the New Testaments, and which were never generally regarded as scripture. To take two definite instances, the reference in verse 9 to Michael, the archangel, disputing with the devil about the body of Moses is taken from a Jewish apocryphal book called *The Assumption of Moses*. In verses 14 and 15 Jude confirms and cements his argument with a quotation from prophecy, as, indeed, is the habit of all the New Testament writers; but Jude's quotation is, in fact, taken from the *Book of Enoch*, which he appears to regard as Scripture and as prophecy. Jerome tells us that it was Jude's habit of using non-scriptural books as Scripture, which made some people regard him with suspicion; and, towards the end of the third century in Alexandria, it was from the very same charge that Didymus defended Jude. It is perhaps the strangest thing in Jude that he uses these non-scriptural books as other New Testament writers use the prophets; and in verses 17 and 18 he makes use of a saying of the apostles which is not identifiable at all.

Jude, then, was one of the books which took a long time to gain an assured place in the New Testament; but by the fourth century its place was secure.

The Date

There are definite indications that *Jude* is not an early book. *Jude* speaks of the faith that was once delivered to the saints (verse 3). That way of speaking definitely seems to look back a long way, and to come from the time when there was a body of belief which was orthodoxy. In verses 17 and 18 he urges his people to remember the words of the apostles of the Lord Jesus Christ which were spoken before. That seems to come from a time when the apostles are no longer there, and when the Church looked back on their teaching. The atmosphere of *Jude* is the atmosphere of a book which looks back.

But beside that we have to set the fact that, as it seems to us, *Second Peter* makes use of *Jude* to a very large extent. Anyone can see that the second chapter of *Second Peter* and *Jude* have the closest possible connection. It is quite certain that one of these writers was borrowing from the other, and incorporating the other's work in his own. On general grounds it is much more likely that the author of *Second Peter* would incorporate *Jude* into his work as a whole, than that *Jude* would, for no apparent reason, take over only one section of *Second Peter*. Now, if we believe that *Second Peter* uses *Jude*, Jude cannot be very late, even if it is not early.

It is true that *Jude* looks back on the apostles; but it is also true that, with the exception of John, all the apostles were dead by A.D. 70. Taking together the fact that *Jude* looks back on the apostles, and the fact that *Second Peter* uses *Jude*, a date round about A.D. 80 to 90 would suit *Jude*.

The Authorship of Jude

Let us go on to ask the question, who was this Jude, or Judas, who wrote this epistle? He calls himself the servant of Jesus Christ, and the brother of James. In the New Testament there are five people called Judas.

(i) There was the Judas of Damascus in whose house Paul was praying after his conversion on the Damascus road (*Acts* 9: 11).

(ii) There was Judas Barsabas, a leading figure in the councils of the Church, who, along with Silas, was the bearer to Antioch of the decision of the Council of Jerusalem, when the door of the Church was opened to the

Gentiles (*Acts* 15: 22, 27, 32). This Judas was also a prophet (*Acts* 15: 32).

(iii) There was Judas Iscariot.

None of these three has ever seriously been considered as the author of this letter.

(iv) There was a second Judas in the apostolic band. John calls him Judas, not Iscariot (*John* 14: 22). In Luke's list of the Twelve there is an apostle whom the Authorized Version calls Judas *the brother* of James (*Luke* 6: 16; *Acts* 1: 13). If we were to depend solely on the Authorized Version we might well think that here we have a very serious candidate for the authorship of this letter, and, indeed, Tertullian does call the writer of this letter the Apostle Judas. But in the Greek this man is simply called *Judas of James*. In the Authorized Version the words *the brother* are printed in italics which is the sign that they are not in the Greek, but have been supplied by the translators. Now this is a very common idiom in Greek and almost always it means not *brother of*, but *son of*; and *Judas of James* in the list of the Twelve is not Judas the *brother* of James, but Judas the *son* of James, as all the newer translations correctly show.

(v) There remains one further Judas in the New Testament, the Judas who was the brother of Jesus (*Matthew* 13: 55; *Mark* 6: 3). And if any of the New Testament Judases is the writer of this letter, it must be this one, for only he could truly be called *the brother of James*, who was also one of the brothers of Jesus.

The question then is, is this little letter to be taken as a letter of the Judas, who was the brother of our Lord? If so, this letter would have a very special interest of its own. What are the objections to believing that Judas, the brother of Jesus was the writer of this letter?

(i) It is asked, if Jude—to give him the form of his name with which we are familiar—was the brother of Jesus, why does he not say so? Why does he identify himself as Jude

the brother of James, and not as Jude the brother of Jesus?
It would surely be explanation enough of that to say that
Jude shrank in humility from taking so great a title of
honour to himself. Even if it was true that he was the
brother of Jesus, he might well prefer in humility to call
himself the servant of Jesus Christ, for Jesus was not only
his brother; Jesus was also his Lord. Further, Jude the
brother of James would in all probability never be outside
Palestine in all his life. The Church he would know would
be the Church at Jerusalem, and of that Church, James
was the undoubted head. If he was writing to Churches
which were in Palestine, then his relationship to James was
the natural thing to stress. It would, when we come to
think of it, be more surprising that Jude should call himself
the brother of Jesus than that he should call himself the
servant of Jesus Christ.

(ii) It is objected that Jude calls himself the servant of
God, and thereby calls himself an apostle. The servants of
God was the Old Testament title for the prophets. God
would not do anything without revealing it first to His
servants the prophets (*Amos* 3: 7). What had been a
prophetic title in the Old Testament became an apostolic
title in the New Testament. Paul speaks of himself as the
servant of Jesus Christ (*Romans* I: I; *Philippians* I: I).
He is spoken of as the servant of God in the Pastoral
Epistles (*Titus* I: I), and that is also the title which James
takes to himself (*James* I: I). There are two answers to
that. First, the title servant of Jesus Christ is not confined
to the Twelve, for it is given by Paul himself to Timothy
(*Philippians* I: I); and, even if it is regarded as a title
confined to the apostles in the wider sense of the word, we
find the brethren of the Lord associated with the eleven
after the Ascension (*Acts* I: 14), and Jude, like James, may
well have been among them; and we learn that the brothers
of Jesus were prominent in the missionary work of the
Church (I *Corinthians* 9: 5). Such evidence as we have
would all tend to prove that Jude, the brother of our Lord,

was one of the apostolic circle, and that the title servant of God is perfectly applicable to him.

(iii) It is argued that the Jude of Palestine, who was the brother of Jesus, could not have written the Greek of this letter for it would be Aramaic that he spoke and not Greek. That is not a safe argument. Jude would certainly know and speak Greek, for Greek was the *lingua franca* of the ancient world, which all men spoke in addition to their own language. The Greek of *Jude* is rugged and forceful; it might well be within the competence of Jude to write it for himself, and, if he could not do so, he may well have had a helper and translator such as Peter had in Silvanus, when he wrote his first letter.

(iv) It might be argued that the heresy which Jude is attacking is Gnosticism, and that Gnosticism is much more a Greek way of thought than it is a Jewish way of thought— and what would Jude of Palestine be doing writing to Greeks? But there is one odd fact about this heresy which Jude attacks—it is the very opposite of orthodox Judaism. The dynamic and controller of all Jewish action was the sacred and the holy law; the first basic belief of Jewish religion was that there was one God; the Jewish belief in angels was highly developed and elaborately wrought out. Now it is by no means difficult to suppose that when certain Jews entered the Christian faith, they swung completely to the other extreme. It is by no means uncommon for a man, when he is, so to speak, released from one thing, to swing entirely to its opposite. It is easy to imagine a Jew who had all his life been in servitude to the law suddenly discovering grace, and plunging into antinomianism as a very reaction against his former legalism. It is by no means impossible to imagine a Jew who had all his life been committed to the belief in one lonely isolated God, suddenly swinging into the very opposite belief as a kind of violent reaction. It is by no means impossible to think of a Jew who had lived in a universe populated and controlled by

angels reacting violently against the belief in angels altogether. It is, in fact, easy to see in the heretics whom Jude
attacks, Jews who had come into the Christian Church
rather as renegades from Judaism than as truly convinced
Christians. They may well have been Jews who had seen in
Christianity, not so much a new way of life, as a violent and
opposite reaction to their own faith.

(v) Lastly, it is argued that, if this letter had been
known to have been the work of Jude the brother of Jesus,
it would not have been so long in gaining an entry into the
New Testament, and that the work of a brother of Jesus
would have gained immediate access to authoritative
Scripture. But the truth is that before the end of the first
century the Church was largely Gentile; the Jews were
regarded as the enemies and the slanderers of the Church.
During His life-time Jesus' brothers had in fact been His
enemies; and it could well have happened that a letter as
Jewish as *Jude* might have had a struggle against prejudice
to get into the New Testament at all.

Jude, the Brother of Jesus

If this letter is not the work of Jude, the brother of
Jesus, what are the alternatives suggested? On the whole,
the alternatives are two.

(i) The letter is, indeed, the work of a man called Jude,
but he is a Jude of which nothing at all is otherwise known.
The difficulty that this theory has to meet is twofold.
First, there would be the coincidence that this Jude is also
the brother of James. Second, it would be hard to explain
how so small a letter ever came to have any authority at
all, if it is the work of some one who is quite unknown.

(ii) It is suggested that the letter is pseudonymous, that
is to say that is was written by someone else, and then
attached to the name of Jude. That kind of custom was
common in the ancient world. Between the Old and New
Testament scores of books were written, and were attached
to, and issued in, the names of Moses, Enoch, Baruch,

Isaiah, Solomon and many an other. No one saw anything wrong in that. But two things are to be noted about *Jude*.

(*a*) In all such publications the name to which the book was attached was a famous name; it was the name of some-one whom all the world knew to be a great prophet or king or hero. It was a name which no one could mistake and which everyone could recognize. Now Jude, the brother of our Lord, was a person who was completely obscure. No one knew, or knows, anything about him. He is not numbered amongst the great names of the early Church; his name means nothing at all. There is a story that in the days of Domitian there was a deliberate attempt to see to it that Christianity did not spread. News came to the Roman authority that certain descendants of Jesus were still alive, amongst them the grandsons of Jude. The Romans felt that it was possible that rebellion might gather around these men, that they might become storm-centres, leaders or, at least, figure-heads, of a Christian revolution. They were ordered to appear before the Roman courts. When they did so, they were seen to be horny-handed sons of toil, and they were dismissed as being quite harmless and quite unimportant. Obviously Jude was Jude the obscure. There could have been no possible reason for attaching a book to the name of a man whom nobody knew.

(*b*) When such a book was written, and when it was attached to the name of a great person, the reader was never left in any doubt as to whose name it was being attached to. It was made abundantly clear—it was under-lined—whose name the book was being attached to. If this book had been issued as the work of Judas the brother of our Lord, quite certainly he would have been given that title in such a way that no one could possibly mistake it; and the plain fact is that it is quite unclear who the author is, which is the reverse of what would have happened had the book been deliberately pseudonymous.

When we read *Jude* it is obviously Jewish; its references are such that only a Jew could understand them, and its allusions are such that only a Jew could catch them. It is simple and rugged; it is vivid and pictorial. It is clearly the work of a simple thinker rather than of a theologian. It fits Jude the brother of our Lord. It is attached to his name, and there could be no reason for so attaching it unless he did in fact write it.

It is our opinion that we will not be wrong if we believe that this little letter is actually the work of Judas, the brother of Jesus.

JUDE

WHAT IT MEANS TO BE A CHRISTIAN

Jude I, 2

> Jude, the servant of Jesus Christ, and the brother of James, sends this letter to the called who are beloved in God, and kept by Jesus Christ. May mercy and peace and love be multiplied to you.

FEW things tell more about a man than the way in which a man speaks of himself. Few things are more revealing than the titles by which a man wishes to be known. Jude calls himself the servant of Jesus Christ and the brother of James. At once this tells us two things about Jude.

(i) Jude was a man well content with the second place. He was not nearly so well known as James; and Jude is content to be known as the *brother of James*. In this he was the same as Andrew. Andrew is Andrew Simon Peter's brother (*John* 6: 8). Andrew, too, was described by his relationship to his far more famous brother. Both Jude and Andrew might well have been jealous and resentful of their far greater brothers, in whose shadow they had to live; but both must have had the great gift of gladly and willingly taking the second place.

(ii) The only term of honour which Jude would allow himself was to call himself *the servant of Jesus Christ*. The Greek is *doulos*, and it means more than *servant*; it means *slave*. Jesus was Master; Jude was servant. That is to say, Jude regarded himself as having only one object and one distinction in life—to be for ever at the disposal of Jesus for service in His cause. The greatest glory which the Christian can conceive of is to be of use to Jesus Christ.

In this introduction Jude uses three words to describe the Christian.

(i) Christians are those who are *called by God*. The Greek for *to call* is *kalein*; and *kalein* has three great areas in which it is used. (*a*) It is the word for summoning a man to *office, to duty, and to responsibility.* It is the word for summoning a man to take office in the service of his city, his community, or his state. The Christian is summoned to a task, to duty, to responsibility in the service of Christ. (*b*) It is the word for summoning a man to a *feast* or a *festival.* It is the word for an invitation to a happy and to a joyous occasion. The Christian is the man who is summoned to joy, the joy of being the guest of God. (*c*) It is the word for summoning a man to *judgment.* It is the word for calling a man to court that he may give account of himself. The Christian is in the end summoned to appear before the judgment seat of Christ. The Christian is the man who is called to responsibility for Christ, called to joy with Christ, and called to judgment by Christ.

(ii) Christians are those who are *beloved in God.* It is this great fact which determines the whole nature of the call. The call to men is the call to be loved and to love. God calls men to duty and to a task, but that duty and task are not a burden, but an honour. God calls men to service, but the service is not the service of tyranny, but of fellowship. In the end God calls men to judgment, but that judgment is not only the judgment of justice, it is also the judgment of love.

(iii) Christians are those who are *kept by Christ.* The Christian is never left alone; Jesus Christ is always the sentinel of his life and the companion of his way. The Christian is not only called; he is also kept.

The Christian is the man who is called by God, beloved in God, and kept by Christ.

THE CALL OF GOD

Jude 1, 2 (*continued*)

BEFORE we leave this opening passage, let us think a little more about this calling of God, and let us try to see something of what this calling means.

(i) Paul speaks about being called to be an *apostle* (*Romans* I: I; I *Corinthians* I: I). In Greek the word *apostle* is *apostolos*; it comes from the verb *apostellein*, which means *to send out*; and an apostle is *one who is sent out*. The apostle is the man who is sent out into the world by Christ and for Christ. That is to say, the Christian is the ambassador of Christ. He is sent out into the world to speak for Christ, to act for Christ, to live for Christ. The honour of Christ is in his hands. By his life he commends, or fails to commend, Christ to others. The Christian is in the world, and among men, as the representative and envoy of Jesus Christ.

(ii) Paul speaks about being called to be *saints* (*Romans* I: 7; I *Corinthians* I: 2). The word for *saint* is *hagios*, which is also very commonly translated *holy*. The root idea of this word is *difference*. The Sabbath is holy because it is different from other days; and God is supremely holy because he is different from men. To be called to be a *saint* is to be called to be *different*. To be a saint is to live a life in which the difference is that every thought and word and action are consciously judged and decided by the standards and the presence of Jesus Christ. The world has its own standards, and its own scale of values. The difference in the Christian life is that for the Christian Christ is the only standard, and loyalty to Christ the only value in the world.

(iii) The Christian is called *according to the purpose of God* (*Romans* 8: 28). God's call goes out to every man, although every man does not accept it; and this means that for every man God has a purpose. It has been said that fate is what we are compelled to do; destiny is what we are meant to do. Every man is a man of destiny, for every man has a place in the purpose of God. And the Christian is the man who submits himself to the purpose of God for him and for his life.

Paul has much to say about this calling of God, and we can only set it down very summarily. The calling of God sets before a man a great hope (*Ephesians* 1: 8; 4: 4). The calling of God should be a unifying influence, for men should be bound together by the conviction that they all have a part in the purpose and the calling of God (*Ephesians* 4: 4). The calling of God is an *upward* calling (*Philippians* 3: 14), a calling that sets a man's feet on the way to the stars; it is a *heavenly* calling (*Hebrews* 3: 1), a calling which makes a man think of the things which are invisible and eternal, and which comes to him from beyond and sets his gaze on the beyond; it is a *holy* calling, a calling, as we have seen, to be different, a call to consecration to God. It is a calling which can cover a man's ordinary every day task. His day's work is part of that to which he is called (1 *Corinthians* 7: 20). It is a calling which comes from God, and God does not alter or change His mind (*Romans* 11: 29). It is a call which knows no human distinctions, and which cuts across the world's classifications and the world's scale of importances (1 *Corinthians* 1: 26). Although it is the call to God, it does not leave a man with nothing to do. The Christian must be worthy of his calling (*Ephesians* 4: 1; 2 *Thessalonians* 1: 11); and all life must be one long effort to make that calling secure (2 *Peter* 1: 10). The calling of God is the privilege, the challenge and the inspiration of the Christian life.

DEFENDING THE FAITH

Jude 3

> Beloved, when I was in the midst of devoting all my energy to writing to you about the faith which we all share, I felt that I was compelled to write a letter to you to urge you to engage upon the struggle to defend the faith which was once and for all delivered to God's consecrated people.

HERE we have the occasion of this letter. Jude has been engaged on writing a treatise about the Christian faith, the faith which all Christians share; but there had come news to him that evil and misguided men had been spreading abroad destructive teaching; so the conviction had come to him that he must lay aside his treatise and that he must write this letter. Jude fully realized the duty to be the watchman of the flock of God. The purity of their faith was threatened and he rushed to their defence and to the defence of the faith. That involved setting aside the work on which he had been engaged; but there are times when it is much better to write a tract for the times than a treatise for the future. It may be that Jude never again got the chance to write the treatise which he had planned; but the fact is that he did more for the Church by writing this urgent little letter than he would have done by leaving a long and detached treatise on the faith. In this passage there are certain truths about the faith which we hold.

(i) The faith is *something which is delivered to us*. The facts of the Christian faith are not something which we have manufactured and discovered for ourselves. In the true sense of the word they are *tradition*, something which has been handed down from generation to generation until they have come to us. They go back in an unbroken chain of tradition to Jesus Christ himself. There is something to be added to that. The facts of the Christian faith are indeed something which we have not discovered for ourselves. It is, therefore, true that the Christian tradition is not something which is handed down in the cold print of books; it is something which is passed on from person to person through the generations. The chain of Christian tradition is a living chain whose links are men and women who have experienced the dynamic and the wonder of the facts.

(ii) The Christian faith is *something which is once and for all delivered to us*. That is to say, there is in the Christian faith an unchangeable quality. That is not to say that each age has not to rediscover, to rethink, and to re-experience the Christian faith; but it does mean to say that there is an unchanging nucleus in it—and the permanent and unchanging centre of it is that Jesus Christ came into the world and lived and died to bring salvation to men.

(iii) The Christian faith is *something which is entrusted to God's consecrated people*. That is to say, the Christian faith is not the possession of any one person; it is the possession of the Church. The Christian faith is not any man's private property; that to which it is entrusted is the Christian fellowship of the Church. It is not a matter of private interpretation. The Christian faith comes down within the Church, is preserved within the Church, and is understood within the Church.

(iv) The Christian faith is *something which must be defended*. There are imperial titles which change as different parts of our empire enter upon their independence, but our kings and queens enjoy one unchanging title—Defender of the Faith. Every Christian must be a defender of the faith. If the Christian tradition comes down from generation to generation, it means that each generation must hand it on, uncorrupted, unperverted, still in its original truth. There are times when that is difficult. The word which Jude uses for to *defend* is the word *epagōnizesthai*, which contains within it the root of our English word *agony*. The defence of the faith may well be a costly thing; but the defence and the preservation of the faith is a duty which falls on every generation of the Church. It is our constant duty to hand on that which we have received.

THE PERIL FROM WITHIN

Jude 4

> For certain men have wormed their way into the Church—long before this they were designated for judgment—impious creatures they are—who twist the grace of God into a justification of blatant immorality, and who deny our only Master and Lord, Jesus Christ.

HERE is the peril which made Jude lay aside the treatise he was about to write, and take up his pen and write this burning letter. The peril came *from within the Church*. It was not the threat of persecution which was the danger; there was a canker at the very heart of the Church.

Certain men, as the Authorized Version has it, had *crept in unawares*. The word in the Greek (*pareisduein*) is a very expressive word. It is used of the specious and seductive words of a clever pleader seeping gradually into the minds of a judge and jury; it is used of an outlaw slipping secretly back into the country from which he has been expelled; it is used of the slow and subtle entry of innovations into the life of state, which in the end undermine and break down the ancestral laws. It always indicates a secret, stealthy, and subtle insinuation of something evil into a society or a situation.

Certain evil men had insinuated themselves into the Church. They were the kind of men for whom judgment was waiting. They were impious creatures, godless in their thought and in their life. Jude picks out two characteristics about them.

(i) They perverted the grace of God into an excuse for blatant immorality. The word in the Greek which we have translated *blatant immorality* is a grim and terrible word. It is the word *aselgeia*. The corresponding adjective is *aselgēs*. Most men, when they sin, seek concealment; they try to hide their sin. They have enough conscience left to have at least some feelings of shame; they have enough respect for common decency not to wish to be found out. But the *aselgēs* is the man who is so lost to honour, to decency, and to shame that he does not care who sees his sin and his immorality. It is not that he arrogantly and proudly flaunts it; it is simply that he can publicly do the most shameless things, because he has ceased to care for shame and decency at all. These men were undoubtedly tinged with Gnosticism. Gnosticism was that line of thought which set out with the idea that only spirit is good, and that matter is essentially evil. If that be so, it means that the body is essentially evil. And if that be so, it does not matter what a man does with his body; since it is evil, its lusts and its desires can be sated and glutted, because it is of no importance what is done with the body. Further, these men believed that, since the grace of God is wide enough to cover any sin, a man can sin as he likes. He will be forgiven anyhow; the more he sins, the greater the grace; therefore, why worry about sin? Grace will look after that. Grace was being perverted into a justification for sin.

(ii) They denied our only Lord and Master, Jesus Christ. There is more than one way in which a man can deny Jesus Christ. (*a*) He can deny Him in the day of persecution, and can abandon Christ for the sake of his own safety. (*b*) He can deny Him for the sake of convenience. There are occasions when it is more convenient to conceal than to reveal the fact that one is a Christian. There are times when a man is tempted conveniently to forget his Christianity. (*c*) He can deny Him by his life and conduct. His lips may say that he believes in Jesus Christ, while his every action, his words, and his whole attitude to life and to others denies it, and gives the lie to his profession. (*d*) He can deny Him by developing false ideas about Him. If these men were Gnostics, they would have two mistaken ideas about Jesus. First, since matter is evil, and since the body is evil, they would hold that Jesus had no real body, that He only *seemed* to have a body, that He was nothing other than a kind of spirit ghost in the apparent shape of a man. The Greek for *to seem* is *dokein*; and these men were called *Docetists*. (There is no letter *c* in Greek; in the word *docetist* the Greek *k* is transliterated by the English *c*, and, therefore, the *c* is pronounced hard like a *k*). These men would deny the manhood and the humanity and the real incarnation of Jesus Christ. Second, they would deny the uniqueness of Jesus. They believed that there were many stages between the evil matter of this world and the perfect spirit which is God; and they believed that Jesus was only one of the many stages on the way.

No wonder Jude was alarmed. He was faced with a situation in which there had wormed their way into the Church men who were twisting the grace of God into a justification, and even a reason, for sinning in the most shameless and blatant way, and who denied both the manhood and the uniqueness of Jesus Christ.

THE DREADFUL EXAMPLES

Jude 5-7

It is my purpose to remind you—although you already possess full and final knowledge of all that matters—that, after the Lord had brought the people out of Egypt in safety, He subsequently destroyed those who were unbelieving; and that He has placed under guard in eternal chains in the abyss of darkness, to await the judgment which shall take place on the great day, the angels who did not keep their own rank, but left their own proper habitation. Just so Sodom and Gomorrah and the surrounding cities, who in the same way as these took their fill of sexual sin, and strayed after perverted sexual immorality, are a warning by the way in which they paid the penalty of eternal fire.

I.—THE FATE OF ISRAEL

JUDE issues a warning to the evil men who were perverting the belief and the conduct of the Church. He tells them that he is, in fact, doing nothing other than remind them of things of which they were perfectly well aware. In a sense it is true to say that all preaching within the Christian Church is not so much bringing to men new truth as it is confronting them with the truth which they already know, but which they have forgotten or are deliberately disregarding. Preaching within the Church is often nothing other than reminding a man of who he is and of what he knows.

To understand the first two examples which Jude cites from history we must understand one thing. The evil men who were corrupting the Church did not regard themselves as enemies of the Church and of Christianity; they regarded themselves as the advanced thinkers, as a cut above the ordinary Christian, as the spiritual aristocracy and élite. They regarded themselves as the leaders and not the corrupters of the Church. Jude chooses his examples to make clear that, even if a man has received the greatest privileges, he may still fall away into disaster, that even those who have received the greatest gifts and privileges from God cannot consider themselves safe, but must still be on constant watch against the mistaken things.

The first example which Jude chooses is from the history of Israel. He goes for his story to *Numbers* 13 and 14. The story is this. The mighty hand of God had delivered the people from slavery in Egypt. What greater act of deliverance could there be than that? The guidance of God had brought the people safely across the desert to the borders of the Promised Land. What greater demonstration of the Providence of God could there be than that? So, at the very borders of the Promised Land, at Kadesh-barnea, spies were sent out to spy out the land before the final invasion was to take place. Then, with the exception of Caleb and Joshua, the spies came back with the news and the opinion that the dangers ahead were so terrible, and the people so great and so strong, that it was hopeless to go forward, and that they could never win their way into the Promised Land. The people rejected the report of Caleb and Joshua, who were for going on, and accepted the report of the others, who insisted that the case was hopeless. This was a clear act of disobedience to God, a clear instance of complete lack of faith in God; and the consequence was that God gave sentence that of these people, with the exception of Joshua and Caleb, every single person of over twenty would never enter the Promised Land, but that they would all wander for forty years in the wilderness until they were dead (*Numbers* 14: 32, 33; 32: 10-13). Here was the dreadful example of those who had been brought out of Egypt, who had been brought across the desert, who had been brought to the very borders of the Promised Land, and who, after all that, were guilty of disobedience and lack of faith, and who, therefore, received death in the wilderness wandering rather than rest in the Promised Land.

This, indeed, was a picture which haunted the mind of both Paul and the writer to the Hebrews (1 *Corinthians* 10: 5-11; *Hebrews* 3: 18—4: 2). Here is the proof that even the man with the greatest privilege can meet with disaster before the end, if he falls away from obedience and lapses from faith. Dr. Johnstone Jeffrey tells of a great man who absolutely refused to have his life-story written before his death. " I have seen," he said, " too many men fall out on the last lap." It was John Wesley's warning, " Let, therefore, none presume on past mercies, as if they were out of danger." In his dream John Bunyan saw that, even from the gates of heaven, there was a way to hell.

It is Jude's warning to these men that, great as their privileges have been, they must still have a care lest disaster come upon them; and his is a warning which each one of us would do well to heed.

THE DREADFUL EXAMPLES

2.—THE FATE OF THE ANGELS

Jude 5-7 (continued)

THE second dreadful example which Jude takes is the example of the fallen angels.

The Jews had a very highly developed doctrine and hierarchy of angels. The angels were the servants of God. In particular the Jews believed that every nation had its presiding angel. In the *Septuagint* the Greek version of the Hebrew Scriptures, *Deuteronomy* 32: 8 reads, " When the Most High divided the nations, when He separated the sons of Adam, He set the bounds of the nations according to the number of the angels of God." That is to say, to each nation there was a presiding angel.

The Jews believed in a fall of the angels, and much is said about this in the *Book of Enoch* which is so often behind the thought of Jude. In regard to this fall of the angels there were two lines of tradition.

(i) The first saw the fall of the angels as due to pride and to rebelliousness; the angels disobeyed God and rebelled against Him. That legend gathered especially round the name of Lucifer, the light-bringer, the son of the morning. Isaiah writes, " How art thou fallen from heaven, O Lucifer, son of the morning! " (*Isaiah* 14: 12). When the seventy returned from their mission and told Jesus of their successes, Jesus warned them against pride. He said, " I beheld Satan as lightning fall from heaven " (*Luke* 10: 18). The idea was that there was civil war in heaven; and that the angels rose against God and were cast out of heaven, and that Lucifer had been the leader of that rebellion.

(ii) The second stream of tradition finds its scriptural echo in *Genesis* 6: 1-4. In this line of thought the angels were attracted by the beauty of mortal women; they left heaven, seduced these mortal women, and so sinned.

In the first case the fall of the angels was due to *pride*; in the second case the fall of the angels was due to *lust* for the forbidden things.

In effect Jude takes the two ideas and puts them together. He says that the angels left their own rank; that is to say, they aimed at a rank and at an office which was not for them. He also says that they left their own proper habitation; that is to say, they left the heavenly places and came to earth to live with the daughters of men.

All this seems strangely recondite and strange to us; it moves in a world of thought, and amidst stories and traditions from which we have moved away.

But Jude's warning is clear. Two things brought ruin to the angels—pride and lust; and, even although they were angels, even although heaven was their dwelling-place, even although they had been in the nearer presence of God, they nonetheless sinned, and for their sin are reserved for judgment. To those who read and heard Jude's word for the first time the whole line of thought was clear, for *Enoch* had much to say about these fallen angels, and their fate, and their reservation for judgment. So Jude was speaking to his people in terms that they could well understand; and he was telling them that, if pride and lust ruined the angels in spite of all their privileges, pride and lust could ruin them. The evil men within the Church were proud enough to rebel against the Church's teaching, and to think that they knew better than the Church's teaching. Their way of life was the way of lust; they perverted the grace of God into a justification for blatant immorality; lust had ruined the angels, and lust could ruin them. Whatever be the ancient background of Jude's words, Jude's warning is still true. The pride which knows better than God, and the desire for the forbidden thing are the way to ruin in time and in eternity.

THE DREADFUL EXAMPLES

3.—SODOM AND GOMORRAH

Jude 5-7 (continued)

THE third of the examples which Jude chose is that of the destruction of Sodom and Gomorrah. Notorious for their sins, these cities were obliterated by the fire of God. Sir George Adam Smith in *The Historical Geography of the Holy Land* points out that no incident in history ever made such an impression on the Jewish people, and that Sodom and Gomorrah are time and time again used in Scripture as the examples *par excellence* of the sin of man and of the judgment of God; they are so used even by Jesus Himself (*Deuteronomy* 29: 23; 32: 32; *Amos* 4: 11; *Isaiah* 1: 9; 3: 9; 13: 19; *Jeremiah* 23: 14; 49: 18; 50: 40;

Zephaniah 2: 9; *Lamentations* 4: 6; *Ezekiel* 16: 46, 49,
53, 55; *Matthew* 10: 15; 11: 24; *Luke* 10: 12; 17: 29;
Romans 9: 29; *2 Peter* 2: 6; *Revelation* 11: 8). " The
glare of Sodom and Gomorrah is flung down the whole
length of Scripture history."

The story of the final wickedness of Sodom and Gomorrah
is told in *Genesis* 19: 1-11, and the tragic tale of their
destruction in the passage immediately following (*Genesis*
19: 12-28). The sin of Sodom is one of the most horrible
stories in history. Ryle has called it a " repulsive incident."
The real horror of the incident is cloaked a little in the
Authorized Version by a Hebrew turn of speech which to
some extent veils the incident in English. Two angelic
visitors had come to Lot. At his pressing invitation they
came into his house to be his guests. When they were there,
the inhabitants of Sodom surrounded the house, demanding
that Lot should bring out his visitors that they should
know them. In Hebrew the verb *to know* is the word for
sexual intercourse. It is said, for instance, that Adam
knew his wife, and she conceived, and bare Cain (*Genesis*
3: 1). What the men of Sodom were bent on was unnatural sexual intercourse, homosexual intercourse, with
Lot's two visitors. They were bent on sodomy, the word in
which their sin is dreadfully commemorated.

It was after this that Sodom and Gomorrah were con-
sumed off the face of the earth. The neighbouring cities
were Zoar, Admah and Zeboim (*Deuteronomy* 29: 23; *Hosea*
11: 8). This disaster was localised in the dreadful desert in
the region of the Dead Sea, a region which Sir George Adam
Smith calls, " This awful hollow, this bit of the infernal
regions come to the surface, this hell with the sun shining
into it." It was there that the cities were said to have
been; and it was said that under that scorched and barren
and twisted earth there still smouldered an eternal fire of
destruction. The soil is bituminous with oil below, and
Sir George Adam Smith conjectures that what happened
was this: " In this bituminous soil took place one of these

terrible explosions and conflagrations, which have broken
out in the similar geology of North America. In such
soil reservoirs of oil and gas are found, and suddenly dis-
charged by their own pressure or by the earthquake.
The gas explodes, carrying high into the air masses of oil
which fall back in fiery rain, and are so inextinguishable
that they float afire on the water." It was by such an erup-
tion of fire and hail of flame that Sodom and Gomorrah
were destroyed. That awful desert was only a day's journey
from Jerusalem. Men never forgot the fate of Sodom and
Gomorrah, and God's judgment on sin.

So, then, Jude reminds these evil men of his own day of
the fate of those who in the ancient times defied the moral
law of God. It is reasonable to suppose that those men
whom Jude attacks had also descended to homosexuality
and to sodomy, and that they were perverting the grace of
God to cover even these shameful sins.

Jude is insisting that these men should remember that
sin and judgment should go hand in hand, that they should
learn from history, and that they should repent in time.

CONTEMPT FOR THE ANGELS

Jude 8, 9

> In the same way these, too, with their dreams, defile
> the flesh, and set at naught the celestial powers, and
> speak evil of the angelic glories. When the archangel
> Michael himself was disputing with the devil about
> the body of Moses, he did not venture to launch
> against him an evil-speaking accusation, but said,
> " The Lord rebuke you! "

JUDE begins this passage by comparing the evil men with
the false prophets whom Scripture condemns. *Deuteronomy*
13: 1-5 sets down what is to be done with " the prophet or
the dreamer of dreams " who corrupts the nations and
who seduces the people from their loyalty to God. Such a
prophet is to be mercilessly killed and exterminated. One

of the titles of the prophet was "the dreamer of dreams," and these men whom Jude attacks are false prophets, dreamers of false dreams, seducers of the people, and must be treated as such. Their false dreams and their false teaching issued in two things.

(i) It made them defile the flesh. We have already seen the twofold direction of the teaching of these men on the flesh. First, the flesh is entirely evil; only spirit matters; therefore, the flesh is of no importance, and the instincts of the body can be given their way without let or hindrance or control. Second, the grace of God is all-forgiving and all-sufficient; therefore, sin does not matter, for grace can and will forgive every sin. Sin is nothing other than the means whereby grace is given its opportunity to operate. These errors of the false thinkers are clear, but what their second error was is not quite so clear.

(ii) They despised angels. Celestial powers and angelic lordships are names for ranks of angels within the angelic hierarchy. This follows immediately after the citing of Sodom and Gomorrah as dreadful examples; and part of the sin of Sodom was the desire of its people to misuse and to maltreat the angelic visitors of Lot (*Genesis* 19: 1-11). The men Jude attacks spoke evil of the angels. To prove how terrible and sinful a thing that was Jude cites an instance, not from Scripture at all, but from an apocryphal book, entitled *The Assumption of Moses*. One of the strange things about Jude is that he so often makes his quotations, not from Scripture, but from the apocryphal books. Such quotations seem very strange to us; but these books were very popular and very widely used at the time when Jude was writing, and to Jude's readers the quotations would be very effective. The story in *The Assumption of Moses* runs as follows. The strange story of the death of Moses is told in *Deuteronomy* 34: 1-6. *The Assumption of Moses* goes on to add to that story the further story that the task of burying the body of Moses was given to the archangel Michael. At this the devil disputed with Michael for the possession of Moses. He based his claim on two grounds. Moses' body was matter; matter is evil; and, therefore, Moses' body belonged to him, for matter was his domain. Second, Moses was a murderer, for had not Moses slain the Egyptian whom he saw smiting the Hebrew? (*Exodus* 2: 11, 12). And, if Moses was a murderer, the devil had a claim on his body. Now the point that Jude is making is this. Michael was an archangel; the devil was the devil; Michael was engaged on a task given him to do by God; the devil was seeking to stop him doing it, and was making claims he had no right to make. But even in a collection of circumstances like that Michael spoke no evil of the devil, brought no accusation against him, but simply said, " The Lord rebuke you ! " Jude's point is that, if the greatest of the good angels refused to speak evil of the greatest of the evil angels, even in circumstances like that, then surely no human being may speak evil of any angel.

What the men Jude was attacking were saying about the angels we do not know. Maybe they were saying that the angels did not exist. Maybe they were saying the angels were evil, and in the service of the evil God. This is a passage which no doubt means very little to us, but equally no doubt it would be a weighty argument and rebuke to those to whom Jude addressed it.

THE GOSPEL OF THE FLESH

Jude 10

> But these people speak evil of everything which they do not understand, whereas they allow themselves to be corrupted by the knowledge which their instincts give them, living at the mercy of their instincts, like beasts without reason.

JUDE says two things about the evil men whom he is attacking.

(i) They criticize everything which they do not understand. Anything which is out of their orbit and their experience they disregard as worthless and irrelevant. Now in their lives spiritual things and values have no place; and, therefore, they regard all spiritual things with scorn and with contempt. " Spiritual things are spiritually discerned " (I Corinthians 2: 14). They have no spiritual discernment, and, therefore, they are blind to, and contemptuous of, all spiritual realities.

(ii) They allow themselves to be corrupted by the things they do understand. What they do understand is the demands of the fleshly instincts which they share with the brute beasts. Their law is the law of the uncontrolled instincts; their way of life is to allow the instincts they share with the beasts to have their way; their values are fleshly values; their gospel is a gospel of the flesh. Jude describes men who have lost all sense of, and awareness of, spiritual things, and for whom the things demanded by the animal instincts of man are the only realities and the only standards.

The terrible thing about this is that the first condition is the direct result of the second. The tragedy of life is that no man is born without a sense of the spiritual things, but that he can lose that sense, until for him the spiritual things cease to exist. A man can lose any faculty, if he refuses to use it. We discover that with such simple things as games and skills. If we give up playing a game, we lose the ability to play it. If we give up practising a skill—such as playing the piano—we lose it. We discover that in such things as abilities. We may at one time know something of a foreign language, but if we never speak or read it, we lose it. Every man can hear the voice of God; every man has some awareness of physical things; and every man has the animal instincts on which, indeed, the future existence of the race depends. But, if a man consistently over a life-time refuses to listen to God, if he shuts his ears and his eyes to all spiritual values and standards and voices, if he makes his instincts the sole standard of his desires, and the sole dynamic of his conduct, then in the end he will come to a time when he cannot hear the voice of God, when the spiritual values are lost, and when he has nothing left to be his master but his clamant desires. In the end a man can come to a state when he cannot even see the necessity of self-control, when he cannot even see the beauty of chastity, when purity has no attraction for him, and when the only thing which matters in his world is the satisfaction of the impulses, instincts and desires which come from his animal nature. And it is a terrible thing to have reached a stage in which a man is deaf to God and blind to goodness; and that is the stage which the men whom Jude attacks had reached.

LESSONS FROM HISTORY

Jude 11

> Woe to them, because they walk in the way of Cain; they fling themselves into the error of Balaam; they perish in Korah's opposition to God.

JUDE now goes to Hebrew history for parallels to the wickedness of the wicked men of his own day; and from it he draws the examples of three notorious sinners.

(i) First, there was Cain, the murderer of his brother Abel (*Genesis* 4: 1-15). In Hebrew tradition Cain stood for two things. (*a*) He was the first murderer in the world's history; and, as *The Wisdom of Solomon* has it, " he himself perished in the fury wherewith he murdered his brother " (*Wisdom* 10: 3). It may well be that Jude is implying that those who delude and seduce others are nothing other than murderers of the souls of men, and that, therefore, they are the spiritual descendants of Cain. (*b*) But in Hebrew tradition and teaching Cain came to stand for something more than that. In Philo, he stands for selfishness and self-love. In the Rabbinic teaching Cain is the type of the cynical and sceptical man. In the Jerusalem *Targum* he is depicted as saying: " There is neither judgment

nor judge; there is no other world; no good reward will
be given to the good, and no vengeance taken on the wicked;
nor is there any pity in the creation or the government
of the world." To the Hebrew thinkers Cain was the
cynical, sceptical, atheistic, materialistic unbeliever, who
believed neither in God or the moral order of the world,
and who, therefore, did exactly as he liked. So Jude is
charging his opponents with defying God, and denying the
moral order of the world. It is still true that the man who
chooses to sin has still to reckon with God, and has still
to learn, always with pain, and sometimes with tragedy,
that no man can defy the moral order of the world with
impunity.

(ii) Second, there was Balaam. In Old Testament thought,
in Jewish teaching and even in the New Testament (*Revelation* 2: 14) Balaam is the great example of those who
taught Israel to sin. In the Old Testament there are two
stories about Balaam. The one is quite clear, and very
vivid and dramatic. The other is more shadowy, but
much more terrible; and it is the second which left its mark
on Hebrew thought and teaching. The first is in *Numbers*
chapter 22 to 24. In these three chapters there is told
the story of how Balak attempted to persuade Balaam
to curse the people of Israel, for he feared their power;
how five times he offered Balaam large rewards to do so.
In this story Balaam refused to be persuaded by Balak, but
in the whole story the covetousness of the man stands out,
and it is clear that only the fear of what God would do to him
kept him from striking a dreadful bargain with Balak. In
this story Balaam did not do what Balak wanted him to do,
but his unholy desire to do it is printed across the whole
narrative. Balaam already emerges as a most detestable
character. In *Numbers* 25 there emerges the second story.
In it Israel is seduced into the worship of Baal with evil
and dreadful and repulsive moral consequences. As we
read later (*Numbers* 31: 8, 16), it was Balaam who was
responsible for that seduction, and he perished miserably

because he taught others to sin. Out of this composite story Balaam stands for two things. (*a*) He stands for the covetous man, who was prepared to sin in order to gain reward. (*b*) He stands for the evil man, who was guilty of the greatest of all sins—the sin of teaching others to sin. So Jude is declaring of the wicked men of his own day that they are ready to leave the way of righteousness to make gain; and that they are teaching others to sin. To sin for the sake of gain is bad; but to rob someone else of his or her innocence, and to teach another to sin, is the most sinful of sins.

(iii) Third, there was Korah. The story of Korah and his company is in *Numbers* 16: 1-35. The sin of Korah was that he rebelled against the guidance of Moses when the sons of Aaron and the tribe of Levi were made the priests of the nation. That was a decision which Korah was not willing to accept; he wished to exercise a function which he had no right to exercise; and when he did so he perished terribly, and all his companions in wickedness with him. So Korah stands for the man who refuses to accept authority, and who reaches out for things which he has no right to take, and no right to have. So Jude is charging his opponents with defying the legitimate authority of the Church, and of, therefore, preferring their own way to the way of God. We have still to remember that there are things which pride incites us to take, but which are not for us, and, if we take them, the consequences can be disastrous.

THE PICTURE OF WICKED MEN

Jude 12-16

These people are hidden rocks which threaten to wreck your Love Feasts. These are the people who at your feasts revel with their own cliques without a qualm. They have no feeling of responsibility to anyone except themselves. They are clouds which drop no water but are blown past by the wind. They are fruitless trees in autumn's harvest time, twice dead, and torn up by the roots. They are wild sea waves, frothing out their own shameless deeds. They are wandering stars and the abyss of darkness has been prepared for them for ever. It was of these, too, that Enoch, who was the seventh from Adam, prophesied when he said:

> Behold the Lord has come with ten thousands of His holy ones, to execute judgment upon all and to convict all the impious for all the deeds of their impiousness, which they have impiously committed, and for the harsh things which impious sinners have said against Him.

For these people are grumblers. They querulously complain against the part in life which God has allotted to them. Their conduct is governed by their desires. Their mouths speak swelling words. They toady to men for what they can get out of it.

THIS is one of the great passages of invective of the New Testament. Here is blazing moral indignation at its hottest and fiercest flame. As Moffatt puts it: " Sky, land and sea are ransacked for illustrations of the character of these men." Here is a series of vivid pictures, every one of them with its meaning and with its significance. Let us take them one by one.

(i) They are like hidden rocks which threaten to wreck the Love Feasts of the Church. This is the one case in which there is doubt about what Jude is actually saying. Of one thing there is no doubt—the evil men are a peril to the Love Feasts. The Love Feast, the *Agapē*, was one of the very earliest features of the Church. The *Agapē* was a meal of fellowship, held on the Lord's Day. It was a meal to which everyone brought what he could, and at which all shared and shared alike. It was a lovely idea that the Christians in each little house Church should sit down on the Lord's Day to eat in fellowship together. No doubt there were some who could bring much, and there were others who could bring little. No doubt for many of the slaves it was the only decent meal in all the weeks.

But very soon the *Agapē* began to go wrong. We can see it going wrong in the Church at Corinth, when Paul declares that at the Corinthian Love Feasts there was nothing but division; they were divided into cliques and sections; some had too much, and others starved; and the meal for some had become a drunken revel (I *Corinthians* II: 17-22). Unless the *Agapē* was a true fellowship, it was a travesty, and very soon it had begun to belie its name.

Jude's opponents were making a travesty of the Love Feasts. But what is it that he calls them? The Authorized Version says that he calls them " spots on your feasts of charity " (verse 12); and that agrees with the parallel passage in *Second Peter*—" spots they are and blemishes " (2 *Peter* 2: 13). We have translated it Jude's expression " hidden rocks." The difficulty is that Peter and Jude do not use the same word, although they use words which are very similar. The word in *Second Peter* is *spilos*, which unquestionably means a *blot* or *spot*; but the word in Jude is *spilas*, which is a very rare word. Just possibly it may mean a *blot*, because in later Greek it can be used for the spots and markings on an opal stone. But in ordinary Greek by far its most common meaning is *a submerged*, or *half-submerged, rock on which a ship can be easily ship-wrecked*. We think that here the second meaning is much more likely. The Love Feast was a love feast; in it people were very close together in heart; in it there was the kiss of peace; and the wicked and evil and immoral men were using these Love Feasts to provoke immorality, and were using them as a cloak to gratify their own lusts. They were making them Love Feasts in entirely the wrong sense of the term. It is a dreadful thing, if men enter into the Church, and use the opportunities which the fellowship of the Church gives for their own perverted ends. These wicked men were like sunken rocks on which the fellowship of the Love Feasts was in danger of being wrecked.

THE SELFISHNESS OF WICKED MEN

Jude 12-16 (*continued*)

(ii) These wicked men revel in their own cliques and have no feeling of responsibility for anyone except themselves. These two things go together for they both stress the essential selfishness of the wicked men.

(*a*) They revel in their own cliques without a qualm. This is exactly the situation which Paul condemns in *First Corinthians*. The Love Feast was supposed to be an act of fellowship; and the fellowship was demonstrated and guaranteed by the sharing of all things. Instead of sharing, the wicked men kept themselves in their own clique, and kept to themselves all they had. In *First Corinthians* Paul actually goes the length of saying that the Love Feast could become a drunken revel, in which every man grabbed at all that he could get (I *Corinthians* 11: 21). No man can ever claim to know what Church membership means, if in the Church he is out for what he can get, and if in the Church he remains within his own little group, and never even seeks to enter into fellowship with a wider circle.

(*b*) We have translated the next phrase: " They have no feeling of responsibility for anyone except themselves." The Greek literally means, " shepherding themselves." The duty of a leader of the Church is to be a shepherd of the flock of God (*Acts* 20: 28). The false shepherd cared far more for himself than for the sheep which were supposed to be within their care. Ezekiel describes the false leaders and the false shepherds, from whom their privileges were to be taken away: " As I live, saith the Lord, surely because my flock became a prey, and my flock became meat to every beast of the field, because there was no shepherd, neither did my shepherds search for the flock, but the shepherds fed themselves, and not the flock . . . behold I am against the shepherds, and I require my flock at their hand, and cause them to cease from feeding the flock "

Ezekiel 34: 8-10). The man who feels no responsibility for the welfare of anyone except himself stands condemned.

So, then, here Jude condemns the selfishness which destroys fellowship, and the lack of the sense of responsibility, of all feeling of obligation for, and duty to, others.

(iii) The wicked men are like clouds, blown past by the wind, which drop no rain, and like trees in harvest time which have no fruit. Here these two phrases again go together, for they describe people who make great claims, but who are essentially useless. There were times in Palestine when people would pray for rain. At such a time a cloud might pass across the sky, bringing with it the promise of rain. But there were times when the promise of rain was only an illusion, and the cloud was blown on, and the rain never came. In any harvest time there were trees which looked as if they were heavy with fruit, but which, when men came to gather from them, gave no fruit at all. These are the pictures of men who make great claims, and who offer fine promises, but who, for all that, are quite useless to the community.

Here at the heart of this there lies one great truth. Promise without performance is a useless thing, and in the New Testament there is nothing which is so unsparingly condemned as uselessness. No amount of outward show, and no amount of fine words, will take the place of usefulness to others. Usefulness is an essential part of fellowship; the goodness which is not useful is an illusory thing. As it has been put: " If a man is not good for something, he is good for nothing."

THE FATE OF DISOBEDIENCE

Jude 12-16 (continued)

JUDE then goes on to use a vivid picture of these evil men. " They are like wild sea waves frothing out their own shameless deeds." The picture is this. When there has been a storm, and when the waves have been lashing the shore with their frothing spray and their spume, after the storm has subsided and the waves have receded, there is always left on the shore a fringe of seaweed and driftwood and all kinds of unsightly litter from the sea. That is always an ugly and an unsightly scene to look upon. But in the case of one sea it was grimmer than in any other. The waters of the Dead Sea can be moved to waves; and these waves, too, cast up the driftwood on the shore; but in the case of the Dead Sea there is one unique circumstance. The waters of the Dead Sea are so impregnated with salt that they strip and consume the bark of any branches or brushwood or driftwood which is in them; and, when such wood is cast up on the shore, it gleams bleak and white, more like dried and whitening bones than wood. The deeds of the wicked men are like the useless and unsightly litter which the waves leave scattered on the beach after a storm; they are like the grim, skeleton-like relics of the Dead Sea storms. It is a picture which vividly portrays and conveys the ugliness and the repulsiveness of the deeds of Jude's opponents.

Jude uses still another picture. The wicked men are like the wandering stars, who are kept in the abyss of darkness for their disobedience. This is a picture directly taken from the Book of Enoch. In that book the stars and the angels are sometimes identified; and there is a picture of the fate of the stars who were disobedient to God, and who left their appointed place and orbit and who were destroyed. In his journey through the earth Enoch came to a place where he saw, " neither a heaven above nor a firmly founded earth, but a place chaotic and horrible." He goes on: " And there I saw seven stars of the heaven bound together in it, like great mountains and burning with fire. Then I said, ' For what sin are they bound, and on account of what have they been cast in hither?' Then said Uriel, one of the holy angels, who was with me, and who was chief over them, ' Enoch, why dost thou ask, and why art thou eager for the truth? These are the numbers of the stars of heaven which have transgressed the commandment of the Lord, and are bound here till ten thousand years, the time entailed by their sins, are consummated'" (*Enoch* 21: 1-6). The fate of the wandering stars is typical of the fate of the man who disobeys God's commandments, and who, as it were, literally takes his own way of things.

Jude then confirms all this with a prophecy; but the prophecy is again taken from *Enoch*. The actual passage in *Enoch* runs: " And behold! He cometh with ten thousands of His holy ones to execute judgment upon all, and to destroy all the ungodly; and to convict all flesh of all the works of their ungodliness which they have ungodly committed, and of all the hard things which ungodly sinners have spoken against Him " (*Enoch* 1: 9).

This quotation has raised many questions in regard to *Jude* and to *Enoch*. There is no doubt that in the days of Jude, and in the days of Jesus, *Enoch* was a very popular Jewish book, which every pious Jew would know and read. Ordinarily, when the New Testament writers wish, as it were, to confirm and guarantee their words, they do so with a quotation from the Old Testament, using it as the word of God. Are we then to regard *Enoch* as sacred Scripture, since Jude uses it exactly as he would have used one of the prophets? Or, are we to take the view of which Jerome speaks? Are we to say that *Jude* cannot be Scripture, because Jude makes the mistake of using as Scripture a book which is, in fact, not Scripture?

We need waste no time at all upon this debate. The fact is that Jude, a pious Jew, knew and loved the Book of Enoch and had grown up in a circle and a sphere where the Book of Enoch was regarded with respect, and even reverence; and he takes his quotation from it perfectly naturally, knowing that his readers would recognize it, and that they would respect it. Jude is simply doing what all the New Testament writers do, and which every writer must do in every age, he is speaking to men in language which they recognized and understood.

THE CHARACTERISTICS OF EVIL MEN

Jude 12-16 (*continued*)

IN verse 16 Jude sets down three last characteristics of the evil men.

(i) They are grumblers, for ever discontented with the life which God has allotted to them. In this picture he uses two words, one of which was very familiar to his Jewish readers, and the other of which was very familiar to his Greek readers.

(*a*) He describes them by the word *goggustēs*. (*Gg* in Greek is pronounced *ng*). The very word describes the sound of the discontented voices of the murmurers. This is the very word which is so often used in the Greek Old Testament for the *murmurings* of the children of Israel against Moses as he led them through the wilderness (*Exodus* 15: 24; 17: 3; *Numbers* 14: 29). Again and again we read that the people *murmured* against Moses. The very word describes with its sound the low mutter of resentful discontent which rose from the sullenly rebellious people. These wicked men in the time of Jude are the modern counterparts of the murmuring children of Israel in the desert, people full of sullen complaints against the guiding hand of God.

(*b*) He uses the word *mempsimoiros*. This word is made up of two Greek words, *memphesthai*, which means *to blame* and *moira*, which means *one's allotted fate or life*. A *mempsimoiros* was a man who was for ever grumbling about life in general. The *mempsimoiros* was a standard Greek character. Theophrastus was the great master of the Greek character sketch, and he has a mocking character study of the *mempsimoiros*, which is worth quoting in full:

> Querulousness is an undue complaining about one's lot; the querulous man will say to him that brings him a portion from his friend's table: " You begrudged me your soup or your collops, or you would have asked me to dine with you in person." When his mistress is kissing him he says, " I wonder whether you kiss me

so warmly from your heart." He is displeased with Zeus, not because he sends no rain, but because he has been so long about sending it. When he finds a purse in the street, it is: " Ah! but I never found a treasure." When he has bought a slave cheap with much importuning the seller, he cries: " I wonder if my bargain's too cheap to be good." When they bring him the good news that he has a son born to him, then it is: " If you add that I have lost half my fortune, you'll speak the truth." Should this man win a suit-at-law by a unanimous verdict, he is sure to find fault with his speech-writer for omitting so many of the pleas. And if a subscription has been got up for him among his friends, and one of them says to him: " You can cheer up now," he will say: " What? when I must repay each man his share, and be beholden to him into the bargain? "

Here, vividly drawn by Theophrastus' subtle pen, there is the picture of a man who can find something to grumble about in any situation. He can find some fault with the best of bargains, the kindest of deeds, the most complete of successes, the best of good fortune. He is the chronic grumbler. " Godliness with contentment is great gain " (I *Timothy* 6: 6); but the evil men are chronically discontented with life and with the place in life that God has given to them. There are few people more unpopular than chronic grumblers, and all such might do well to remember that such grumbling is in its own way an insult to God, who allotted their lives to them.

(ii) Jude reiterates a point about these wicked men, which he has made again and again—their conduct is governed by their desires. To them self-discipline and self-control are nothing; to them the moral law is only a burden and a nuisance; honour and duty have no claim upon them; they have no desire to serve and no sense of responsibility. Their one value is pleasure, and their one dynamic is desire. We have only to think what the world would be like, if all men were like that, to see what complete chaos would ensue.

(iii) They speak with pride and with arrogance, yet at

the same time they are ready to toady and pander to the great and the important, if they think that they get anything out of it. It is perfectly possible for a man at one and the same time to be a bombastic creature towards the people he wishes to impress, and a flattering lick-spittle to the people whom he thinks important. Jude's opponents are glorifiers of themselves and flatterers of others, as they think the occasion demands, and their descendants are sometimes still among us to this day.

THE CHARACTERISTICS OF ERROR

Jude 17-19

> But you, beloved, you must remember the words which were once spoken by the apostles of our Lord Jesus Christ; you must remember that they said to us: " In the last time there will be mockers, whose conduct is governed by their own impious desires." These are the people who set up divisions—fleshly creatures, without the Spirit.

JUDE points out to his own people that nothing has happened which they might not have expected. The apostles had given warning that in the last times just such evil men as are now among them would come. The actual words of Jude's quotation are not in any New Testament book. Jude may be doing any one of three things. He may be quoting some apostolic book which has gone lost, and which we no longer possess. He may be quoting, not any book at all, but some oral tradition of the apostolic preaching, which has been handed down, or even some sermon which he himself had heard from the apostles. He may be giving the general sense of a passage like I *Timothy* 4: 1-3. In any event he is telling his people that error was only to be expected in the Church. From this passage we can see certain of the characteristics of these evil men.

(i) They mock at goodness, and their conduct is governed by their own evil desires. The two things go together.

These opponents of Jude had two characteristics, as we have already seen. They believed that only spirit was good, and that matter was essentially and altogether evil. That meant that the body is altogether evil; and that could be used as an argument that it does not matter what a man does with his body; the body is of no importance; and, therefore, it makes no difference at all if a man gives it its way and gluts and sates its desires. What is done with the body—so they said—is completely unimportant. Further, they argued that, since grace can forgive any sin, sin does not matter. If a man sins, grace is always there. To sin merely gives grace a chance to operate; therefore, again sin does not matter. Now, added to this these heretics had a third characteristic. They believed that they were the advanced thinkers; they believed that they were a step ahead of everyone else. And they regarded those who believed in, and observed, the old moral standards as narrow, old-fashioned, and out-of-date. They were long past purity, chastity, morality; and those who worried about such things, and who thought such things important, were living on a lower level of thought and religion.

That point of view is by no means dead. There are still those today who believe that the accepted standards of morality and fidelity, especially in matters of sex, are quite out-of-date. There are those who have no hesitation in being promiscuous. Kingsley Martin, writing in a symposium called *What I believe*, has much to say about the modern relationship between the sexes as he sees it. The older code, he says, was founded on two beliefs—the belief that sexual intercourse is for child-begetting and bearing, and the necessary dependence of women. He goes on to say that once women have become independent and have earned the right to earn their own living, and once methods of contraception have been developed and perfected, the old standards of sexual morality are out-of-date and must be abandoned. He writes: " The result in our day is a new sexual code. . . . The new code tends to make it the accepted thing that men and women can live together as they will, but to demand marriage of them if they decide to have children." In other words unlimited sexual intercourse is perfectly acceptable as a moral standard, so long as marriage is not entered into and children begotten. Here is an up-to-date morality which puts chastity and purity amongst the outworn things which have been overpassed.

In the time of Jude there were those who regarded themselves as beyond the accepted standards, and who looked with contempt on those who still observed the old laws, and who regarded such people as old-fashioned and antiquated. But there is a terrible text in the Old Testament: " The fool hath said in his heart, There is no God " (*Psalm* 53: 1). It must be noted that in that text the word *fool* does not mean the intellectual fool, the brainless man; it means the moral fool, the man who, in the modern phrase, is playing the fool. And the fact that he says there is no God is entirely due to wishful thinking. He knows that, if there is a God he is wrong, and that he can look for judgment; therefore, he eliminates God. In the last analysis those who eliminate the moral law, those who give free rein to their own passions and desires, those who say that the moral law is out-of-date, do so because they want it to be out-of-date in order that they may do as they like. They have listened to themselves instead of listening to God—and they have forgotten that there comes a day when they will be compelled to listen to God.

THE CHARACTERISTICS OF ERROR

Jude 17-19 (*continued*)

(ii) These evil men have a second characteristic. They set up divisions—they are fleshly creatures, without the Spirit. Here is a most significant thought—to set up divisions within the Church is always sin. To be responsible for divisions within the Church is necessarily to transgress the will and the purpose of God. These men set up divisions in two ways.

(a) As we have already seen, even at the Love Feasts, they had their own little cliques. By their conduct they were steadily destroying fellowship within the Church. They were drawing a circle to shut men out instead of drawing a circle to take men in. Exclusiveness is always a sin, and nowhere is it more a sin than within what ought to be the Christian fellowship.

(b) But they went further than that. There were certain thinkers in the early Church who had a way of looking at human nature which set up a radical division between man and man; and which basically and essentially split men into two classes. To understand this we must know something of Greek psychology, something of the normal Greek view of human nature. To the Greek man was body (*sōma*), soul (*psuchē*) and spirit (*pneuma*). The meaning of the word *body* is obvious; the body is simply man's physical construction and constitution. The word soul (*psuchē*) is more difficult to understand, for the Greeks used it in a way in which we do not use it. To the Greeks *soul*, *psuchē*, was simply *physical life*. As they saw it, everything that lives and breathes has *psuchē*. Not only men have *psuchē*; an animal has *psuchē* and even a plant can be said to have *psuchē*. *Psuchē*, then, is only the principle of physical life. *Pneuma, spirit*, is quite different; *pneuma* belongs to man alone, and is that which makes a man a thinking creature, kin to God, able to speak to God, and able to hear God speak to him.

Now, these thinkers went on to argue in this way. They argued that all men possessed *psuchē*, physical life; but they argued that very few really possessed *pneuma*, spirit. Only the really intellectual, only the chosen few, the élite, possessed *pneuma*; and, therefore, only the very few could rise to real religion and real knowledge of God. The rest must be content to walk on the lower levels of religious experience, for that was all for which they were fit. They, therefore, divided men into two classes. There were the *psuchikoi*, who were physically alive, but who were intellectually and spiritually dead, so to speak, with no hope of any advance. We might call them *the fleshly creatures*; all they possess is flesh and blood life; intellectual progress and spiritual experience are beyond them. There were the *pneumatikoi*, the people who really had spirit, the people who were capable of real intellectual knowledge, real knowledge of God, and real spiritual experience. Here was a radical division and cleavage; here was the creation of an intellectual and spiritual aristocracy over against the common herd of men.

Still further, these people who believed themselves to be the *pneumatikoi*, the spiritual and intellectual aristocracy believed that they were exempt from all the ordinary laws which govern a man's conduct. Ordinary people, the common herd, might have to observe the moral laws and the accepted standards, but they were above that. For them sin did not exist; they were so advanced that they could do anything, and take no taint, and be none the worse. We may well remember that there are still people who believe that they are above the laws, who, when they see what happens to others who sin, say in their heart of hearts that it could never happen to them, who believe, to use the colloquial phrase, that they can get away with anything. There are still people like that.

We can now see how cleverly Jude deals with these people. These self-styled intellectual and spiritual aristocrats say that the rest of the world are the *psuchikoi*, the merely fleshly, while they are the *pneumatikoi*, the truly spiritual. Jude takes the words and reverses them; he turns the descriptions upside down. "It is you," he thunders at them, "who are the *psuchikoi*, the fleshly and flesh-dominated; it is you who possess no *pneuma*, no real knowledge and no experience of God." Jude is saying to these people that, although they think themselves the only truly religious people, they have no real religion at all. They think themselves superior, but their superiority is an illusion and a snare. Those whom they despise are, in fact, much better than they are themselves.

The truth about these so-called intellectual and spiritual people was that they desired to sin, and they twisted religion into a justification for sin.

THE CHARACTERISTICS OF GOODNESS

Jude 20, 21

> But you, beloved, you must build yourselves up on the foundation of your most holy faith; you must pray in the Holy Spirit; you must keep yourselves in the love of God; while you wait for the mercy of our Lord Jesus Christ which will bring you to life eternal.

As in the previous passage Jude described the characteristics of error, so here he describes the characteristics of goodness.

(i) The good man builds up his life on the foundation of the most holy faith. The life of the Christian is founded on the faith. That is to say, the life of the Christian is founded, not on something which he manufactured himself, but on something which he received. There is a ladder and chain in the transmission of the faith. The faith came from Jesus to the apostles; it came from the apostles to the Church; and it comes from the Church to us. There is something tremendous here. It means that the faith which we hold is not merely someone's personal opinion; it is a revelation which came from Jesus Christ, and which is preserved and transmitted within His Church, always under the care and the guidance of the Holy Spirit, from generation to generation. The good man rests his life, not on any one's uncertain opinions, not on any one's fantasies of thought, not on any temporary or local heresies, but on the revelation which came from Jesus Christ, and which is preserved for ever in the Church, so long as the Church is sensitive and obedient to the guidance of the Holy Spirit.

That faith is a *most holy faith*. Again and again we have seen the meaning of this word *holy*. Its root meaning is *separate* or *different*. That which is *holy* is *different* from other things, as the priest is different from other men, the Temple different from other buildings, the Sabbath different from other days, and God supremely different from men.

Our faith is different in two ways. (*a*) It is different from other faiths and from philosophies in that it is not man-made but God-given; it is not opinion, it is revelation; it is not guessing, it is certainty. (*b*) It is different from other faiths in that it has the power to make those who believe it different. It is not only a mind-changer, it is a life-changer. It is not only an intellectual belief, it is a moral dynamic. The Christian faith is different because in itself it is unique revelation, and because in its effect on others it is unique power.

(ii) The good man is a man of prayer. It has been put this way: " Real religion means *dependence*." The essence of religion is the realization and the admission of our total dependence on God; and prayer is the acknowledging of our dependence on God, and the going to God for the help we need. As Moffatt has it in a magnificent definition: " Prayer is love in need appealing to love in power." The Christian must be a man of prayer for at least two reasons. (*a*) He knows that he must test everything by the will of God, and, therefore, he must take everything to God for God's approval. (*b*) He knows that of himself he can do nothing, but that with God all things are possible, and, therefore, he must ever be taking his insufficiency to God's all sufficiency.

Prayer, says Jude, is to be *in the Holy Spirit*. What Jude means is this. Our human prayers are at least sometimes bound to be selfish and blind. It is only when the Holy Spirit takes full possession of us that our desires are so cleansed and purified that our prayers are right. The truth is that as Christians we are bound to pray to God, but that God alone can teach us how to pray and what to pray for.

(iii) The good man is the man who keeps himself in the love of God. What Jude is thinking of here is the old covenant relationship between God and His people as described in *Exodus* 24: 1-8. In the covenant God came to His people promising that He would be their God, and they would be His people; but that relationship depended on the people accepting and obeying the law which God gave them. If they were to keep themselves within the covenant relationship, they must keep themselves within obedience to God. " God's love," Moffatt comments, " has its own terms of communion." It is true in one sense that we can never drift beyond God's love and care; but it is also true that, if we desire to remain in close and intimate communion with God, we must give to God the perfect love and the perfect obedience, which must ever go hand in hand.

(iv) The good man is the man who waits with expectation. He waits for the coming of Jesus Christ in mercy, love and power; for he knows that the purpose of Jesus Christ for him is to lead him and to bring him to life eternal, which is nothing other than the life of God Himself.

RECLAIMING THE LOST

Jude 22, 23

> Some of them you must argue out of their error, while they are still wavering. Others you must rescue by snatching them out of the fire. Others you must pity and fear at the same time, hating the garment stained by the flesh.

WE may simply note that different translators give differing translations of this passage. The reason is that there is much doubt as to what the true Greek text is. We ourselves have given the translation, which we believe to be nearest to the sense of the passage.

Even to the worst heretic, even to those most far gone in error, even to those whose beliefs are most menacing and dangerous, the Christian has a duty that is binding. The Christian's duty must always be, not to destroy, but to save such men. His aim must be, not to banish them from the Christian Church, but to win them back into the Christian fellowship. His aim must be, not to have nothing to do with them, but to establish with them relationships in which he can win them back to truth and to Christ. James Denney said that, to put the matter at its simplest, Jesus Christ came to make bad men good. Sir John Seeley said: "When the power of reclaiming the lost dies out of the Church, it ceases to be the Church." As we have taken this passage, Jude divides the troublers of the Church into three classes, to each of whom a different approach is necessary.

(i) There are those who are flirting with falsehood, and playing with fire. There are those who are obviously attracted by the wrong way, who are on the verge of destructive heresy, who are on the brink of committing themselves to error, but who are still hesitating, and still wavering, and who have not yet taken the final step. Those must be convinced, convicted, argued out of their error, while yet there is time. From this two things emerge as a duty. (a) We must study to be able to defend the faith, to give a reason for the hope that is in us, to commend our faith to others. We must know what we ourselves believe, so that we can meet error with truth, and heresy with the right way. And we must make ourselves such that we can defend the faith in such a way that by our graciousness and our sincerity we may win others to it. To do this we must banish all uncertainty from our own minds, and all arrogance and intolerance from our approach to others. We must have steadfastness of faith and winsomeness to defend and to commend the faith. (b) We must be ready to speak in time. Many a person would have been saved from error of thought and error of action, if someone else had only spoken in time. Sometimes we hesitate to speak, but there are times, and they are many, when silence is a cowardly thing, and when silence can cause more harm than speech can ever cause. One of the greatest tragedies in life is when someone comes to us and says, " I would never have been in the mess I am now in, if someone—if you—had only spoken to me."

(ii) There are those who have to be, as it were, snatched from the fire. There are those who have committed themselves to error, who have actually started out on the wrong way, and who have to be stopped, as it were, forcibly, and even against their will. They have to be pulled out of the situation which they are creating for themselves. It is all very well to say that we must leave a man his freedom, that he must be free to make his own decisions, that he has a right to do what he likes. All these things are in one sense true, but there are times for action, when a man must be even forcibly saved from himself.

(iii) There are those whom we must pity and fear at one and the same time. Here Jude is thinking of something which is always true. There is danger to the sinner; but there is also danger to the rescuer. He who would cure an infectious disease always runs the risk of infection. Jude says that we must hate the garment stained by the flesh. Almost certainly he is thinking here of the regulations in *Leviticus* 13: 47-52, where it is laid down that the garment which has been worn by a person, who had been discovered to be suffering from leprosy, must be burned in the fire. The old saying remains true—we must love the sinner but hate the sin. Before a man can rescue others, he must himself be strong in the faith. His own feet must be firm on the dry land before he can throw a lifebelt to the man who is likely to be swept away; he must himself be a sturdy swimmer before he can save others who are in danger of being submerged in error. The simple fact is that the rescue of those in error is not for everyone to attempt. Those who would win others for Christ must themselves be very sure of Christ; and those who would fight the disease of sin must themselves have the strong antiseptic of a healthy faith. Ignorance can never be met with ignorance, not even with half-knowledge; it can be met only by the man who can say, " I know whom I have believed."

THE FINAL ASCRIPTION OF PRAISE

Jude 24, 25

> Unto Him who is able to keep you from slipping, and to make you stand blameless and exultant in the presence of His glory, to the only God, our Saviour, through Jesus Christ our Lord, be glory, majesty, dominion and power, before all time, at this present time, and for all time. Amen.

IT is probable that these are the only two verses of *Jude* that many people know. Jude comes to an end of his letter with this tremendous ascription of praise.

Three times in the New Testament praise is given to *the God who is able*. In *Romans* 16: 25 Paul gives praise to the God who is able to stablish us. God is the one person who can give us a foundation for life which nothing and no one can ever shake. In *Ephesians* 3: 20 Paul gives praise to the God who is able to do far more than we can ever ask or even dream of. God is the God whose grace no man has every exhausted, and on whom no claim can ever be too much.

Here once again Jude offers his praise to the God who is able.

(i) God is able to keep us from slipping. The word is *aptaistos*. It is used both of a sure-footed horse which does not stumble and of a man who is a good man and who does not fall into error. " He will not suffer thy foot to be moved," or as the Scottish metrical version has it, " Thy foot He'll not let slide " (*Psalm* 121: 3). To walk with God is to walk in safety even on the most dangerous and the most slippery path. In mountaineering climbers are roped together so that even if the amateur and the inexperienced climber should slip, the skilled mountaineer can take his weight and save him. Even so, when we bind ourselves to God, God keeps us safe.

(ii) He can make us stand blameless in the presence of His own glory. The word for blameless is *amōmos*. This is characteristically a sacrificial word; and it is commonly and technically used of an animal which is without spot or blemish, and which is therefore fit to be offered to Gods The amazing thing is that when we submit ourselves to God, the grace of God can make our lives nothing less than a sacrifice which is fit to offer to Him.

(iii) He can bring us into His presence exultant. Surely the natural way to think of entry into the presence of God is to think of entry in fear and in trembling, in shame and in disgrace. But by the work of Jesus Christ, and in the grace of God, we know that we can go to God with eagerness and with joy, and with all fear banished. Through Jesus Christ, God the stern Judge has become known to us as God the loving Father.

We may note one last thing. Usually we associate the word *Saviour* with Jesus Christ, but here Jude gives it to God. Jude is not alone in this for God is often called Saviour in the New Testament (*Luke* 1: 47; I *Timothy* 1: 1; 2: 3; 4: 10; *Titus* 1: 3; 2: 10; 3: 4). So we end with the great and the comforting certainty that at the back of everything there is a God whose name is Saviour. The Christian has the joyous certainty that in this world he lives in the love of God, and that in the next world he goes to the love of God. The love of God is at once the atmosphere and the goal of all his living.